THE AMERICAN REVOLUTION AND EIGHTEENTH-CENTURY CULTURE

AMS Studies in the Eighteenth Century: No. 5
ISSN: 0196-6561

Other titles in this series:

No. 1.   Modern Language Association of America. *Proceedings of the 1967-68 Neoclassicism Conferences.* Edited and with a Selected Bibliography 1920-68 by Paul J. Korshin. 1970.

No. 2.   Francesco Cordasco. *Tobias George Smollett: A Bibliographical Guide.* 1978.

No. 3.   Paula R. Backscheider, editor. *Probability, Time, and Space in Eighteenth-Century Literature.* 1979.

No. 4.   Ruth Perry. *Women, Letters, and the Novel.* 1980.

No. 6.   G. S. Rousseau, editor. *The Letters and Papers of Sir John Hill.* 1982.

No. 7.   Paula R. Backscheider. *A Being More Intense: A Study of the Prose Works of Bunyan, Swift, and Defoe.* 1984.

THE AMERICAN REVOLUTION

AND

EIGHTEENTH-CENTURY

CULTURE

ESSAYS FROM THE 1976
BICENTENNIAL CONFERENCE
OF THE
AMERICAN SOCIETY FOR
EIGHTEENTH-CENTURY STUDIES

EDITED BY
PAUL J. KORSHIN

AMS PRESS
NEW YORK

Library of Congress Cataloging-in Publication Data

American Society for Eighteenth-Century Studies.
   Bicentennial Conference (1976 : University of
   Pennsylvania)
   The American Revolution and eighteenth-century
culture.

   (AMS studies in the eighteenth century ; no. 5)
   Includes index.
   Bibliography: p.
   1. United States—Civilization—To 1783—Congresses.
2. United States—Politics and government—Revolution,
1775-1783—Congresses. 3. Europe—Civilization—To
1783—Congresses. I. Korshin, Paul J., 1939-
II. Title. III. Series.

E163.A47   1976   973   83–45275
ISBN 0-404-61471-X

AMS Press, Inc.
56 East 13th Street, New York, N.Y. 10003, U.S.A.

Manufactured in the United States of America

CONTENTS

ILLUSTRATIONS

PREFACE

THE nine essays in this book, which now appear in print together for the first time, were originally part of the program of the Bicentennial Conference of the American Society for Eighteenth-Century Studies (ASECS) at the University of Pennsylvania in November 1976. The bicentennial of American independence, as scholars of the period will remember, received more attention from the academic world in the United States than such anniversaries ordinarily do. The circumstances of and the reasons for that attention are worthy of our notice today for, in the early 1970s, the still young National Endowment for the Humanities established a special program for conferences on "The Bicentennial." In a decade free from national efforts to reduce federally funded programs and at a time when the humanities were a source of national pride rather than a subject of the suspicion of zealots, the National Endowment's program attracted much attention, and many fine proposals received financial help, including the one for the ASECS Bicentennial Conference. Thus the NEH helped to make the two hundredth anniversary of American independence the most widely celebrated scholarly event in recent memory.

Indeed, one might well say that there was an over-celebration of the occasion for many conferences—and, over the next three or four years volumes of conference proceedings—produced, for some a saturation of studies on American independence, its causes, and its consequences. As a result of the events of the Bicentennial Year, certain locations in the country acquired a notoriety not always deserved. Of all places, Philadelphia, the site of the conference that gives rise to this book, probably suffered more than any other city as a result of the outbreak of legionnaires' disease in the city's Hotel Bellevue Stratford in summer 1976. The scholarly gatherings in the city after that event had to labor in the shadow of that shocking epidemic, which epidemiologists still do not fully understand. But its beginnings in the late 1960s, the ASECS dealt—as it does to-day—mainly with European civilization; its Bicentennial Conference reflected these interests at the same time that it undertook to strengthen the scholarly associations between European and American studies. 1976 was a great year for creating such ties, but how strong they have become in the ensuing decade is a matter for some argument today.

The following nine essays fall into two clearly separate goups, those that deal with aspects of politics and freedom and those that cover the emergence of new literary and artistic ides in the world around the American Revolution. M. M. Goldsmith's "Faction Detected," for example, is actually a study of the fall of Sir Robert Walpole's ministry from power in the early 1740s, but its context is the ideological consequences of that fall. What reforms did Walpole's opponents, who had campaigned against his government for twenty years, institute when they assumed power? As Professor Goldsmith shows, very few indeed; libertarian rhetoric did not necessarily lead to change, just as reforming zeal does not always produce reform. Donald Greene, writing about "Libertarian Rhetoric and Practive in Eighteenth-Century Britain," studies some of the very rhetoric that Goldsmith is concerned with, much of it in popular songs and ballads, most of it long forgotten today, and shows conclusively that, rhetoric notwithstanding, the politicians who called for liberty when in opposition but produced no change once in office helped bring the idea of patriotism into disrepute in Great Britain. Greene, too, studies the mechanics of the end of the Walpole government, and argues that some of the civil liberties that the American Bill of Rights would indemnify later in the eighteenth century derive from that tumultuos period.

Jeffrey Barnouw's fascinating essay, "American Independence: Revolution of the Republican Ideal," carries forward an intense scholarly debate on the origins of the American Revolution. In recent decades, scholars have proposed that the new nation emerged from a tradition of republicanism, of pro-commonwealth thought, that derives from Aristotle's *Politics* and the writings of Polybius, the concept of the Roman republic, the civic humanism of the Italian Renaissance and Machiavelli, the English political theorists of the seventeenth century, particularly the ASECS Bicentennial Conference took place as scheduled in the week of the U. S. national elections; all the papers that I have collected here their authors read in person at that time to appreciative audiences.

For such a collection to appear in 1985, five or six years after the flood tide of Bicentennial conference proceedings has receded from its height, requires an explanation. At first, indeed, the American Society for Eighteenth-Century Studies contracted to publish the papers as an extra volume in its annual series of conference proceedings, and even accepted payment from several hundred subscribers for it, but that organization lost its willingness—and forgot its contract—shortly after the Bicentennial celebrations were over. No matter, and perhaps all for the best, for the following essays really have very little to do with the vast majority of publications that sprang from the scholarly gatherings of 1976. Most Bicentennial-style collections related to independence, the American Revolution, and their collective effects throughout colonial society. Such is not the case with this volume, for the planners of the ASECS Bicentennial Conference gave it the title of "The American Revolution and Eighteenth-Century Culture," with the intention of promoting discourse not on independence and the colonial experience but rather on significant ideas that were current at the time and that related to U. S. independence indirectly.

Hence the conference's meetings focused on such subjects as Anglo-French intellectual relationships and influences, taste and the arts at the time of the Revolution, American inspiration for the German Enlightenment, political thought in the second half of the eighteenth century, the ideas of slavery and freedom in Great Britain and American, and American literature at the time of independence. A dozen other smaller groups covered, *inter alia*, Anglo-American pessimism, eighteenth-century architecture, food and cuisine in eighteenth-century thought, radicalism and conservatism, and the industrial revolution as an eighteenth-century phenomenon. Some of these topics—such as political thought—can easily relate to the major themes of the Bicentennial, but most of them deal with the broader milieux of eighteenth-century studies, which had always been the mission of the American Society for Eighteenth-Century Studies. Since

James Harrington, and the aristocratic and other opponents of the regime of Sir Robert Walpole. The parents of the new American state, according to this view, owed their Declaration of Independence and later their Constitution to this rich background, which J. G. A. Pocock calls "The Atlantic Republican Tradition." Professor Barnouw's long argument, which rehearses the high points—and weaknesses—of this school of thought, suggests instead that independence came about not for reasons of ideology alone but also because of self-interest, economic and commercial factors, and a widespread desire for exploitation of the new continent that was just then being opened to exploration. The ideology that helped form the American nation-state, Barnouw argues, comes not from that Atlantic republican tradition, but from that tradition and the thought of Thomas Hobbes; the state that emerged was not an ideal of civic virtue but one that successfully embodied the notion of economic expansion.

Just as Professor Barnouw presents radical interpretations of traditional ideas, so Isaac Kramnick, in "Tommy Paine and the Idea of America," studies how one of the greatest radicals of the eighteenth century has, thanks to misunderstandings and some willful misinterpretation of his *Common Sense*, come to be a figure who appeals to the traditionalists. Despite his atheistic radicalism, which shocked many of his contemporaries, Paine thrives today as a deradicalized icon for the ruling class; his face has even appeared on a United States postage stamp and phrases from his writings have entered dictionaries of quotations (for where else would the likes of President Gerald Ford—or his handlers—have discovered the snippets of Paine that found their way into presidential speeches?). The late Roger T. Anstey, the great historian of abolitionism, in his essay on British abolitionism in the eighteenth and nineteenth centuries, also discusses ideas of liberty and freedom, but in the much more practical sense that relates to the ownership of slaves, the greatest debate in the new American state during its founding years and first century. At the time of the country's first centennial, in 1876, slavery was still an unsolved problem; hence for a study of the patterns of abolitionism to grace a bicentennial meeting could not have been more appropriate. Anstey's subject, like that of sev-

eral other contributors, is origins, but in his case the origins are
those of the antislavery movement in Great Britain in the period
of the American Revolution and how Evangelical thought helped
to make the cause respectable over a period of thirty years until
the abolition of the British slave trade in 1807. Anstey is sensitive to the fact that the Quakers had been prominent not only in
the founding of Pennsylvania and the very university in whose
lecture hall he delivered his paper but also in American abolitionism, perhaps the most impressive case in our national history
of an essentially religious movement producing substantial social change.

While Professor Anstey writes of the influence of religious
life and ideas on the political stage, Irma Jaffe, in the first of the
essays in this book on literature and the arts, studies the religious background of one of the most famous of all eighteenth-
century American paintings, This is the enormous work by John
Singleton Copley, *Watson and the Shark* (1778). Professor Jaffe's
interpretation of it shows how Copley embodied ideas from the
Bible, contemporary preaching, the history paintings of Raphael and Rubens, and eighteenth-century notions of Old and
New Worlds in his splendid view of young Broók Watson escaping, although severely injured, from a shark while he was
swimming in Havana harbor in 1749. Until now, Jaffe observes,
we have not fully understood this great painting. She augments
our knowledge of it by demonstrating that Copley, although he
painted it in England and the subjects of it are British, was nevertheless quintessentially American (after hearing George III's
speech recognizing the United States, in 1782, Copley went into
his London studio and added an American flag to a ship in the
background of a portrait he was then painting of Elkanah Watson). Durand Echeverria also writes about the Old World and the
New, this time from the perspective of France and "The French
Image of American Society." The image, he shows, was cul-
tivated by generations of romantic idealizing of the imagined
Roman virtue of the American yeoman, the primitivism of the
natives, the heroism of the pioneers, and the exoticism of the
New World. But Professor Echeverria also looks at the more
practical side of French admiration: it was always tempered by
economic considerations and varied from Americophilia to

Americophobia according to the French expectations of economic exploitation. The French, to be blunt, admired America more when they thought there was something in it for them, less when their commercial ventures did not prosper. The long shadow of Hobbes, Jeffrey Barnouw would agree, touched more than England and America in the eighteenth century.

On the more strictly literary side of the contents, Karl Keller's "Literary Excess as Indigenous Aesthetic in Eighteenth-Century America" takes a standard feature of nineteenth-century American literature, hyperbole, and seeks its origins in the previous century. What Keller calls "an aesthetic of outragousness" dominates early American writing, and he finds its sources in the extremes of literary expression that were so popular in colonialtimes.These extremes themselves go back to English metaphysical poetry and Puritan spiritual self-flagellation, but the baroque excess of much early American writing will come as no surprise to anyone who has spent much time reading it. Despite the radicalism of some American political thought, most genres of literature in the country's first century are conservative: the taste for imaginative literature did not arrive on the shores of the new continent in the first boat. As Kenneth Silverman shows in his contribution, "The Economic Debate over the Theater in Revolutionary America," there was a longstanding Puritan prejudice against stage performances of which we may still perceive vestiges in blue laws that continue to exist today. Professor Silverman shows that some of the arguments against the theater were economic as well, while many people feared that the presence of the stage would lead to corruption of morals, a rash of new brothels, and the ruin of young men and women. Such generalizations are always amusing; in contrast, I might note the French assertion, about the same time, that not a single case of adultery had ever been known in the city of Philadelphia (one of the centers of early American theater, in fact). The theater, as Professor Silverman relates, won out after all and so, perhaps incredibly, did American literature and society, despite all attempts from Europe at ridicule, exploitation, and economic domination.

The University of Pennsylvania provided a splendid venue for a Bicentennial Conference on eighteenth-century ideas and topics, for it is North America's first university and was the first academic institution on the new continent to cultivate ties with Enlightenment Europe (in the case of the University of Pennsylvania, with Scotland and its Enlightenment). Even now, so many years after the events of 1976 and the delivering of the papers that we now publish here, it is good to look back at the decade of the 1970s and to acknowledge again the generosity of the National Endowment for the Humanities and its Division of Research Programs, the support of the then new Faculty of Arts and Sciences at the University, and finally the energy and vision of that body's first dean, Vartan Gregorian, who made possible the ASECS Bicentennial Conference and, ultimately, this book.

—PAUL J. KORSHIN

Faction Detected:
Ideological Consequences of
Robert Walpole's Decline and Fall

M. M. GOLDSMITH

BETWEEN the party battles of Queen Anne's reign and the disturbances—internal, imperial, and European—of George III's, Britons reposed, so we usually think, in eighteenth-century harmony. Despite occasional discords produced by the South Sea Bubble, the Excise Bill and the '45, the Augustans held a common set of values. Throughout this period of Whig political domination by Sir Robert Walpole and his successors, their minds remained classical and somewhat complacent, notwithstanding their fears of commerce and corruption. But the political conceptions of Hanoverian Britons did not remain static, for the events of Walpole's decline and fall—the Opposition campaign of 1739-41, the motion for Walpole's removal, Walpole's eventual retirement and its aftermath—contributed to the formation and the acceptance of more skeptical disillusioned views about politics than had previously been current.

In 1735, despite a decade of strenuous effort, the successes of the Opposition had been literary and artistic rather than political. An Opposition press had been created; every week the *Craftsman* fulminated against the evils of Sir Robert Walpole's administration. It was lampooned and caricatured in engravings and prints; it was sung against in ballads and in Gay's *Beggars' Opera*. Pope, the greatest poet of the age, and Swift, its most as-

1

tringent satirist, both exercised their pens against the Great Man.[1]
To him Bolingbroke ironically dedicated his *Dissertation on Parties* when it appeared in book form in March 1735. Yet
Bolingbroke had failed to weld together an opposition campaign capable of unseating Walpole, who had ridden the storm
over the excise in 1733 and successfully managed the election of
1734. Moreover, Bolingbroke's own position had become precarious. Denounced as the "anti-minister," distrusted by such
important Opposition leaders as William Pulteney, subjected to
a campaign of vilification in the government press, entangled in
intrigue with foreign agents, and reduced in fortune, Bolingbroke retreated to exile in France.[2]

Nevertheless, we should not underestimate the difficulties
faced by an opposition at this time, nor undervalue Bolingbroke's contribution to the creation of a "formed," or systematic,
opposition. One of the principal problems for an opposition was
to legitimize its actions. After all, it had to object to, and even obstruct, the King's ministers in the performance of their duties.
Fortunately, there was available an ideology which justified opposing at least some of the ministry's actions: the neo-Machiavellian, neo-Harringtonian, Country ideas that were so
widely diffused in the eighteenth century.[3] All those against
Walpole could unite on the main elements of this ideology: that
Britain had a mixed constitution, with monarchic, aristocratic,
and democratic elements carefully balanced; that this constitution provided for liberty—and sometimes other goods such as
prosperity and the flourishing of the arts and sciences; nevertheless that such a constitution needed constant vigilance since
if the balance were disturbed, it might be destroyed, corrupted;
that the causes of decay or corruption were endemic in men, for
they sought naturally the satisfaction of their own desires for
wealth and power; that these causes could only be checked by
maintaining the constitution. Given such principles, Tories could
combine with dissident Whigs on a Country party program of
hostility to a standing army, promotion of place and pension bills,
and agitation against ministerial corruption harmful to the liberties or interests of Britain. Thus Bolingbroke was at some pains
to deny that the existing parties retained the old differences in
principles which had divided Whig and Tory. In fact the min-

isterial party were hypocritical; they professed Whig principles while actually behaving as an unprincipled and anti-constitutional faction, greedily pursuing personal gain at the expense of the nation and its liberties.[4]

But ministerial writers insisted that party principles were at issue. "Tory" principles, they urged, involved accepting hereditary divine right. Tories were therefore opposed to the present dynasty and the present constitutional order. It followed that the Opposition was a faction of disloyal malcontents. Or rather it was a set of factions: firstly, the Jacobites, openly opposed to the King and the constitution; secondly, the Tories who were really crypto-Jacobites—and here Bolingbroke's past was an embarrassment; and thirdly, discontented Whigs, who were prepared to work with their treasonous partners in order to serve their own private ends, that is, get into places.[5]

The ministerial line cleverly exploited the fissures within the Opposition. Dissident Whigs like Pulteney and Carteret were sensitive to the accusation that they were hostile to the regime. For being against the Hanoverian dynasty would doom them to exclusion from office forever. Since they wished to regain office, the threat of exclusion was real. But if they were to regain office they had to embarrass the government, and so they had to work with "Tories." Bolingbroke's argument that the Opposition were the constitution's and the dynasty's loyal defenders was thus welcome to them as it was to most Tories. it was a Country ideology for a Country party—for most parliamentary "Tories" were country gentlemen, frequently representatives of their counties. And backing up the landed interest was the mercantile, for the Tories had support in London and other mercantile centers. Only William Shippen and his small group of Jacobites could agree with the ministerial view of what differences existed in principle—in favor of the present regime or against it. For the Jacobites, a mere change of ministers could have little appeal. In fact, all the Tories, Hanoverian as well as Jacobite, were necessarily suspicious that they were being used by the dissident Whigs as nothing more than a footstool for climbing back into power.[6] Nonetheless, the Tories, mainly backbench country gentlemen who did not necessarily aspire to ministerial heights but only to political, and especially local, rehabilitation, needed the parliamentary eloquence of the Opposition Whigs just as those Whigs needed their backing. If they could work together they had some chance of success—the unasked question was whether the successful overthrow of Walpole would be followed by a new ministry in which Tories shared. But for all, opposition could only be justified, and not treasonous, if opposing was defending the constitution against corruption, an expression of the spirit of liberty against the spirit of faction. To fight ministerial influence, bribery, jobbery, and tyranny, Country ideology was a necessity.[7]

Against this attack the Ministry deployed no contrary ideology. Instead, they claimed to be the true adherents of Whig principles. The accusation of corruption was a chimera conjured up by the leaders of the Opposition to dupe their followers. After all, the ministers, and the members of Parliament who voted for them, were gentlemen of independent means—taking bribes was not worth their while—and they too valued English liberty, which had in fact increased under the government's auspices. Indeed, the lenity of the government toward the treasonous malcontents might be regarded as excessive. The Ministry presented itself as able and public-spirited; the truly corrupt are those who hunger for ministerial office and perhaps those outside Parliament who are possessed by a licentious, factious enthusiasm. Thus the objections to the actions of the Ministry are treasonous, or self-interested, or perhaps just simply the over-hasty passionately distorted judgments of men who accuse the Ministry of inevitable misfortunes which they have done all they could do to prevent.[8]

Bolingbroke's withdrawal in 1735 could hardly be said to have deprived the Opposition of all its pens. Some noticeable new writers were appearing. Henry Fielding ridiculed the Ministry on the stage. *The Historical Register for 1736*, with its sly "Ode to the New Year," its council of ministers in Corsica, of which the deepest minister never speaks, and which manages only to agree on a new tax, its auction of political virtues, and its suggestion that some patriots, at least, could be bought off by "Quidam," that is, Walpole, was only one of his efforts.[9] *Eurydice Hiss'd* makes an obvious parallel between Pillage, a great man in farces, and a certain other Great Man. The parallel between the theatre and politics is neatly drawn—both great men care only for money. Pillage comes to grief in the end—an end Fielding must have wished for Walpole too.[10] In the published versions of the "Dedication to the Public," Fielding underlines his point by claiming that the *Gazeteer* has misrepresented his plays: if mankind weren't so blind, he "need not have publicly informed them that The Register is a ministerial pamphlet, calculated to infuse into the minds of the people a great opinion of their ministry, and thereby procure an employment for the author, who has been often promised one, whenever he would write on that side." To drive home his point Fielding relates an ironic parable against the ministerial writers. The tale concerns two gentlemen, one of whom tells the other, aptly named "Bob" (and somewhat short-sighted), that the sign on an inn, depicting an ass, is in fact Bob's likeness.[11]

The theater was to provide the scene of another patriotic effusion that annoyed the ministry—Henry Brooke's *Gustavus Vasa, The Deliverer of his Country*.[12] Gustavus is a patriot prince—the later 1730s were replete with patriot princes as well as patriot kings, for Bolingbroke was not the only writer who saw Frederick, Prince of Wales, as a useful prop for the Opposition.[13] Returning from exile, Gustavus leads the poor, virtuous, simple, liberty-loving Dalecartians against the tyrannical Danish conqueror of Sweden, Cristiern, and his corrupt minister, Trollio. In Act IV, Scene 1 they discuss the arts of government. Cristiern observes that "men are machines," to be manipulated by touching the springs of their favorite passions. Trollio, his mentor in corruption, expounds:

> Let Heav'n spy out for Virtue, and then starve it.
> But Vice and Frailty are the Stateman's Quarry,
> The Objects of our search and of our Science;
> Mark'd by our Smiles, and cherish'd by our Bounty.
> 'Tis hence you lord o'er your servile Senates.

It is only necessary to bait their lusts, and even patriots can be suborned. Cristiern responds that "virtue is the Bane of Government," a libel on the state to be suppressed. On good Country party, patriotic principles, such views are truly the uttermost depths of wickedness. Appropriately, the Swedes regain their liberty, Trollio comes to grief, and the king repents. *Gustavus Vasa* was the first play to which the Lord Chamberlain, exercising his new statutory powers, denied a license.

This suppression elicited a scathing response from a writer named Samuel Johnson. Johnson had already shown some evidences of the spirit of liberty. In 1738 he had published *London: A Poem in Imitation of the Third Satire of Juvenal*, which contains several reflections on the current state of affaris. Indeed, there are passages in which every line scourges the Ministry:

> Here let those reign, whom pensions can incite
> To vote a patriot black, a courtier white;
> Explain their country's dear-bought rights away,
> And plead for pirates in the face of day.
> Let such raise palaces, and manors buy,
> Collect a tax, or farm a lottery
> With warbling eunuchs fill a silenc'd stage,
> And lull to servitude a thoughtless age.

In this society rebellious virtue is overthrown and the thirst for gold unchecked. Corruption abounds and merit is smothered. *"SLOW RISES WORTH BY POVERTY DEPRESS'D"*—but we ought not to overlook the lines following that one:

> But here more slow, where all are slaves to gold,
> Where looks are merchandise, and smiles are sold;
> Where won by bribes, by flatteries implor'd
> The groom retails the favours of his Lord.

The last is of course a parallel to Walpole's situation. In fact Johnson attacked Walpole directly in *Marmor Norfolciense*—a supposed prophetic inscription taking a strong line against a foreign policy subordinating the interest of Britain to those of Hanover. Thus his *Compleat Vindication of the Licensers of the Stage* is by no means out of character.[14]

But despite the contributions of Fielding, Johnson, and others, the Opposition writers had become ossified into stereotyped repetition. Ministerial hints that action might be taken against the excessive license allowed to the scurrilous press raised a clamor defending liberty of the press—reports of Peter Zenger's trial in New York even appeared.[15] But that the Opposition press was beginning to evoke a certain *ennui* even among those favorably disposed was evident. The barometer of the age, the *Gentleman's Magazine*, printed in January 1739 an article entitled "Reflections on Periodical Writers." While emphasizing the importance of political writing, the reflector denounced mercenary writers as "abandon'd prostitutes of the Pen." While it was certainly a duty to warn against any encroachment on liberty, the writer noticed that from one set of political commentators the reader could expect a weekly satire, from another, a daily panegyric. Although there was likely to be a bit more truth in the first than in the second, the author was clearly skeptical of those who depicted any human being as wholly good or entirely evil. Clearly the periodical writers' inspiration had dried up and so the *Gentleman's Magazine* was justified in not republishing their endlessly repetitive essays.[16] The author of these "Reflections" may well have been Samuel Johnson, who was by now working for Cave on the *Gentleman's Magazine*. That publication was reporting parliamentary debates thinly disguised as occurring in "Magna Lilliputia," which, according to Captain Gulliver's grandson, had a constitution once similar to the mixed constitution of Britain, but which is now somewhat corrupted. The introduction to these debates, which appeared in June 1738, was also written by Johnson; and he wrote many of the speeches (especially those published from July 1741 to March 1744).[17]

At the beginning of 1739 Sir Robert Walpole and his Ministry seemed firmly seated in power. The Opposition in parliament, despite the existence of Cobham's cubs, the young adherents of the Prince, hardly seemed formidable; the theatre was licensed and thus controlled; the Opposition press was moribund; and one may even detect the beginnings of a skeptical disillusion, as exhibited in the critical strictures of the *Gentleman's Magazine* on periodical writers, with at least the more enthusiastic party effusions.

However, in politics a few weeks is a long time. By April the Opposition had mounted a new campaign against the government. It was directed against the Convention with Spain, which they alleged sacrificed British honor and commercial interests. By November Walpole's attempt to find a peaceful solution to the conflict with Spain had collapsed and Britain was at war. The

Opposition had now the advantage of having advocated British honor and interests against the insults of Spain and also the advantages of being able to criticize the Ministry's war measures. Walpole was accused of having no intention of using the increased armed forces for fighting—they were merely for increasing the places at his disposal for corrupting members of Parliament.[18] The Opposition was greatly encouraged when in 1740 that old standby, a place bill, was defeated by only 16 votes, 222-206.[19]

In the press as well as in Parliament, the campaign against Walpole was pursued with renewed vigor. *Are these Things So?* exploited Alexander Pope's known anti-ministerial position to present the "Englishman in his grotto," an independent, liberty-loving poet, confronting the "Great Man at Court" with some hard questions: did "*Gaul* or *Spain*" now "*limit* out her [Britain's] *Sea?*"; what had been done with the millions voted in taxes?; had a brave admiral [Vernon] been curbed?; was the Great Man sole cause of Britain's internal corruption and external shame? The question was pursued and a number of different answers given in a flurry of pamphlets.[20]

Moreover the periodical press had revived as well. Henry Fielding had joined James Ralph in writing *The Champion*. In its early days the paper was not as devoted to political subjects as it was later to become; nevertheless, in it Fielding, as Hercules Vinegar, scorned the *Gazeteer*, discussed the art of political fishing, castigated the prime minister, and even found space for a short examination of the names Robert, Robin, and Bob—names somewhat connected with thievery.[21] Even the established papers found some new things to say. It is during the years of Walpole's decline that there is a first glimpse of the possiblities of a campaign for parliamentary reform not limited to the hackneyed program of eliminating placemen and holding annual parliaments. There are several inklings of John Brewer's "alternative structure of politics."[22] *Common Sense* was prepared to support the right of the people to complain about the actions of their representatives. (The opposition sought to stimulate public pressure on members of Parliament while the Ministry defended its actions by instancing the support of independent, substantial M.P.s. For the Opposition, of course, any member

voting with the Ministry had to be suspected of having been se-
duced by place or pension, actual or prospective.) Although
Common Sense admitted that ministers needed influence in order
to be able to carry on public business, the paper denied that the
people had entirely delegated their power to their representatives. To support this contention, it quoted extensively from
Richard Overton's *A Remonstrance of Many Thousand Citizens*,
which reminded parliament men that their power had been entrusted to them by the people to use for the people's good and
their freedom: "We are your principals, and you our agents."[23]

By 1740, the opposition newspapers were defending the
right of constituents to instruct members of Parliament, another
issue that was to be important later. Moreover, the problem of
the right relation of representatives to the represented could
prompt some rather radical sentiments:

> When Trade and Manufactures sink in any Town, the Peo-
> ple leave it of Course, and the Right of Electing does not
> follow the People. Several *Cornish* and *Wiltshire* Boroughs,
> quite deserted, send two Members each to Parliament: while
> one of these Towns, it is said, values itself on being a Bor-
> ough, *Birmingham, Leeds, Wakefield*, and other large Towns
> don't send one. A Member for the county of *York* represents
> ten thousand Free-holders; yet his vote counts for no more
> than that of a Man who represents twenty (I won't say Ex-
> cise men, or Custom-house officers, but) poor Labourers. If
> the People were more equally represented, perhaps there
> would be no Occasion for a Place Bill.[24]

Thus in 1740-41, with an eye on the approaching elections,
the Opposition mounted a campaign in Parliament along with
the campaign of instructions and anti-ministerial propaganda
outside it. Although the staple of this campaign was the traditional place bill, the Opposition, aided by the fact that the war
was going badly, found much to criticize in the Ministry's prosecution of the war, in its arrangements for enlarging the army,
and its proposal of a register of seamen. The debate on the latter
was written up by Johnson for the *Gentleman's Magazine* (appearing somewhat after the event, mainly in 1741).[25] If his report
has any foundation in fact, tempers were short. The bill, the Opposition alleged, would make slaves of anyone who might be

classified as a sailor—a theme which lent itself to rhetoric about English liberty. It is the first debate in which Pitt is reported to have taken a prominent part, typically in defense of the rights of Englishmen.[26]

The campaign was carried forward from December to February in the Lords by a series of motions requesting papers relating to the conduct of the war and by protests when these motions were defeated. The climax of the campagin came on 13 February when motions were tabled in both houses asking for an address to the King "to remove the Right Honourable Sir Robert Walpole . . . from His Majesty's Presence and Councils for ever." "The Motion" so startled the *Gentleman's Magazine* that a short account found its way into the February issue (rather than having to wait, as was usual, for later publication).[27] Significant minor anomalies highlight the political importance of "the Motion": the report of the debate in the House of Lords was given fairly soon (from May to August), but the debate having begun in the Parliament of Great Britain is unaccountably shifted to the Senate of Lilliput; moreover, it is only after this that the Prime Minister, always previously referred to by that title, is given a proper name, variously Sir Rub. Walelup or Walelop.

But instead of destroying Walpole, the vote, in both Houses, shattered the Opposition. In the Commons, the Motion was lost by 290-106. The *Gentleman's Magazine* duly named those who unaccountably voted against "a late motion" and those who were "sneakers," that is, had absented themselves to avoid voting.[28] The reasons for this massive defeat were various. Clearly many Opposition members feared that they would be destroying Walpole for the benefit of Pulteney and Carteret, neither of whom was greatly liked. The Motion and the debate turned on the accusations against Walpole personally, accusations which were not proved; ministerial speakers argued that they were punishing a man against whom no crime had been proved. Perhaps too, the Motion was regarded as encroaching upon the Kings's prerogative to choose his servants; obviously 1741 is too early for a justfication for "storming the closet."

Walpole eventually went a year later; the worsening of Britain's position in the war and somewhat unfavorable results in the elections resulted in the deterioration of his support in the Commons. His going did not introduce the millennium, but a rather unseemly scramble from which there emerged a revised Whig administration—one lacking Walpole but one retaining his followers—to which were added Pulteney, Carteret and other dissident Whigs, some of the Prince's patriots and a very few Tories. To those left behind, what had happened was clearly a "sell-out," or in the language of the time, a desertion. And John Lord Perceval's *Faction Detected* was the clever, but cynical justification of the deserters. Perceval argued that principles are rarely if ever held by an opposition—the motives are usually personal and extreme oppositions are always dangerous. But Whig oppositions are less dangerous than Tory oppositions, which are basically Jacobite and so treasonous factions. The last opposition was a Whig opposition joined by a Tory faction—it would have been disastrous to allow the Tories to force their way into power, and the separation from them—called by some a desertion or betrayal—was entirely correct.[29] Perceval goes out of his way to denigrate the present Opposition. "Broad-bottomed" in figure and in policy, they mean to force the Tories in. Moreover there is no need to worry about corruption or influence, for power follows property; the property of the people had been increasing; therefore, if the balance of the constitution is to be maintained, the influence at the disposal of the crown must also increase.[30]

Thus, on Perceval's account, it is always justifiable for dissident Whigs to oppose, and it is also always justifiable for them to desert, to abandon their allies in opposition in order to accept a call to office. The Tories cannot be legitimate as a party; individual Tories many repent (and so become Whigs).

Walpole's resignation did not revolutionize the politics of Hanoverian Britain. Realignments occurred, but the Walpolian system remained to be administered by Walpole's chosen successor Henry Pelham and his half brother Thomas Pelham-Holles, Duke of Newcastle. But the events of Walpole's decline and fall did have an effect. These events—the Opposition campaign of 1739-41, the debacle of "the Motion" in February '41, Walpole's resignation in February '42 and the resulting maneuvering which led to the ministry so cynically justified in *Faction Detected*—all contributed to establishing more skeptical, more disillusioned views of politics than had previously prevailed. This is not to say that any one of these events caused the development, nor even that all of them cumulatively caused it. Each of these events encouraged such views and anyone tempted to a skeptical disillusioned view by any of these events would have found no reasons in the succeeding events to think he had been mistaken.

To support this hypothesis there are several prominent examples. First, there is Henry Fielding, whom we have already noticed writing Oppositon propaganda. But in 1741 Fielding withdrew from *The Champion*. Moreover late in December 1741 there appeared *The Opposition: A Vision*.[31] In it the Opposition is depicted as a contentious, faction-ridden rabble in a wagon; they are so little unified, they even sit back to back as well as disagree about which way to go. Their great trunk of grievances contains only a few newspapers, on one is "the word champion, and on another was the word __onsense, the letter N being, I suppose folded down" (an acerbic jest on *Common Sense*). In the box marked "Public Spirit," everyone's private goods are carried. Two of the asses pulling this unpleasant assortment are called Vinegar and Ralph. The motly crew is put to rout by a fat, pleasant gentleman in a coach and six, for one of the asses objects to being driven and some passengers refuse to drag the gentleman out of his coach. The asses are turned out to graze; the Opposition wagon remains in the mire; the coach pursues the high road to the country.

Hercules Vinegar had rounded on his former allies in a bitter attack. *The Opposition: A Vision* took its imagery from the Government's "Motion" prints; it exhibited Walpole (the fat gentleman in the coach), triumphing over a petty, personally vindictive, divided, self-seeking, morally and intellectually despicable crew. But Fielding's subsequent conduct makes it unlikely that he had simply changed sides. He did not follow *The Opposition* with other works supporting the Ministry but he did subsequently publish works which reiterated his former views and repeated his attack on Walpole. The most notable example is *Jonathan Wild*, originally published in 1743 in Volume Three of the *Miscellanies*. In *Jonathan Wild*, Fielding exploits the clichés of anti-Walpolism vividly, cleverly, amusingly, and remorselessly. For Wild is a Great Man, and his greatness is prime ministerial; all his friendships are based firmly on interest—that is, his own advantage. He never foolishly benefits anyone for any other motive; he controls his passions, never being carried away into uncalculating malice, never even doing more mischief than is necessary for his purpose.[32]

To make sense of Fielding's have written *The Opposition: A Vision* and subsequently publishing *Jonathan Wild*, it is not necessary to postulate the author's having been converted to Walpole's side and then reconverted to the Opposition—an apostasy followed by a return to faith. In Fielding's writings during this period there is evidence that he became disillusioned; he ceased to believe in the Opposition without adopting a faith in Walpole. *Joseph Andrews*, published in 1742, contains a number of anti-ministerial strokes: the sly reference to *"Prime Ministering"* as a trade with its own "Mysteries or Secrets"; Parson Adam's approval of the anti-government opinions of a blustering Patriot and his own Country party politics; the alehouse-keeper's strictures on *Gazeteers*, put into the mouth of a character who testifies to having personally suffered the indignities to British shipping complained of by the Opposition; and, of course Beau Didapper, who "Tho' he was born to an immense Fortune, he chose, for the pitiful and dirty Consideration of Place of little consequence, to depend entirely on the Will of a Fellow, who they call a Great-Man".[33]

But *Joseph Andrews* also attacks the Opposition: the blustering Patriot who rails against the cowardly ministerial army is himself discovered to be a coward.[34] Parson Adams's attempt to back a suitable Country candidate have been unsuccessful. Esquire Fickle proved not to be the supporter of the Church he claimed to be; what is more, he accepted a place and solicited Adams's support for his former rival, Colonel Courtly. Sir Oliver Hearty, while he was alive, was "a worthy Man" and befriended Adams, but being addicted to hunting, "in Five years together, he went but twice up to Parliament; and one of those Times, I have been told, never was within sight of the House." The incumbent, Sir Thomas Booby, does speak in the House but cannot persuade it. Thus the Opposition, in Adams's experience, includes deserters, absentees, and some good, but powerless, members.[35] A further slight upon the Opposition was added for the second edition, which appeared in June 1742 almost four months after the original publication. Adams, disregarding the cowardly Patriot, succeeds in rescuing Fanny from an assailant. The night being dark and Adams silent, Fanny "began to fear as great an Enemy in her Deliverer, as he had delivered her from; and as she had not Light enough to discover the Age of *Adams* and the Benevolence visible in his Countenance, she suspected he had used her as some very honest Men have used their Country; and had rescued her out of the hands of one Rifler, in order to rifle her himself."[36]

The evidence of *Joseph Andrews* indicates that Fielding had lost faith in the Opposition without becoming a believer in Walpole. And there are even a few indications of Fielding's disillusion in *Jonathan Wild*. The Great Man's address to his assembled gang in favor of concord between those of different principles, i.e., those who wear their hats fiercely cocked and those who prefer trencher hats, calls upon all wearers of hats, i.e., men of different party principles, to unite in their depredations on the public while maintaining the outward show of distinctions among them. Later, Wild, whose greatness usually makes him an analogue of Walpole, appears in Newgate as leader of the Opposition. He forms a party and persuades the inmates to depose their chief on the grounds that he is "in Reality undermining the Liberties of Newgate." Elected the new leader, Wild soon appears in the finery which he had attacked his predecessor for wearing.[37] One must, it seems, suspect those loudest in denouncing the corruption of existing ministers of desiring merely to acquire their positions and perquisites.

Yet, however disillusioned and skeptical he may have become about both Ministry and Opposition, Fielding still clung to some of his political principles—for only by doing so could he condemn their actions. In Newgate "a very grave man" points out that there is no advantage in overthrowing one wolf, or great man, to replace him with another. This does not mean that one should tamely submit to the existing plunderer; rather "it is better to shake the plunder off than to exchange the plunderer." Further, the plundered sheep are to ally themselves, considering all "as members of one community, to the public good of which we are to sacrifice our private views."[38] Instead of pursuing their private interests, men must adhere to the public good, but Fielding had lost faith in existing politicians adhering to that principle.

Another skeptical onlooker of Walpole's decline and fall was Samuel Johnson. One might infer a disillusioned detachment from politics on Johnson's part during these years from his failure to continue to write Opposition poems and pamphlets such as he had produced in 1737-39. Johnson's position is also indicated by his extensive treatment of the debate on the motion for Walpole's removal. Although the debate in the Lords was written up almost immediately, the debate in the Commons did not appear in the *Gentleman's Magazine* until February, March, and April, 1743. By then Walpole had been Earl of Orford for a year, and the debate could be reconstructed in the knowledge of what had happened since. But Johnson seems to have lost the passionate conviction of *Marmor Norfolciense* and the *Compleat Vindication*. Walpole is thoroughly castigated by the Opposition. Sandys, moving the Motion, exhibits Britain as in a state of corruption, subject to the insults of enemies and unassisted by allies. His review of British foreign policy indicts Walpole for having abandoned Britain's traditional alliance with the emperor and pursued the delusion of a French alliance, which has had the effect of aggrandizing her greatest enemy. At home Walpole has attempted to create a standing army; the policy assumes that the people are so hostile that they might prefer the Pretender. Furthermore, he has undermined the constitution by establishing a system of corruption and dependence.[39] Both Pitt and Pulteney speak for the Motion. Pulteney alleges that Walpole "has long enjoyed all that Power and Influence with which the Prime Viziers of arbitrary Monarchs are invested, and exerted them with the same Licensciousness," that he has engrossed places, riches, and honors, transferring them at his pleasure, and especially to his own family. He has used this wealth to create palaces with gardens and foundations where both soil and water were lacking (the notorious situation of Houghton).[40]

Instead of the detailed defense of his actions, especially in foreign policy, actually made by the Prime Minister, Johnson put into his mouth a brief and dignified rebuttal, "a plain unstudy'd Defence." It agrees in only a few points with other accounts of what Walpole said; he seems to have denied that he committed any crime, or has even been accused of any, that he had any sole power, asserting that he always acted with others in council and that these decisions were approved in Parliament. But Johnson also has him deny that the advancement of his family is a crime, reject the accusation that he is rapacious or avaricious—all he has is the places he is known to possess and a "little House at a small Distance from this City, worth about seven hundred [pounds], which I obtained that I might enjoy the Quiet of Retirement, without remitting my attendance on my Office." He alludes, touchingly, to his decoration, the Order of the Garter, and concludes:

> Having now, Sir, with due Submission offered my Defence, I shall wait the Decision of the House without any other Solicitude than for the Honour of their Counsels, which cannot but be impaired if Passion should precipitate, or Interest pervert them. For my Part, that Innocence which has supported me against the Clamour of Opposition, will establish my Happiness in Obscurity, nor shall I lose by the Censure which is now threatened any other Pleasure than that of serving my Country.[41]

Johnson's report of Walpole's speech differs substantially from what others reported Walpole as having said. For example, in Richard Chandler's report, Walpole ends his speech by appealing to the Constitution: removing a minister without alleging a particular crime is an encroachment on the prerogative of the Crown.[42] This is an appeal consistent with the conventions of the mid-eighteenth-century constitution.

The improving of Walpole's vindication indicates that during the years of Walpole's decline and fall Johnson lost some of his former Country party enthusiasm. This conclusion is strengthened by several other bits of evidence. One of them is evidence of omission: he wrote no more political tracts until 1756. Second, he added at the end of the debate on the Motion a succinct account of the Tory justification for their not voting against Walpole: they had acted in accordance with long-held principles; the proposal was unprecedented; the attainder of Strafford, the bill against Clarendon, and the imprisonment of Oxford were

similarly wrong; no one should be punished without being con-
victed of a crime; and the deprivation of employments and the
incapacity to be employed were a punishment and public mark
of ignominy.[43] Third, in the Preface to the 1743 issue of the *Gentleman's Magazine*, Johnson tells us:

> It has been for many Years lamented, by those who are most
> eminent among us for their Understanding and Politeness,
> that the Struggles of opposite Parties have engrossed the
> Attention of the Publick, and that all Subjects of Conversa-
> tion, and all kinds of Learning have given way to Politicks.
>
> Though under a Form of Government like ours, which
> makes almost every Man a secondary Legislator, Politicks
> may justly claim a more general attention than where Peo-
> ple have no other Duty to practice than Obedience, and
> where to examine the Conduct of their Superiors, would be
> to disturb their own Quiet without Advantage, yet it must
> be owned, that Life requires many other Considerations, and
> that Politicks may be said to Usurp the Mind when they leave
> no Room for any other Subject.[44]

The view that politics, public affairs, can usurp a citizen's attention is only possible for someone who has already withdrawn
from political partisanship.

That Fielding and Johnson were not peculiar in withdrawing from Country party enthusiasm and adopting a skeptical,
disillusioned attitude is evidenced by the reception accorded to
the contributions of a man well known for his detached, disillusioned skepticism and his advocacy of moderation in politics,
David Hume. The first edition of the first volume of his *Essays,
Moral and Political* appeared in Edinburgh in June or July 1741.[45]
Hume must have composed these essays during the period in
which the Opposition campaign against Walpole reached its
peak. In them, he attempted a cool analysis of issues which were
being hotly debated between the Ministry and the Opposition.
In "That Politics may be reduced to a Science," he declared himself "a friend of moderation," although he was not so moderate
as to regard all forms of government as equally good since he
held that settled rules and procedures were valuable. This was
"a sufficient inducement to maintain, with the utmost zeal, in every free state, those forms and institutions by which liberty is

secured, the public good consulted, and the avarice or ambition of particular men restrained and punished," but there were enough zealots fomenting faction. He wished to promote moderation, the best way being to promote zeal for the public, for the partisans on both sides were too extreme: if the Opposition's view of the splendors of Britain's mixed constitution was correct, they could hardly justify their passionate conviction that Walpole had been undermining it for twenty years. The constitution must be a very faulty one if it allows such a bad minister as he allegedly is to hold power despite their opposition. Similarly inappropriate are the immoderate panegyrics of the ministerial party. No change of ministry could be so dreadful or as harmful as they assert.[46]

In the *Essays*, Hume frequently attemps a fresh analysis of recent issues. In "Of the Liberty of the Press," he argues that liberty is extraordinarily great in Britain, but does little harm since it is essential to maintaining the republican aspects of the British constitution against the monarchical ones—"all the learning, wit and genius of the nation" may thus be employed to defend liberty. Since general laws against sedition and libel are as strong as they may be, the only further restraints possible would be discretionary punishments or prior censorship, "such a barefaced violation of liberty, that they will probably be the last efforts of a despotic government." Paradoxically, what the Opposition presented as a danger to Britain's free constitution was only possible if that constitution were already destroyed. Liberty of the press, though valuable, was in little danger.[47] Hume partly admitted the Court argument that some influence (which the Opposition called corruption) in the form of the disposal of places, but not bribery, was necessary to make British mixed government work. The Opposition, he suggested, had argued too rigidly against this, yet the essay ends by suggesting that some monarchs or ministers may be objectionable by having too much influence.[48]

Skepticism pervades Hume's views on party. He believed that parties from interest, a court party and a country party, are endemic to a government like the British government. What is more, in their origins and their original principles the Tories were naturally a court party, the Whigs a country party. Denying that Bolingbroke is correct in his view that since the Revolution Whigs and Tories are no more, Hume followed the ministerial line in asserting that there are Tories and that they do retain some loyalty to the House of Stuart. And yet these Tories do not, it seems, form a substantial part of the Opposition at Westminster where the enemies of the minister call the courtiers the true Tories and themselves Old Whigs. Indeed the Tories "have been so long obliged to talk in the republican style, that they seem to have made converts of themselves by their hypocrisy, and embraced the sentiments [i.e., in favor of liberty] as well as language of their adversaries."[49]

Hume's *Essays, Moral and Political* took up the issues which excited partisan animosity during 1739-41, and they discuss these issues in terms which are recognizably related to the prevailing ideology of the period. Hume considered the causes of the establishment and decline of liberty, prosperity, and the arts and sciences; he re-examined Machiavelli's views about monarchy; he commended Bolingbroke, Lyttelton, and Marchmont while he condemned the Ministry's hired pens.[50] On these issues, Hume claimed to be presenting a philosophic, detached, public-spirited, and moderate point of view. Nevertheless, his views were not seen as impartial—equally favorable to both parties or indifferent between them, for the manner of their publication undermined the claim of impartiality.

Hume's *Essays* appear initially in Edinburgh in June-July 1741. But notice of their publication in England first occurred in February-March 1742.[51] By then two of the essays were known to the public. On 10 October 1741 in the *Craftsman*, No. 747, there appeared an essay entitled "Whether the British Government inclines more to Absolute Monarchy, or to a Republic." The essay reflects the eighteenth-century civic humanist preoccupation with the tendency of governments, even free governments with mixed constitutions, to degenerate into absolutism or anarchy. Referring to Harrington's maxim that power follows property, Hume argued that wealth concentrated in one man's hands was more efficacious than if it were diffused. Having outlined an Opposition case against increased wealth (and therefore power to corrupt) in the hands of the Ministry, and a counter argument, Hume concluded that the power of the crown was on the increase—although very slowly. The long-term prospects—as to how Britain might terminate—were either a tumultuous republic followed by absolute monarchy or a peaceably established absolute monarchy, "the true *Euthanasia* of the British constitution." From this Hume said he drew a lesson of moderation—the danger of a republic being more terrible, the danger of monarchy more imminent. No doubt the *Craftsman* and its readers could equally conclude that it was advisable and justifiable to struggle against the imminent danger.⁵² The essay was reprinted in the *Gentleman's Magazine* for October 1741 with a commendatory note: "The above judicious Essay is given without alteration or Abridgement."

The second volume of Hume's *Essays* appeared in Edinburgh in January 1742. In it was "A Character of Sir Robert Walpole." Again, Hume claimed impartiality; he admitted that Walpole had ability, but not genius, that he was "good-natured, not virtuous." He had some virtues, but he would have been more "worthy of his high station, had he never possessed it; and is better qualified for the second than for the first place in any government." He was moderate in exercising power but not equitable in engrossing it. With the Opposition, Hume thought Walpole's ministry had benefited his family more than the public.

> During his time trade has flourished, liberty declined, and learning gone to ruin. As I am a man I love him; as I am a scholar, I hate him; as I am a *Briton*, I calmly wish his fall. And were I a member of either House, I would give my vote for removing him from St. James's; but should be glad to see him retire to *Houghton-Hall*, to pass the remainder of his days in ease and pleasure.

Hume's impartiality, it seems, would not have prevented him from voting with the Opposition for the motion to remove Walpole; he would not have been either on the ministerial side or a Tory sneaker.⁵³

The "Character of Sir R —— W ——" was widely reprinted; it appeared in the *Scots Magazine*, the *London Magazine* and the *Gentleman's Magazine* in March 1742. The *Gentleman's Magazine* introduced it as follows: *The following Character, taken from a Vol-*

ume of Essays lately published at Edinburgh, *was inserted in most of the News-papers of* Great Britain," but found it wanting in clearness and consistency. Like the *Scots Magazine*, it included a list of queries from the *Newcastle Journal* of 13 February 1742. Hume may have answered these queries, for the author's answers were never denied by him. Among the aspects in which liberty had declined are mentioned the increased of the civil list, votes of credit and too large a standing army, all of which concerned Hume.[54]

In these two instances at least, Hume's views, however moderate, were favorable to the Opposition. They were widely distributed and favorably received. The *Essays* as a whole were more skeptical and detached than the "Character" and the "British Government"; some of the views expressed in the other essays were more favorable to the Ministry. Indeed, in the "Advertisement" prefixed to the second volume (published January 1742) Hume confessed that he was now inclined to think more favorably of Walpole when "he seems to be upon the Decline." Nonetheless the true Hume, skeptical, detached from party zeal, and moderate, had a considerable literary success. In a letter to Henry Home dated 13 June 1742, he reports that "The Essays are all sold in London; as I am inform'd by two Letters from English Gentlemen of my Acquaintance. There is a Demand for them; & as one of them tells me, Innys the great Bookseller in Paul's Church Yard wonders there is not a new Edition, for that he cannot find Copies for his Customers."[55] When editions of Hume sell out in a few months then one is inclined to believe that skepticism is sweeping the country.

The nature of party in a mixed constitution was not a subject exclusive to Hume. In 1743 Edward Spelman published *A Fragment out of the Sixth Book of Polybius* in which the Polybian theory of the mixed constitution was applied to England. In his preface he put forward the view that "in all free governments there ever were and will be Parties," for parties "are not only the Effect but the Support of Liberty."[56] Those in power will not be pleased, for the leaders of other parties "are properly their Rivals." The followers may aim at reforming an abuse of power, but the leaders will aim "at the Power it self, without considering the Abuse, unless it be to continue it." Thus the followers are concerned about measures, but the leaders about men and places (Hume also had pointed out that party leaders were motivated by interest). Spelman regarded this situation as beneficial, since the opposers would scrutinize the actions of the ministers, motivated by their "Thirst of Power." Each party would appeal to the people to judge, and thus the whole apparatus would arrange itself to produce ease, plenty, and security for millions.[57] Spelman, like Hume, seems more concerned with a detached understanding of the British constitution than with contributing to party strife.

Nevertheless, political controversy did not disappear once Walpole had fallen, nor did the millennium arrive. A reorganized Opposition, including some former champions such as James Ralph, continued the struggle for virtue and liberty. But the party battles surrounding Walpole's decline and fall had irreversible effects on political thought in eighteenth-century Britain. The ideological consequences of Walpole's decline and fall were first, disillusionment—some of those who had been true patriots of the Country party lost their faith; second, cynicism—especially with regard to the motives of those who might aspire for office (note that Pulteney was trapped by his previous disclaimers of ambition just as Pitt later was); and third, skepticism—both about the doctrines of the country ideology and about the possibility of a virtuous, patriotic government doing away with influence or "corruption." As a result, there was a new acceptance of party in the context of a new examination of the British constitution and of politics, most notably by Spelman and by Hume. And, at least in Hume's case, this examination was connected with the notion that ends of government are security and prosperity rather than virtue.

NOTES

1. Political aspects of the works of Pope, Swift, and Gay are discussed in Isaac Kramnick, *Bolingbroke and His Circle: The Politics of Nostalgia in the Age of Walpole* (Cambridge, Mass. Harvard University Press, 1968), esp. pp. 205-35; Maynard Mack, *The Garden and the City: Retirement and Politics in the Later Poetry of Pope, 1731-1743* (Toronto: University of Toronto Press, 1969), pp. 116-87, 274-78; C. H. Firth, "The Political Significance of Gulliver's

Travels," *Proceedings of the British Academy, 9* (1920), 237-59.

Mack, *The Garden and the City,* reproduces and discusses some of the Opposition prints and caricatures as well as some anti-Walpole popular ballads. Further information on prints as a form of opposition propaganda can be gleaned from H. M. Atherton, *Political Prints in the Age of Hogarth* (Oxford: Clarendon Press, 1972); see pp. 69-71 for a discussion of some anti-Walpole prints of 1731 and the government's prosecution of William Rayner for them. For ballads, see *Political Ballads Illustrating the Administration of Sir Robert Walpole,* ed. Milton Percival (Oxford: Clarendon Press, 1961).

Another artistic form that might involve the symbolic expression of Opposition ideology was the garden; for example, Lord Cobham's garden at Stowe had a Temple of British Worthies (1733) and a "gothic" Temple of Liberty; see J. Burke, *English Art, 1714-1800* (Oxford: Clarendon Press, 1976), pp. 53 ff.

2. H. T. Dickinson, *Bolingbroke* (London: Constable, 1970), pp. 212-46.

3. Quentin Skinner has exhibited Bolingbroke's exploitation of this ideology to legitimize opposition in "The Principles and Practice of Opposition: The Case of Bolingbroke versus Walpole," *Historical Perspectives: Studies in English Thought and Society in Honour of J. H. Plumb,* ed. N. McKendrick (London: Europa, 1974), pp. 93-128.

See also Caroline Robbins, *The Eighteenth-Century Commonwealthman* (Cambridge, Mass.: Harvard University Press, 1959); J. G. A. Pocock, *The Machiavellian Moment* (Princeton: Princeton University Press, 1975), pp. 401-505, and "Machiavelli, Harrington and English Political Ideologies in the Eighteenth Century," in *Politics, Language and Time* (New York: Atheneum, 1971); Kramnick, pp. 56-83, 137-87; and Dickinson, pp. 184-211.

4. See, for example, *A Dissertation upon Parties* (London, 1735), esp. Letter I (p. 5): "The Bulk of *both Parties* are really united; on Principles of Liberty, in Opposition to an oscure Remnant of *one Party,* who disown those Principles, and a mercenary Detachment from the *other,* who betray them"; earlier (pp. 1-2) it is suggested that the ministry operates by fomenting illusionary divisions and by corruption; Letter XIX (p. 239), " and nothing can be more ridiculous than to preserve the nominal Division of *Whig* and *Tory Parties,* which subsisted before the *Revolution,* when the Difference of *Principles,* that could alone make the Distinction real, exists no longer; so nothing can be more reasonable than to admit the nominal Division of *Constitutionalists* and *Anti-Constitutionalists,* or of a *Court* and a *Country Party,* at this Time, when an avow'd Difference of Principles makes this Distinction real."

5. The Government's arguments appear frequently in parliamentary debates during the '30s; see the reports in the *Gentleman's Magazine* and the *London Magazine.* Some excerpts from the Ministry's pamphlets and journals can be found in J. A. W. Gunn, *Factions No More: Attitudes to Party in Government and Opposition in Eighteenth-Century England* (London: F. Cass, 1971), pp. 11-32: see also the introduction, pp. 1-34. Walpolian positions are set out by Kramnick, pp. 111-36. The first four chapters of John Brewer's *Party Ideology and Popular Politics at the Accession of George III* (Cambridge: Cambridge University Press, 1976) provide a perceptive summary of the politics and political argument of the period.

It is interesting to note that Walpole's biographer, J. H. Plumb, asserts that Walpole not only used the Jacobite threat in debate but actually believed in it; see *Sir Robert Walpole: The King's Minister* (London: Cresset, 1960), esp. pp. 46, 147, 306. Plumb also notes the rifts in the Opposition, pp. 122-36, 139-54, 302-12.

A Jacobite threat was required by the ministerial Whigs in order to justify their monopoly of office and its emoluments (here I agree with Brewer, p. 46). Skinner's point, that to concentrate on Bolingbroke's sincerity ("Principles and Practice of Opposition," p. 94) mistakes the relation of political principles and practice, applies equally to Walpole.

6. Bolingbroke later asserted that "it was plain that some persons meant that the opposition should serve as *their* scaffolding, nothing else," quoted in Plumb, p. 310. Plumb notes that this suggestion appears in *Letters on the Spirit of Patriotism*; see *The Works of Lord Bolingbroke* (4 vols.; London, 1844), II, 363; see also Dickinson, pp. 247-76. Needless to say, Bolingbroke was not alone in his misgivings.

7. For some examples, see Gunn, pp. 95-109.

8. Thomas Gordon, Cato turned supporter of Walpole, uses this last ploy in his "Dedication to Sir Robert Walpole" to *The Works of Tacitus*, Vol. I (London, 1728).

    See also, for examples: *London Journal*, No. 979, 20 May 1738; the Debates on the Place Bill of 1740, Supplement to the *Gentleman's Magazine*, 1740; Walpole's speech on the Place Bill of 1740, *Parliamentary History*, XI, col. 363-66, quoted in Gunn, pp. 127-30.

9. The ode explicitly parodies the yearly effort of that ministerial poet, Colley Cibber. In the "Dedication to the Public" of the printed version, Fielding says that the ode proves, plainly, that the *Historical Register* is a ministerial pamphlet, for the uniqueness of the day (and according to his footnote, one may read "man" for "day") never seen before and never to be seen again "the present age are clearly obliged to the ministry," "Dedication," lines 79-93, in Henry Fielding, *The Historical Register for 1736* and *Eurydice Hissed*, ed. W. W. Appleton (London: Edward Arnold, 1967), p. 6. (For the other passages mentioned, see Act I, lines 157-61, 195-232; II, 130-271; III, 181-277, ibid., pp. 18, 20-21, 29-31, 46-49)

10. See, for example, *Eurydice Hissed*, lines 34-137, ibid., pp. 55-59.

11. *Historical Register*, "Dedication," lines 76-83, 105-25: ibid., pp. 6, 7.

    The parable adopts a typical Opposition pose of injured innocence: that the plays are actually directed against Walpole and the Ministry is presented as a bizarre fantasy of ministerial hack writers. A similar pretense about any parallel between the crimes of Wolsey, Gaveston, or Roman imperial tyrants and any contemporary rulers is typical of Opposition journals.

    I agree with Martin Battestin that in these plays "Walpole . . . suffered the burden of ridicule" but not that they "lampooned the corruption and duplicity of both parties," "Fielding's Changing Politics and *Joseph Andrews*," *Philological Quarterly*, 39 (1960), 40.

12. London, 1739.

13. See, for example, *The Reveur*, 10, 20 January 1738; reported in *Gentleman's Magazine*, VIII (1738), 38. Better-known contributions to the genre in-

clude Richard Glover, *Leonidas* (1737); James Thomson, *Liberty* (1735-36) and *Edward and Eleanor* (1739); David Mallet, *Mustapha* (1740) and, even earlier, John Gay, *Fables* (London, 1727, 1738, rpt. Menston, Yorks: Scolar Pess, 1973), pp. 1-3.

Bolingbroke's *The Idea of a Patriot King*, although first published in 1749, was written c. 1738. See also Dickinson, pp. 256-67.

14. See Samuel Johnson, *Poems*, Yale Edition of Johnson's *Works*, ed. E. L. McAdam, Jr., with George Milne (New Haven and London: Yale University Press, 1964), VI, 47-60 for "London." See also *Marmor Norfolciense* (April, 1739) and the *Compleat indication* (May, 1739).

Johnson's political views at this time are discussed by Donald J. Greene, *The Politics of Samuel Johnson* (New Haven: Yale University Press, 1960), pp. 81-108; see also James L. Clifford, *Young Samuel Johnson* (London: William Heinemann, 1955), esp. pp. 169-212.

15. For example, in the *Craftsman*, 21 January 1738, and reported in the *Gentleman's Magazine*, VIII (1738), 35.

16. *Gentleman's Magazine*, IX (1739), 3-7.

17. Greene, pp. 112-40. At this time Johnson held typically "Country party" views; if he was a Tory, he was similar in this to most Tories. Greene had to wrestle this relatively straightforward truth from obscurity—an obscurity caused by the identification of mid-eighteenth century Toryism with the seventeenth-century creed of divine right and passive obedience and thus Jacobitism. This identification was fostered by Walpole's propaganda machine, but it also attracted late eighteenth-century romanticizers like Boswell.

18. See, for example, the reports of parliamentary debates in the *Gentleman's Magazine* for August 1740 and December 1741.

19. For a full account of the political, especially parliamentary, activities of this period, see J. B. Owen, *The Rise of the Pelhams* (London: Methuen, 1957).

20. *Are these Things So?* (London, 1740), pp. 2-6. See also the introduction by Ian Gordon to the Augustan Reprint Society edition which includes *The Great Man's Answer*. For the controversy see Mack, pp. 194-200. See also Pope's *Epilogue to the Satires: The Year One Thousand Seven Hundred and Thirty Eight, passim*.

21. *The Champion*, 4 December 1739, 5 January 1740, 15 December 1739, 8 May 1740, and 7 June 1740, respectively.

22. The alternative politics which emerged in the 1760s was characterized by radical ideology, extra-parliamentary organization, and popular protest; see Brewer, esp. pp. 139-269.

23. *Common Sense*, No. 141, 13 October 1739, and reported in *Gentleman's Magazine*, IX (October 1739), quoting Richard Overton, *A Remstrance of Many Thousand Citizens* (London, 1646). The tract is reprinted on *Leveller Manifestoes*, ed D. M. Wolfe (London: T. Nelson, & Sons, 1944). The passages quoted are in Wolfe, pp. 113-17; some passages have been slightly changed in wording, and *Common Sense* omits particulars relating to 1646 and excises both some complaints about kingly tyranny and also Overton's objections to the powers of the House of Lords, especially their veto.

It is a strikingly radical quotation, and indeed, so far as I know, the only instance so far discovered of a direct link between eighteenth-century radicals and their seventeenth-century predecessors.

24. *Common Sense*, No. 3, 10 January 1741, reported in *Gentleman's Magazine*, January 1741.

25. See esp. October and November 1741.

26. Pitt, early in his political career, successfully presented himself as a "patriot." The opportunities and limitations Pitt faced as a consequence of his having adopted this role are explored by Brewer, pp. 96-111.

27. The account appears in the "Historical Chronicle" instead of in the parliamentary report from Lilliput; *Gentleman's Magazine*, XI (1741), 106.

28. *Gentleman's Magazine*, XI (1741), 232. See also Owen, pp. 1-40. "The Motion" lent itself to visual representation and resulted in a fusillade of caricatures; for examples, see Atherton, pp. 121-28, and D. George, *English Political Caricature* (2 vols.; Oxford: Clarendon Press, 1959), I, 89-91.

29. *Faction Detected* (London, 1743), pp. 3-16.

30. Ibid., pp. 41-46. Perceval denies that the desertion was any kind of betrayal or treason (p. 71) and asserts that it is too soon for there to be any new opposition based upon measures. The remnant of the opposition "formed themselves, for the present, under the title of the Broad-Bottoms; a Cant Word, which, corresponding equally with the Personal Figure of some of their Leaders, and the Nature of their Pretensions, was understood to imply, a Party united to force the Tories, into the Administration" (pp. 45-46).

31. In January 1741 Fielding published *Of True Greatness* and the *Vernoniad*. Both are Opposition pieces: the first is addressed to Bubb Doddington; the second praises Admiral Vernon, then an Opposition shibboleth. In April there appeared *The Crisis*, in time for the election, its title perhaps evoking Richard Steele's shade on the part of the Opposition and true Whig principles. Fielding attended a meeting of the partners in *The Champion* on 29 June 1741; he dated his break from June 1741. See Fielding's *Miscellanies*, ed. Henry Knight Miller (Wesleyan Edition; Oxford: Clarendon Press, 1972), I, 14. His partners, however, dated his withdrawal earlier. In reassigning his author's shares to James Ralph in March 1742 they justified this on the grounds that Fielding had "withdrawn himself . . . for above Twelve Months past." See G. M. Godden, *Henry Fielding: A Memoir* (London: Low, 1910), pp. 115-16, 138-39. *The Opposition: A Vision* was advertised in *The Champion* on 17 December 1741. It was acknowledged in *Miscellanies*," Preface" (Wesleyan edition), I, 15.

Fielding's situation and actions in 1741 are discussed by Martin C. Battestin, "Fielding's Changing Politics" pp. 39-44.

32. *The Life of Mr. Jonathan Wild The Great* in *The Complete Works of Henry Fielding, Esq.*, ed W. E. Henley (New York: Groscup, 1902-03), I, iv, v, xi, xiv; II, viii; III, xi; IV, xv, 14, 15-19, 34, 48, 79, 82, 130-32, 201-03.

33. *Joseph Andrews*, ed. Martin C. Battestin (Wesleyan Edition; Oxford: Clarendon Press, 1967), II, i, vii, viii, xvii; IV, ix, 89, 131-32, 132-35; 179, 182-83, 312-13.

34. Ibid., II, vii, ix, 131-32, 135-37.

35. Ibid., II, viii, 132-135.

36. Ibid., III, x, 140. *Joseph Andrews* was written mainly during the later half of 1741. It was in the press in January 1742 and was published 22 February. The second edition appeared on 10 June. See Martin C. Battestin's "General Introduction", ibid., pp. xxvii-xxxii. Fielding's politics are discussed, ibid., pp. xvii-xxi, and in "Fielding's Changing Politics," pp. 39-55. My account of the change in Fielding's politics agrees with Battestin's in most respects; it differs somewhat in interpreting the meaning of the change and assessing the evidence about Fielding's views. See also W. B. Coley, "Henry Fielding and the Two Walpoles," *P.Q* 45 (1966), 157-78, who suggests that Fielding's continued allegiance to part of the Opposition, Chesterfield and Lyttelton, was quite compatible with distrust of Pulteney and Carteret. But *The Champion* was not connected with Pulteney and Carteret; it and Fielding's co-author, James Ralph, were attached to Chesterfield and Lyttelton.

Was Fielding paid to change sides in 1741? If so, he was paid only for *The Opposition*, or not enough and not continuously.

Some indication of the complexity of Fielding's irony in his fictions can be found in J. Paul Hunter, *Occasional Form* (Baltimore and London: Johns Hopkins University Press, 1975).

37. *Jonathan Wild*, II, vi; IV, iii, 73-75, 152-57. Martin Battestin holds in "Fielding's Changing Politics," pp. 48-49 and n. 12, that the hypothesis that *Jonathan Wild* was begun in 1740 and revised in 1742 is sound. Certainly much of *Jonathan Wild* is consistent with its originating as a straightforward anti-Walpole satire. Both of the chapters mentioned above seem to qualify as later additions. See also the tales of Mrs. Heartfree's remarkable and Fanny-like series of deliverances, IV, vii-ix, xi, 165-81, 183-88: (1) from Jonathan Wild by the amorous captain of the French privateers; (2) from him by the bestial captain of the English man-of-war; (3) from him in turn by befuddling him with drink, whereupon the lieutenant puts her on a brig for Cork which is wrecked in a storm, after which she is protected by a gentleman (who turns out to be the count) who in turns attempts to seduce her; (4) from whom she is rescued by a French hermit, who is just about to succumb to her charms when (5) the sailors return to escort her to the nearby city, which she reaches unharmed despite their considering whether they should attempt her virtue; (6) once in the city she is propositioned by its ruler. She declines and is rewarded by this virtuous magistrate with a valuable jewel. Fielding here takes the "double rape" theme almost to absurdity; the moral seems to be that almost every rescuer is a prospective ravisher but that virtue is eventually rewarded.

38. Ibid., IV, iii, 155-56. See Battestin, "Fielding's Changing Politics," p. 53.

39. *Gentleman's Magazine*, XIII (March 1743), 59-74.

40. Ibid. (May 1743), 176-79.

41. Ibid., 179-81. See also Greene, *The Politics of Samuel Johnson*, pp. 125-33, for substantial quotation and discussion of this speech.

42. Richard Chandler, *History and Proceedings of the House of Commons from the Restoration to the Present Time* (London, 1742), XII, 114-21.

43. *Gentleman's Magazine*, XIII (May 1743), 181; see Greene, p. 130.

44. *Gentleman's Magazine*, XIII (1743), Preface; see Greene, p. 142.

45. *Essays, Moral and Political* (Edinburgh: Printed by R. Fleming and A. Alison for A. Kincaid . . ., 1741). In the *Caledonian Mercury* on 7, 13, and 16 July 1741 there appeared the following advertisement: "This Day is Published, Essays on various Subjects, viz. of the Delicacy of Taste and Passion . . . Printed for A. Kincaid a little above the Cross." (I owe this reference to the kindess of B. P. Hillyard, Assistant Keeper, Department of Printed Books, National Library of Scotland.) The June issue of the *Scots Magazine*, III (1741), 280, lists "Essays on various subjects 2s 6d." In view of the other advertisement it seems likely that this one announces the publication of Hume's *Essays* as well.

    This publication date has not been clearly established in the literature: E. C. Mossner, *The Life of David Hume* (Edinburgh: Nelson, 1954), pp. 138-39, says the *Essays* "were brought out at Edinburgh late in 1741" and unaccountably (and incorrectly) adds in a note that the title page is dated 1742. W. B. Todd in "David Hume. A Preliminary Bibliography," *Hume and the Enlightenment: Essays presented to Ernest Campbell Mossner*, ed. W. B. Todd (Edinburgh and Austin: University of Texas Press, 1974), p. 191, says, "Imprint date is apparently old-style. The book, seemingly disregarded in the Edinburgh newspapers, is first noticed at London on 25 February 1742 as there issued bound for 2s. 6d. and sold by J. and P. Knapton, C. Hitch and A. Millar, (*Daily Post*; also *Daily Advertiser*, 1 March, London Evening Post, 2—4 March)." Thus he also incorrectly puts the first issue of the book in 1742 by confusing the Edinburgh publication with its appearance in London. Duncan Forbes, *Hume's Philosophical Politics* (Cambridge: Cambridge University Press, 1975), p. 193, thinks the *Essays* were "published in the autumn of 1741."

46. For the sake of convenience I shall cite the most available edition although it is not a critical edition: *Essays: Moral, Political and Literary* (Oxford: Clarendon Press, 1963), pp. 13, 23-27.

47. *Essays* pp. 8-12.

48. "Of the Independency of Parliament," ibid., pp. 40-47. Corrupt influence was a frequent Opposition theme, 1739-41: it was one of the issues in the "Secession" of 1739; see the queries in the *Gentleman's Magazine*, IX (May 1739); *Common Sense*, 9 June 1739; *Common Sense*, 13 October 1739; and the discussions in the papers and in Parliament on the Place Bill of 1740.

49. "Of the Parties of Great Britain," *Essays*, pp. 63-74.

50. See, for example, *Essays*, pp. 19-22, 25, 42, 48-50, 93-97, 112-38.

51. In addition to the advertisements noted by Todd, quoted above in note 45, see *The Champion*, No. 360 (2 March 1742), which notes the publication of two volumes of *Essays, Moral and Political* for Knapton, Hitch, and Millar. They also appear in the lists of new books in both the *London Magazine* and the *Gentleman's Magazine* in March 1742; I have been able to find no announcement of the publication of Hume's *Essays* in any English periodical in 1741.

52. *Essays*, pp. 48-53. Duncan Forbes, *Hume's Philosophical Politics*, p. 221, noticing the *Craftsman's* reprinting, argues that "in fact Hume's own conclusion does not really support the opposition case." The point, of course, is that a principal Opposition paper thought that the essay did support that case.

It is worth noting that neither the *Craftsman* nor the *Gentleman's Magazine* mentioned any previous publication of this essay. Hume's letters for this period are sparse and he does not mention this incident. It is possible that he submitted the essay himself; after all, he orginally designed the essays as periodical contributions; see Mossner, *Life*, p. 138.

53. *Essays*, pp. 27-28. In 1748, Hume made the "Character" into a note and later dropped it entirely.

54. See Mossner, *Life*, pp. 143-44. Note that the previous publication in Edinburgh of the "Character" is explicity mentioned in contrast to the presentation of the "British Government." This suggests that neither volume of the *Essays* appeared in London until late February or March, 1742.

Forbes, *Hume's Philosophical Politics*, rightly emphasises the complexity of Hume's political thought. He contrasts Hume's views with "vulgar Whiggism" and presents a view of Hume in 1741-42 rather different from the one presented here; see esp. pp. 125-223. In establishing a contemporary context for Hume's thought, he turns principally to Bolingbroke and the *Craftsman*. Almost all of his illustrations and quotations come from the period before 1738. This bias tends to lead him to overlook Hume's (however moderate) anti-Walpolism and other aspects of the *Essays* specifically related to 1739-41. For example, Forbes never mentions that Hume asserts that he would vote for Walpole's removal. Again, when Hume identifies the Tory party as favoring alliance with France (*Essays*, p. 71), no contemporary reader would have supposed Hume to be referring to the existing Opposition which had been denouncing Walpole for allying Britain with France instead of maintaining the old alliance with Austria (cf. Forbes, pp. 193-94).

For other useful discussions of Hume's political views, see John B. Stewart, *The Moral and Political Philosophy of David Hume* (New York and London: Columbia University Press, 1963,) esp. pp. 196-255; James Moore, "Hume's Political Science and the Classical Republican Tradition," *Canadian Journal of Political Science*, 10 (1977), 809-39.

55. *New Letters of David Hume*, ed. Raymond Klibansky and Ernest C. Mossner (Oxford: Clarendon Press, 1954), p. 10 (Letter 5).

56. Edward Spelman, *A Fragment out of the Sixth Book of Polybius* (London, 1743), pp. vii-viii. For a brief note with a few short extracts from this, see Peter Campbell, "An Early Defence of Party," *Political Studies*, 3 (1955), 166-67; see also J. A. W. Gunn, *Factions No More*, pp. 151-53.

57. Spelman, pp. vii-xxii.

American Independence
Revolution of the Republican Ideal
A Response to Pocock's Construction
of
"The Atlantic Republican Tradition"

JEFFREY BARNOUW

A PROVOCATIVE ARGUMENT about the convictions which motivated and triggered the American Revolution has been put
forward recently by J. G. A. Pocock in terms of what he calls the
"paradigm of republican virtue." In *The Machiavellian Moment* this
paradigm is traced from various classical sources through the
civic humanism of the Italian Renaissance and Machiavelli to
Harrington, and then by way of various writers whom he dubs
"neo-Harringtonian," including the first Earl of Shaftesbury,
Bolingbroke and the "Country" party generally, to the leaders
of the American Revolution. This latter span is said to constitute
the Atlantic Republican Tradition.

A prominent feature of Pocock's conception of republican
virtue—one crucial to his extension of this paradigm to the
American Revolution—is the fundamental opposition between
virtue and commerce, between the autonomy of the individual
and economic interdependence. The American Revolution, Pocock claims, was a manifestation of resistance to, or even flight
from, modernity and, specifically, early modern capitalism. The

colonists supposedly regarded the market economy, together with the sphere of finance and its involvement in political life, as inevitably leading to "corruption" of a sort that must destroy the polity and with it the possibility of individual integrity.

Given their (psychological) participation in Pocock's rigorist paradigm, the Colonists had to see the growth of commerce as a threat to their liberty, and it was this perception, and not the perception of threats to the liberty and growth of their commerce, that impelled them to revolution. Allegedly the Machiavellian assumptions which the paradigm contained were "self-actuating"; the Revolution was paradigmatically determined.

I propose to counter this interpretation of the conceptions that informed the American Revolution and their intellectual historical background by showing that the Atlantic Republican Tradition was rather characterized by Hobbesian features, above all, by emphasis on the founding of sovereignty and the role of self-interest in that foundation. After an initial outline of this contrary interpretation, I will analyze several links in Pocock's republican tradition, which means scrutinizing the way he constructs his paradigm and the continuity of its transmission.

I will concentrate on the rigoristic, Spartan and Stoic, aspects of his republicanism which are finally essential in its application to the American Revolution, which he construes as the result of paranoia following from the paradigm. I mean to show that his paradigm does not fit Harrington, his key link from Machiavelli to America, at all, and fundamentally distorts the motivation of the American Revolution.

1. "THE HOBBESIAN MOMENT" OF AMERICAN INDEPENDENCE

The American Revolution was a revolution not in the classical sense of a return to the first principles of its constitution, but as the deliberate constitution of a polity on fundamentally new principles. Independence was only negatively made possible by severing the political ties to the British Empire. The positive reality of national independence, which was seen as both a consequence and a guarantee of individual freedom, had to be secured by the establishment of political unity and autonomy, that is, sovereignty. It is for constituting of political sovereignty on a new basis that American independence was revolutionary in a perspective of world history.

This new foundation was a conviction of the independence of individual citizens which, although it had developed gradually through the course of Colonial American history and had been anticipated in theories and practices in classical Athens and seventeenth-century England, nevertheless constituted a break with the traditional conception of citizenship. This new sense of the freedom of the individual, which gave prominence to particular and private pursuits, under the heading "pursuit of happiness," should not be construed negatively, as if its implicit rejection of the classical ideal of citizenship that had been based on the subordination (not to say sacrifice) of personal to public welfare brought with it a withdrawal or alienation from civic life.

The liberal conception of political participation can be fully as active and positive as the classical republican conception precisely because it denies any necessary opposition between individual interests and the common good. The determination of what is good for the whole can only emerge from the critical interaction of particular pursuits. The establishing of sovereignty in the Revolutionary United States was both an instance and a lasting basis of such political engagement on the grounds of enlightened self-interest.

In the actual title of the document known as the *Declaration of Independence*, "The unanimous Declaration of the thirteen united States of America," "united" is not capitalized. That only emphasizes it the more for us, and should enable us to see that this was precisely a declaration of unity, from which the United States was to emerge. Its opening paragraph epitomizes this Hobbesian moment:

> When, in the course of human events, it becomes necessary for one people to dissolve the political bands which have connected them with another, and to assume among the powers of the earth the separate and equal station to which the Laws of Nature and Nature's God entitle them, a decent respect to the opinions of mankind requires that they should declare the causes which impel them to the separation.

The laws of nature are invoked here as the grounds of right for a people not only to dissolve political ties connecting them with another people, but also for them to claim a position "among the powers of the earth."

"Respect to the opinions of mankind requires" that they justify their action by detailing their grievances, which is done in the balance of the *Declaration*. No appeal is made directly to other "powers of the earth," though this was clearly one purpose of declaring independence. The appeal is rather to the "opinions of mankind" as a moral force exerting influence in the state of nature that prevails in the relations between nations. It is appealed to as a tribunal or witness, and as a source of that sense of right which vindicates the justice of this people's grievances and their positive claims.

This appeal thus refer back to the implicit argument of the opening words, that in the course of human events actions can become necessary from impelling causes, and further that such actions can be justified by their felt or acknowledged necessity. Prominent among the causes that the colonists saw as impelling them to separation and to the assertion of an independent national basis of authority were the threats to colonial commercial life. In his "Summary View of the Rights of British America," written in response to British retaliation after the Boston Tea Party, Jefferson invoked a "natural right" of the colonies to "the exercise of a free trade with all parts of the world,"[1] and the power to protect and further the nation's commercial interests was central to the idea of sovereignty asserted in the *Declaration*.

Here, in the act that constitutes a new nation politically, the right of self-preservation, which Hobbes saw as the basis of all natural right, is implicitly being invoked not at the level of individual survival or interests, but for that of the community and as grounds for national self-rule. The experience of necessitation can dissolve established political bands by showing that they do not secure social and economic life from the "state of nature." But this dissolution does not throw the people back into an atomistic anarchy; the same impelling necessity leads them, as a people, to assert their unanimity and claim the sovereignty that makes this unity a practical reality, a power.

Practical necessity in human events describes the locus of the rights of nature at their most basic level. The right of communities to self-preservation had been invoked by Henry Parker at the outset of the English Revolution, in 1642, as part of an argument that the sovereign's protection should serve "not only to shield us from all kind of evil, but to promote us also to all kind of political happiness."[2] *Salus populi suprema lex esto* was claimed as a principle governing the security of private pursuits and property interests which were postively connected to, or even cumulatively constitutive of, the public interest. This fundamental assumption or assertion was shared by Hobbes and by the Levellers.[3] A similar understanding of the laws of nature is invoked in the *Declaration of Independence* to justify a people's claim to national sovereignty.[4] It is the founding of sovereignty in the self-interest of each citizen that I would call "the Hobbesian moment" in the American Revolution.

In this first section various arguments for the pertinence of Hobbes to the American Revolution and the republicanism that emerged from it will be put forward, with regard both to his theory of civil order or sovereignty and to his psychology of appetitive man, which I take to be important to later trends of political and economic liberalism respectively. This should put us in a position to examine the rival claims of a very different perspective which construes the Revolution—indeed much of American history as a whole—in terms of a paradigm of republican virtue and a corresponding "Machiavellian moment."

In her article "Republicanism and Radicalism in the American Revolution: An Old-Fashioned Interpretation,"[5] Cecilia M. Kenyon persuasively defended the revolutionary character of the Revolution as consciously introducing "a new phase in the political evolution of mankind." For her the "radicalism"—as opposed to "conservatism"—of the Revolution has to do with "the rapid shift in opinion and belief" brought about by the decision for independence, which led Americans from an earlier conviction "that the ends of government—liberty, justice, happiness, and the public good—could be secured within the framework of monarchy," to an exclusive identification of good government and republicanism.

At the same time Americans were forced to determine exactly what they meant or might mean by "republic." The colonies had enjoyed a large degree of self-government before the Revolution. It was the redefinition of republicanism in terms of the continuation of this form of political life, projected on a national scale (which became a commitment to representative democracy), and the resultant association of republicanism with the American conceptions of individual independence and the right to pursue happiness, which, according to Kenyon, turned what could have remained a parochial affair of the British Empire "into a symbol for the liberation of mankind."

"Republicanism," she says, "was an integral part of the symbol, and both contributed to and drew strength from it." The other major factor was what she calls "the modified Lockeian ideals of the Declaration of Independence." By "modified" she means a "radicalization of the doctrine of the *Second Treatise*" that seems to reaffirm its Hobbesian origin. The state of nature, she argues, was a familiar concept in American Puritan thought before Locke's treatise and it retained a Hobbesian rather than Lockeian cast into the eighteenth century. This tended to blur the distinction between the state of nature and the civil state, so that the Hobbesian perspective came to be taken as describing "the innate selfishness of man and the consequently hostile competition of society in which men lived without the external restraint of law and government." This provided a prime argument for the necessity of law and government.

Because of their experience of relatively republican governments within the loose outer structure of the Empire and their experience of competitive economic life as a major factor in the social context of that quasi-self-rule, "the Americans had advanced far beyond the point where they could view the problems of liberty and its opposite *simply* in terms of the people against the government." They were aware of the positive connections between individual liberties or interests and a governmental authority based on or responsive to popular participation. Furthermore, they "emphasized the necessity of securing the rights derived from the state of nature" against even "majority oppression."

This sense of the rights of minorities and of the individual was closely connected with a different transformation of Locke expressed in the *Declaration*: the individualism and relativism

implicit in the right of a "pursuit of happiness." As contrasted
with the third term of Locke's then familiar triad, "life, liberty,
and property," the pursuit of happiness had egalitarian yet div-
ersitarian implications, whereas Locke's *Second Treatise* seems to
have intended the preservation of a *status quo* of property in land,
protecting possession and not opportunity. The pursuit of happiness pertained to that same social life determined by the
commercial economy with its striving and competition, and
tended to set it, where it was bounded by rule of law, in a more
favorable light. Kenyon continues, "without abandoning completely the concept of a common good or public interest or justice,
they tended to regard the purusit of self-interest as legitimate and
sought primarily to avoid an overwhelming concentration of
power behind a single interest."

Together with the so-called relativism of subjective judgment that was seen as inherent in the pursuit of happiness, this
individualism of self-interest "was not new in theory," she says.
"It was clearly explicit in the *Leviathan*, present though somewhat obscured in the *Second Treatise*, and had been an increasing
element in both colonial thought and practice." This element was
recognized for its importance to civic life in Madison's "Tenth
Federalist," which explicitly informs Kenyon's view of the Revolution.

There Madison confronts objections to the proposed Constitution that arise from fear of divisive interests and factions. He
rejects one classical response to this danger, according to which
"theoretic politicians . . . have erroneously supposed that by re-
ducing mankind to perfect equality in their political rights, they
would, at the same time, be perfectly equalized and assimilated
in their possessions, their opinions, and their passions." He, on
the contrary, has just shown that he considers the diversity of
passions and their interdependence with reason not only as inevitable in modern society, but also as a positive resource of the
stability of the state and as a positive value which the state is in-
stituted to preserve.

The idea of a public interest that could be consistently determined and maintained in opposition to the particular interests
of the citizens is treated as a chimera. The proliferation and di-
versification of individual pursuits is taken as an argument for

the need and the possibility of republican rule. "A republic," Madison writes, "by which I mean a government in which the scheme of representation takes place, opens a different prospect." The conception of representative democracy makes possible the extension of republican government over a large geographical area, and the greater extent of the territory renders "factious combinations" less likely and less dangerous. The rejection of the restricted classical idea of a republic depends on a reversal of the argument that republicanism requires a limited territory, but the shift is basically dependent on a socially and economically motivated opening up of the restricted sphere of political life in the classical conception.

Republicanism is thus redefined for modern society in the light of a new conception of economic life and of human psychology, which reflects fundamental historical changes in both. To read the terms of Madison's Tenth *Federalist* back into the generative impulses of the American Revolution does not involve an anachronism, if it can be shown that this sense of the relation of public to private good, of sovereignty to self-interest, was already articulated before the Revolution, even though it had yet to be put into practice in the deliberate constitution of a polity. Hence the relevance, above all others, of Hobbes.

The connection which Hobbes first adumbrated between scientific rationality and moral, political, and legal rationality was grounded in an empirical psychology which brought out the conative dimension of experience: drives, needs, desires, and will, as the necessary basis for the development of reason. The rise of the nation-state constituted as a sovereignty that depended on the identification or psychological participation of its citizens corresponded to the rise of a commercial society which made up to some degree the content of that political form. The security which Hobbes sought from the Leviathan state was for the sake of peaceful enjoyment of the private sphere, commodious living in which human drives and appetites might find ample scope.[6]

The interpretation of the intellectual historical background of the American Revolution which has been put forward here was regarded already by Cecilia Kenyon as "old-fashioned;" she felt the need to reaffirm it because of the emergence of contrary

views that construed the Revolution as a conservative movement. In a similar way Pocock's innovative and controversial
hypothesis is the occasion for yet another reaffirmation, but one
that can also draw on current work in social and economic as well
as intellectual history.

In a number of essays Joyce Appleby has recently argued
for a coalescence of economic and political liberalism as the decisive ideology of the American Revolution. "The transformation
of values which accompanied the intrusion of the market into
social relations can scarcely be distinguished from the liberal
philosophy which found expression in revolutionary rhetoric."[7]
Ongoing research in colonial history suggests "that it was the experience of the free market economy that produced the longing
for freedom and autonomy."[8] This is an argument that in effect
provides a socio-economic and ideological basis for Bernard
Bailyn's construction of the crisis mentality that led to the Revolution, in precisely opposite terms to what Pocock has read into
Bailyn's work.

Economic liberalism, as Appleby defines it, first developed
as a coherent theory in response to a revolution of the market
economy in the late seventeenth century in England in which the
role of the common domestic consumer was thrust into prominence. Already in the debates on foreign exchange in the 1620s
Thomas Mun had drawn attention to the influence of demand
on prices, and shortly after the Restoration, William Petty had
advocated transferring wealth through taxation "from the
Landed and Lazy, to the Crafty and Industrious,"[9] as a stimulus
to the economy. But it was only with the provocation of the craze
for calico and chintz, to the detriment of the market in domestic
woolens, in the 1680s, and then with the controversy surrounding the proposed recoinage in 1696, that full recognition of the
importance of the domestic market emerged.

The so-called mercantilist or balance-of-trade theory, which
emphasized foreign trade and saw its purpose in the attraction
and accumulation of specie, was exposed to severe, indeed intellectually devastating, criticism in the last decades of the
seventeenth century. The attention of many economic writers
was forcibly shifted from production to consumption, and the
mentality of consumers became the new focus of economic ideas.

In 1690 Nicholas Barbon wrote, "The Wants of the Mind are infinite, Man naturally Aspires, and as his Mind is elevated, his Senses grow more refined, and more capable of Delight; his Desires are inlarged,and his Wants increase with his Wishes, which is for every thing that is rare, can gratifie his Senses, adorn his Body and promote the Ease, Pleasure, and Pomp of Life."[10]

In that same *Discourse of Trade*, Barbon accordingly praised England's constitution because "men are most industrious where they are most free, and secure to injoy the Effects of their Labours." A year later Dudley North made the same connection in more specific terms: "The main spur to Trade, or rather to Industry and Ingenuity, is the exorbitant Appetites of Men, which they will take pains to gratifie, and so be disposed to work, when nothing else will incline them to it; for did Men content themselves with bare Necessities, we should have a poor World."[11]

This appropriation of the Hobbesian conception of man and the psychology of appetite for the understanding of economic behavior in an expanding commercial society was apparently blocked in its progress, however, by a complex of what Appleby calls "ideological imperatives" related to the need for social stability and order as felt by the class that had traditionally exercised authority. In her view, mercantilism was able—with Locke's help—to reassert itself,

> not because it explained the market to contemporaries—it had ceased to do this by 1680—nor for want of better explanation, but because it offered a rationale for coercing the poor, controlling the direction of growth, and subordinating the competition among groups to the goals of economic nationalism . . . A consumption-oriented model of economic growth, on the other hand, threatened major interests of the ruling class that had coalesced in Restoration England. Dangerous leveling tendencies lurked behind the idea of personal improvement through imitative buying. The notion that the wealth of nations began with stimulating wants rather than organizing production robbed intrusive social legislation of a supporting rationale.[13]

Economic liberalism was stunted in its growth in England after 1700, until the appearance of *The Wealth of Nations* in the year of the *Declaration of Independence*, but found a far more propitious social setting in the Colonies, where "the continued prosperity of the merchant elite depended in large measure upon the ambition and industry of ordinary people responding to profit incentives by growing marketable crops. There was thus neither opportunity nor incentive for any powerful economic group to check the inherent tendency of the market to permeate the entire society."[14] As a further consequence with ideological significance, this permeation "fostered the spread of economic rationality and encouraged the expression of social theories based upon the relationships maintained by the market."

Whether or not this social practical orientation required a "crisis of modernization" in order to sharpen it to the point of motivating and directing revolutionary action against British control,[15] and whether or not the Revolution itself first supplied this orientation a coherence with political aims and a good conscience,[16] it is clear that resistance to British Imperial policies of regulation and then of repression not only infused the assertion of economic rights with patriotism, but led to the consolidation of an American liberal ideology, based on a new idea of autonomy which was derived from the functional rational model of "economic man." "The capacity to act as an independent agent was central to the operation of the market economy."[17] Popular participation in commerce was seen not as a threat to autonomy and liberty, but as a basis and exercise of liberty.

Economic interest and self-assertion were "redeemed" under the aspect of "an inalienable right to pursue happiness," which provided resistance to "the intrusive social power of family, church and government." "Most often couched in political terms this new philosphy of natural rights rested squarely upon the economy, for the limitation of authority was made possible by the alternate social integration of the market which in turn depended upon the consistently self-interested, materially-oriented behavior of the colonists. A pervasive economic rationalism undergirt the rationale for the revolution."[18]

Nothing could be more directly opposed to Pocock's interpretation of the rationale, or irrational impulsion, of the Revolution, as we shall see. Yet, despite their basic differences, Pocock and Appleby seem to agree on two main points: that there is a surprising lack of literate expression of this liberal orientation in eighteenth-century England, and that the phenomenal expansion of the commercial economy undermined traditional conceptions of politics and republicanism. On the first point, I think a great deal of literate expression of liberal values is to be found in the best literature of that period, which needs only to be studied further in that light.[19]

On the second point, the crucial question is when this break was taking place. Like Pocock I believe that Harrington is a significant figure for the American Revolution, but I would characterize much of his influence as tending in the same direction as that of Hobbes. Harrington's idea of a republic has moved much farther from the classical humanist or Machiavellian conception than Pocock recognizes. The same might be said, for example, of certain Commonwealthmen of eighteenth-century England, such as Trenchard and Gordon, whom Pocock has tried to assimilate to the "Country" ideology.[20] In them, as in Hume, we can see continuation of Hobbes as well as Harrington, and an expression of liberal concepts and convictions that are relevant to the American Revolution and the republicanism it engendered. If this constitutes an Atlantic Republican Tradition, it is decidely not that of Pocock.

2. THE BASIS OF POCOCK'S RIGORIST REPUBLICAN TRADITION

The Machiavellian Moment presents a many-faceted construction of the intellectual history of a certain strain of republicanism. A considerable part of this interpretation seems to me to be well-founded and insightful. But there is one strand of Pocock's argument which I find basically mistaken. It is not an element easily isolated because it is deeply involved with his heuristic framework, with the very notion of a "Machiavellian moment."

> The "Machiavellian moment" of the eighteenth century, like that of the sixteenth, confronted civic virtue with corrpu-tion, and saw the latter in terms of a chaos of appetites, productive of dependence and loss of personal autonomy . . . to save personality, [the Country ideology] urged an ideal of virtue which at times reached unreal Stoical heights of moral autonomy, . . . and since its economics tended to ground that personality on a form of property held to have

existed in a pre-commercial past, it tended to see history as a movement away from value which only heroic, not social, action could reverse. But though it was increasingly susceptible to elegiac pessimism, it was endowed with all the riches of the complex and articulate vocabulary of civic humanism with which to expound the science and sociology of virtue. Its paradigms therefore tended to dominate discourse. (486)[21]

Civic virtue, taken as devotion to the general good but with further moral and metaphysical overtones, a stance which in seventeenth- and eighteenth-century England was supposedly possible only on the basis of an economic independence secured through possession of landed property, is here opposed to a realm of uncontrolled appetite associated with individual interests, mobile property and money, with a commercial and consumer society.

If this model appears to dominate discourse in Pocock's view, I believe it is because of its one-sided predominance in his perspective. Pocock's paradigmatic vision not only works to skew his general perception of the body of literature in question, but repeatedly leads him to read his paradigm into texts that he has taken as crucial to his construction of the republican tradition. It is noteworthy that, in passages where the tendency I am trying to isolate and refute becomes most pronounced, Pocock sees the Machiavellian moment as equally "Rousseauan," as when—à propos Jefferson!—he refers to "a dimension of historical pessimism in American thought at its most utopian, which stems from the confrontation of virtue and commerce and threatens to reduce all American history to a Machiavellian or Rousseauan moment," (541) and goes on to claim "that the foundation of independent America was seen, and stated, as taking place at a Machiavellian—even a Rousseauan—moment." (545)

Rousseau, Pocock tells us, "was the Machiavelli of the eighteenth century, in the sense that he dramatically and scandalously pointed out a contradiction that others were trying to live with . . . the contradiction between virtue and culture." (504) Rousseau's rejection of the idea of representation in a republic is also referred to, in a contrast with the fundmamental role which Hobbes attributes to representation,[22] but Rousseau is otherwise scarcely mentioned in *The Machiavellian Moment*. Nonetheless, his tacit presence can be felt at many points where the moral and metaphysical dimensions of republican virtue are brought into play. Pocock's overreading is characteristically the result of a projection of Rousseau's theme of endangered moral personality into texts themselves quite innocent of the notion.

As the opposition to commerce implies, Pocock's paradigm is not only Stoic but Spartan as well. Writing of a "fundamental ambiguity between particular and universal good" in classical republicanism, that is, whether particular and universal good are to be seen as mutually supportive or mutually exclusive, Pocock arrives at a fateful determination:

> The citizen might be thought of as an Athenian, the diversity of whose particular attainments heightened his capacity to act in the public interest, or as a Spartan, sacrificing every particular form of self-development in order to act as a citizen and out of civic solidarity alone. Aristotle on the whole concluded against the Spartan ideal, whatever might be said of Plato; but in Renaissance Europe, from the fifteenth to the eighteenth centuries, the preponderant voice was in favor of the grim patriots of the Eurotas. (74)

This last assertion is supported here only by a footnote reference to *The Spartan Tradition in European Thought* by Elizabeth Rawson.

It is true that, in her introduction, Rawson writes, "between the end of the fifth century B.C. and the eighteenth century A.D. Athens, or at least Athenian democracy, was as a political ideal in almost permanent eclipse."[23] But in her detailed interpretation of the Renaissance humanist revival of classical republicanism, she shows that interest in and identification with Athens preceded and took precedence over that with Sparta, particularly in Leonardo Bruni, who emphasized the association of republican values with cultural and commercial achievement.[24] Sparta became the prevalent classical model (together with Rome) with Machiavelli, through his stress on citizen militia as forming character, a theme which she points out was taken over by Rousseau in a "more absolute condemnation of his own time."

Just as most early references to Sparta are from Athenians using it to criticize their own republic, so the vogue of Sparta from Machiavelli on was largely oppositional, not concerned with constitutional problems in a positive way. After Machiavelli, moreover, beginning with Bodin and Botero, Rawson writes, "Sparta is increasingly despised or ignored." This is in part the result of "a newly strong insistence that the modern world has nothing to learn from the ancient," but it also reflects a resurgence of esteem for Athens.[25]

When Pocock determines that Sparta was the predominant classical Greek model of a republic from the Renaissance to the American Revolution, he settles exclusively on a deliberately strict or rigoristic conception that defines virtue and the common good through its very opposition to particular interests or private good. Yet such virtue is at the same time essentially for the benefit of the individual, meant to secure his quasi-ethical autonomy. Rawson reminds us of this anachronistic view of Sparta in Rousseau, who "regarded all this state machinery as existing entirely for the sake of the individual."[26] Analogously, the social contract for Rousseau was as much a structure for the psychological constitution of the citizen as it was for the political constitution of a state.

The self-subordination of the Spartan citizen-soldier to the good of the whole, i.e. the state, is thus more a metaphor for a Stoic mastery of one's own particular desires which finds support or even implementation in a political structure. What is ethical about such self-rule remains to be shown. On Pocock's own evidence, nothing could be further from Aristotle's idea of a republic, in which "any value to which a man might give priority . . . might become one mode of his participation in the determination and distribution of general values," that is, the ongoing definition of what is to constitute the common good. (71).

Yet it is important to his later argument that Pocock be able to refer to his paradigm of republicanism as Aristotelian even where he forces a rigorist Spartan cast to its various versions in the seventeenth and eighteenth centuries. A crucial point is that his extension of the paradigm to the paranoiac motivation of the American Revolution will only have whatever apparent plausibility it does if the Spartan verion appears to have ousted the Athenian altogether.

It is not only this so-called moral dimension of classical republicanism, pitting virtue against the particular interests and interdependencies of commerce, that leads to a preference of the Spartan military model over the Athenian commercial model. There is also metaphysical dimension to Pocock's paradigm, which pits virtue against fortune and "corruption" in the sense of that decay and loss of stability that necessarily comes with change and thus with time. "'The Machiavellian moment' . . . is a name for the moment in conceptualized time in which the republic was seen as confronting its own temporal finitude." (viii)

Pocock says that to study Machiavelli's and other republicans' thought in terms of such a struggle with temporality "may diminish the amount of magniloquent and unspecific interpretation to which it has been subjected," (viii) but it is precisely this moral metaphysical theme that makes his own argument seem at times vatic and vacuous. His most frequent way of characterizing the concern with the temporal finitude of the state is in terms of "universality." In the opening pargaraph of the first chapter we read:

> The republic or Aristotelian polis, as that concept reemerged in the civic humanist thought of the fifteenth century, was at once universal, in the sense that it existed to realize for its citizens all the values which men were capable of realizing in this life, and particular, in the sense that it was finite and located in space and time. (3)

We have already seen that the concept which Pocock later claims was revived in the Renaissance was decidedly antagonistic to such Aristotelian universalism. It was exclusive rather than inclusive of individual pursuits. What Pocock will mean by the universality of the republic within the rigoristic classical model that he comes to insist upon is rather just the attempted denial of its mere particularity, its subjection to time. This too, as Pocock will later be seen to concede, is a concern which has no roots in Aristotle.

Pocock sometimes suggests that universality in the republic is itself an "epistemological" concern, in a broad and loose sense. He even goes so far as to derive the finitude of temporality from particularity as a problem of the theory of knowledge, as when he makes explicit a set of assumptions underlying his first several chapters: "that the late medieval and Renaissance intellect found the particular less intelligible and less rational than the universal; [by definition, one would think,] that since the particular was finite, it was local both in space and time, so that time became a dimension of its being and consequently shared in the diminished rationality and intelligibility of the particular." (4)

The epistemological question is rather how the rationality attained through universal terms relates to particulars. But Pocock's point is simply that republicanism can be seen as a vocabulary which was meant to provide a "means of rendering time and the particular intelligible on the assumption that they were less than perfectly rational." (4)

The universality of the polis, however, or the universality that is to be attained through political participation, is not primarily a matter of knowing. Augustine had radically separated the city of God from the earthly city, denying that civil life and history have anything to offer for salvation. It was this, rather than simply the classical ontological distinction between realms appropriate to demonstrative knowledge or science and probable customary knowledge or prudence, that put in question the universality which rigorist civic virtue aimed at. If justice were to be achieved by Christians under secular law, "a public *fortuna* must be shown as subject to the operations of grace. The revival of the Aristotelian doctrine that political association was natural to man therefore logically entailed the reunion of political history with eschatology." (43)[27]

As I will soon show, however, that "revival" in terms of grace, or conversely salvation becoming social as a matter of the interdependence of the virtue of all individual citizens, is a "politicization of virtue" which in effect denies the Aristotelian doctrine of man as naturally political, and the "reunion" of civic life and eschatology presupposes an original union that cannot be found in Aristotle.

In the actual revival of the republic as a reality, in the Florence of Salutati and Bruni, moreover, there seems to have been no felt need for such universality to begin with. "The republic . . . was so organized as to assert its sovereignty and autonomy, and therefore its individuality and particularity." "That the republican ideal accepted the fact of the republic's mortality is symbolized by the choice as hero of the unsuccessful rebel Brutus." (53) A Machiavellian moment in which the republic confronts its own temporal finitude would lack motivation at this stage. How did the susceptibility for such a moment arise? It seems to have emerged only with Savonarola, "the crucial conjuncture was that between Savonarola's apocalyptic utterances and the resurgence of the republican *popolo*: between prophecy and citizenship." (105)

This conjuncture sparked the revival of that Spartan conception of the citizen which Aristotle had "concluded against," in which the individual is thought of as "sacrificing every particular form of self-development in order to act . . . out of civic solidarity alone." (74) The Aristotelian sense of republican universality had been renewed in Bruni, who idealized "Florentine civility along lines consciously modeled on the Funeral Oration of Pericles; the citizen is he who can develop as many forms of human excellence as possible." "The excellence of one could only flourish when developed in collaboration with the diverse excellence of others." (88)

From Savonarola on such striving for excellence was supplanted by that Spartan drive "to pursue the perfection of complete self-identification with the common good." (74) This in itself constitutes the rigorist universality of the republic, although Pocock adds what should be an embarrassing question for him: "Yet what was the common good if it led to the abnegation of all particular goods?" His answer must be that the common good is precisely that which enables individuals to disengage themselves from particular desires and private goods. "The dereliction of one citizen . . . reduced the other's chances of attaining and maintaining virtue, since virtue was now politicized." (75)

Politicized virtue "consisted in a partnership of ruling and being ruled with others who must be as morally autonomous as oneself. In embracing the civic ideal, therefore, the humanist staked his future as a moral person on the political health of his city." (75) How such autonomy acquired its moral dimension is not clear, but Pocock's phrase, "the politicization of virtue," implies that a quasi-stoic notion which was orginally foreign to the polis has acquired a political means of realization, or rather political life itself as the means to a non-political end, an idea which does not suit well with the Aristotelian conception of man as a political animal, which Pocock would like to maintain as a permanent source of his republicanism.

This bind is again the result of reversing the Augustinian separation (and thus of presupposing it), of fusing or confusing a quasi-Christian other worldly orientation with the values of life in the earthly city. "Once the justice which was part of Christian virtue was identified with the distributive justice of the polis, salvation became to some degree social, in some degree dependent upon others." (75)

As if it were by now self-evident, Pocock adds in the following sentence, "To the Renaisance mind, this problem was bound to present itself as a problem in time." It is this metaphysical dimension of the Machiavellian moment, the opposition of virtue to fortune and corruption as tendencies inherent in time itself, that leads Pocock beyond the Athenian idea of "the republic as a universal because a comprehensive and therefore stable, harmonization of particular values." (75) "The politicization of virtue introduced a dramatic change. The operations of fortune were no longer external to one's virtue but intrinsically part of it; . . . it became of urgent moral importance to examine the polis as a structure of particulars seeking to maintain its stability—and its universality—in time." (76)

In the immediately following passage Pocock grants that there is little along this line in Aristotle: "For reasons which must be presumed to inhere in the character of Athenian temporal consciousness, Aristotle has not been overwhelmingly concerned with the image of time as the dimension of instability," and Pocock offers instead the sixth book of Polybius's *Histories* as "at least one pre-Christian classic in which this concept was applied to political and constitutional thought." (77)

He points out that Polybius was a Stoic and that his idea of a wheel of fortune in the revolutions of successive types of polity: aristocracy, monarchy, democracy, was a variant of the Stoic attempt to overcome the irrationality of fortune by construing it cyclically. "It was implicit in the whole concept of change as irrational that change contained no principle of growth and could produce nothing new; therefore there could be no understanding of growth or change as history." (78)

In an essay, "Civic Humanism and Its Role in Anglo-American Thought," Pocock epitomizes this conception most tellingly, "In the Polybian 'mixed government' we recognize the universality of the Aristotelian polis. We recognize also that the aim of politics is to escape from time; that time is the dimension of imperfection and that change must necessarily be degenerative."[28] In the later presentation in *The Machiavellian Moment* Pocock, as we have seen, admits that Aristotelian universality is incompatible with the rigoristic universality that construes the aim of politics as escaping from time. But the earlier essay shows in great clarity the connection between the latter and Pocock's idea of the motivation of the American Revolution.

It is against the corruption instrinsic to time that universality in the Spartan-Stoic sense is to be achieved by the citizens rising virtuously above their particular interests. This metaphysical quasi-moral sense of corruption he attempts to identify with the apprehension of political corruption that was so important to the ideology of the American colonists as they moved toward their Revolution, as he suggests attributing their readiness to rebel,

> not to a newly-enlightened belief in progress, but to their possession of a conceptual vocabulary, Renaissance in origin, which made it very hard for them to conceive of certain changes except as "corruption," or to conceive of corruption as anything but total, involving the necessary disintegration of the political and moral fabric as a whole.[29]

We will examine this paradigm-paranoia psychology, in which people are in effect possessed by a "conceptual vocabulary," in the concluding section, and will show that it is quite different from Bailyn's "logic of the rebellion" in terms of conspiracy theories, which Pocock claims as support for his interpretation.

The distortion inherent in this paradigm of republican virtue taken as a perspective on early modern history is palpable in the closing paragraphs of the first part of *The Machiavellian Mo-*

ment where the Stoic legacy of Polybius is projected forward as a presage of doom:

> The pursuit of particular satisfactions would become fiercer, until no system of restraints could contain it. [Polybius] was not only predicting—so at least it would appear to his readers in later centuries—the disintegration of the Roman republic under the strains and temptations of Mediterranean empire; he was stating that, even—or especially—under the most prosperous of historical conditions, the pursuit of particular goods would prove incompatible with the maintenance of civic virtue. The republic was self-doomed. (80)

This vision, Pocock's rather than Polybius's, is circular or solipsistic. It is unable to escape the restrictions imposed by conceptions of virtue and the republic that are marked by anything but prosperous historical conditions. What is doomed is that paradigm of republic virtue, derived from scarcity and military discipline and reinforced by anxiety and metaphysical alienation from the goods, that is, goals, and good fortune of this world.

With regard to the propagation of the republican paradigm from Florence to Pocock's Atlantic tradition the most important figure is, of course, Machiavelli, above all for his application of the model of Spartan military virtue to the popular base of the state. This Pocock sees as the crucial link in Machiavelli's reception by Harrington: the connection between civic virtue and the bearing of arms. Machiavelli uses "the concept of armed *virtù* to transform the question of the participation of the many in citizenship," (202) shifting it from a problem "of knowledge to one of will." (212)

"In the mainstream of Aristotelian theory, the many possessed a knowledge based on experience, which made them capable of electing their superiors and exercising a judgment of policies," but Machiavelli made their role "a matter of the autonomy of personalities mobilized for the public good," in effect, "the militarization of citizenship." (213) To see how Machiavelli's "hatred of mercenaries and his exaltation of the civic militia" is related "to Aristotelian theory of citizenship is the vital point if we wish to understand his political thought." (200) It is a question of seeing not only that only the citizen can be a good soldier, from the republic's point of view, but also "that only the soldier can be a good citizen." (201)

The apparent anticipation of Harrington is deceptive, as paradoxical as the continuity of Pocock's Machiavelli with Aristotle. His vision of the citizen as "a man trained by civic religion and military discipline to devote himself to the patria"(203) is but Sparta writ large, with the added factor that the republic is to be "dynamic" or expansive, using war to increase its territory. The transformation of the problem of popular participation seems in fact to have suppressed the political sphere as far as the people are concerned; Aristotle's idea of citizenship disappears in its "militarization" just as it did in its Polybian "universalization."

Pocock does make clear that Machiavelli has broken with "the usual way of defending a *governo largo*," as opposed to a *governo stretto*, a strict, that is, narrow or exclusive state based on a closed aristocracy and small territory. It was usual, he writes, "to assert that the many were peaceable, desired little more than the enjoyment of a private liberty, had common sense enough to reject what was not for their own good and moral sagacity enough to elect and defer to their natural superiors in the civic elite." (202) Now this quiescent private liberty has become a vice which civic virtue must be used to uproot. Discipline rather than deference will now regulate the relations of the many to the few.

Civic virtue in a *governo largo* "became dependent upon the republic's ability to conquer others." (213) For Machiavelli "civic virtues flourished best when there was no mercy to enemies and the defeat of a city meant death or slavery to its inhabitants." (214) To Pocock this means that the "dimension of grace" was lost, "the republic and its virtue ceased to be universal." (215) But this is not really a loss with respect to the rigorist paradigm, for Machiavelli holds that there is simply a limited amount of virtue in the world, and thus there is competition for it. His "abandonment of the dimension of grace" is simply the complement of "his decision to regard virtue as existing only in republics." "Virtue itself . . . has now become cannibal." (217)

Nonetheless Pocock will continue to refer to and use the Machiavellian paradigm of republican virtue in ways that set its alleged moral overtones vibrating. What is equally surprising is that this is all he chooses to find in Machiavelli, whose "contributions to republican theory were extraordinarily original, but were based on and limited to his decision that military dynamism was to be preferred before the search for stability. It was this decision that led him to investigate the military and social bases of political action and personality." This was Machiavelli's legacy to the "the classical republican tradition of early modern England and America." (218)

3. HARRINGTON'S TRUE LIBERAL CONTRIBUTION TO REPUBLICANISM

In *The Ancient Constitution and the Feudal Law* Pocock included a chapter on Harrington's *Oceana* in which he played down the claim often made for him as one of the first to relate economic analysis to the study of political structure:

> His sole comment on the economic relations between men—and the sole foundation of all that he has to say about property as the basis of power—is "an army is a beast that hath a great belly and must be fed"; he that has the land can feed the soldiers. Harrington, we must keep in mind, was a Machiavellian, and the starting-point of his thought was Machiavelli's perception that in a republic the soldiers must be citizens and the citizens soldiers; if the soldiers follow private men for reward, then the republic cannot survive.[30]

Pocock insists that Harrington was not interested in understanding economic change but simply took the apparently recent preponderance of freeholders, common people holding free title to their land, as a given which could provide the basis for a return to "ancient prudence." His "doctrine that the distribution of land determines political power" means little more, Pocock says, "than that it determines whether a soldier shall fight as a citizen for the public power or as a dependent for his patron or lord."[31]

This is the interpretation of Harrington that Pocock elaborates in *The Machiavellian Movement*. In order to see how much the theme of bearing arms is blown out of proportion there, we need to go back to Harrington's text.

> Fundamental laws are such as state what it is that a man may
> call his own, that is to say, property, and what the means be
> whereby a man may enjoy his own, that is to say, protection;
> the first is also called dominion, and the second, empire or
> sovereign power, whereof this (as has been shown) is the
> natural product of the former, for such as is the balance of
> the dominion in a nation, such is the nature of her empire.[32]

The idea that property "produces" sovereignty, or that power
follows property, is a fundamental political conception, to which
the idea that the distribution of property determines the support and thus the character of the army is only a corollary. The
central concern of Harrington's work, as of Hobbes's political
writings, is the establishment of a stable political order responsive to the needs and interests of the nation, above all, protection
for the enjoyment of what each individual may call his own.

Harrington's conception of sovereignty is close to that of
Hobbes, but his attention to the material basis of its indivisibility
is greater:

> Where the sovereign power is not as entire and absolute as
> in monarchy itself, there can be no government at all. It is
> not the limitation of sovereign power that is the cause of a
> commonwealth, but such a *libration or poise of orders, that there
> can be in the same no number of men, having the interest, that can
> have the power, nor any number of men, having the power, that can
> have the interest, to invade or disturb the government.* (H 657–8)

This maxim explains and completes the maxim concerning the
relation of property and power. It is the maxim of true lawgiving, that is, erecting "necessary superstructures," as opposed to
those which are arbitrary in relation to the foundation in the balance of property and therefore require violence. Lawgiving
should raise superstructures "such as are conformable unto the
balance or foundation; which, being purely natural, requireth
that all interposition of force be removed." (H 603)

The "libration" here, or balance in the sense of "constitution," refers not to any contervalence of mutually limiting
powers, standing for separate estates or classes, but rather to an
equilibrium between the distribution of social and economic
power on the one hand and political power on the other. The

crucial factor in the relation between property and power—far more important than determination of the nature of the army by the distribution of property, but systematically obscured by the exaggeration of the latter in Pocock's presentation—is the political role accorded to economic interest.

Those who own property, particularly land in which they invest their own industry, have a stake in the preservation of the state. This may well be expressed, among other ways, in a readiness to bear arms in defense of their country (and all that they call their own), but it is more important that those citizens who might have the power to disturb the government should be dissuaded from it by understanding and following their own best interest. This maxim is repeated and varied throughout Harrington's writing. The orders of a commonwealth should be "such as they neither would resist if they could nor could if they would." (H 204, cf. 179 top)

"All government is interest, and the predominant interest gives the matter or foundation of the government," Harrington writes in *a System of Politics*, which means that the type of government is determined by whether a single man, a few, or many men have the largest proportion of property: absolute monarchy, aristocracy (or, since "pure aristocracy" in practice is but civil war, regulated monarchy), and democracy. (H 836) "The interest of arbitrary monarchy is the absoluteness of the monarch; the interest of regulated monarchy is the greatness of the noblity; the interest of democracy is the felicity of the people; for in democracy the government is for the use of the people." (H 839)

He goes on to assert that in monarchy the people are for the use of the government, but the striking thing about his claim is not the polemic edge but the simple assumption that government should be seen as serving a purpose, as a means to a happiness which is not itself necessarily political but includes social and economic aspects of human life. The felicity of the people reflects an interest bound up with their owning property and making it productive by their own endeavor. Harrington undeniably has a dynamic view of property, in which it is linked as much with motivation of initiative as with possession, and thus with the "interest" of felicity, or pursuit of happiness. Later in the same work he writes, "Industry of all things is the most accumulative; and accumulation of all things hates leveling. The revenue, therefore, of the people being the revenue of industry, though some nobility (as that of Israel or that of Lacedaemon [Sparta]) may be found to have been levelers, yet not any people in the world." (H 840)

In *Oceana* Harrington seems at first to take over the emphasis on interest, indeed an equation of interest and reason, from Hobbes in a dialectical manner, i.e. for the sake of debate or in order to refute it; "for be it so that reason is nothing but interest, there be divers interests, and so divers reasons," these being private reason or the interest of the individual, reason of state, and "that reason which is the interest of mankind or of the whole." (H 171) Here he marshalls Hooker and Grotius against Hobbes to argue that there is "a common right, law of nature," which moral agents acknowledge is "more excellent . . . than the right or interest of the parts only." And with an ironic nod at Hobbes's idea of thinking as computation, he reasons from this common right: "Now compute well, for if the interest of popular government come the nearest unto the interest of mankind, then the reason of popular government must come the nearest unto right reason." (H 172)

Harrington does not claim, however, that he has made his case against Hobbes: "But it may be said that the difficulty remains yet. For be the interest of popular government right reason, a man does not look upon reason as it is right or wrong in itself, but as it makes for him or against him." This was just the point of the passage from Hobbes which he had taken as his point of departure here.[33] Harrington grants he must "show such orders of a government as . . . shall be able to constrain this or that creature to shake off that inclination which is more peculiar to it and take up that which regards the common good or interest." The demonstration of such orders is the heart of his constitutional thought, beginning here with the basic notion of separating the functions of "dividing and choosing," as when two girls share a cake fairly by having one girl cut it in half and the other pick her half first.

Hobbes thought of sovereignty as "a Common Power, to keep [the citizens] in awe, and to direct their actions to the Common Benefit."[34] By the threat of punishment, the common power could make it dangerous not to—and, most important, thereby make it safe to—keep convenants and observe the laws of nature, which in a state of nature could only be inclinations it would be dangerous to follow. Harrington's approach to the political mechanisms which should constrain the self-interest of each in the common interest (and that means, in the long-range interest of the individual as well) is very different from that of Hobbes, but compatible with it. The end in view is akin in the two approaches. Hobbes says, "the finall Cause, End or Designe of men, (who naturally love liberty, and Dominion over others,) in the introduction of that restraint upon themselves, (in which we see them live in Commonwealths,) is the foresight of their own preservation, and of a more contented life thereby."[35]

Immediately preceding this discussion of reason as interest in *Oceana* Harrington had written that the law in a republic was "framed by every private man to no other end (or they may thank themselves) than to protect the liberty of every private man, which by that means comes to be the liberty of the commonwealth." (H 171) The same is true of private interest. "The government whereof this nation is capable, once seen, taketh in all interests." (H 205) The fundamental importance of interest is not an idea simply taken up from Hobbes for the purposes of debate. He resumes this theme in a non-polemic context, introducing it with the statement, "the people, taken apart, are but so many private interests, but if you take them together, they are the public interest," (H 280) which at the same time refers to their capacity to choose rationally, where this function is kept distinct from debate and dividing.

The continuity of private with public interest is what p-rovides the cohesion of Harrington's republic. His Madisonian formulation, that the republic takes in all interests, does not mean that the political realm is the result of an interplay of interests, where stability would arise from the predominance of one class. Particular interest, on the contrary, should work to reinforce indivisible sovereignty, the objectivity and efficacy of the laws, while the content of the common interest is determined by the process of legislation. Harrington agrees with Matthew Wren (and Hobbes), "*that the law proceeds from the will of man (whether a mon-*

arch or a people), *that this will must have a mover, and that this mover is interest"* (H 715, italicized in the original).

There is a striking series of aphorisms in *A System of Politics* which brings out the intimate positive relation between interest and justice. It ascribes an instinct of self-preservation to governments in the same sense that the *Declaration* will invoke this as a right for the American people.

> 2. Let equity or justice be what it will, yet if a man be to judge or resolve in his own case, he resolves upon his own interest.
> 3. Every government, being not obnoxious [i.e. open to harm, censure or punishment] to any superior, resolves in her own case.
> 4. The ultimate result [i.e. decision of the sovereign will] in every government is the law in that government. . .
> 10. Law in democracy holds such a disproportion to natural equity, as the interest of a nation to the interest of all mankind.
> 11. One government has much nearer approaches to natural equity than another; but in case natural equity and self-preservation come in competition, so natural is self-preservation to every creature, that in that case no one government has any more regard to natural equity than another. (H 848)

Here Harrington is evidently drawing on Machiavelli, yet his affinity to Hobbes is equally apparent. The close association of interest, decision, and law is reinforced by an aphorism of distinctly Hobbesian cast: "Wheresoever the power of making law is, there only is the power of interpreting the law so made." This clearly suggests that Harrington was on the side of Bacon and Hobbes in the intermittent controversy with Coke and Hale, in which they challenged the common-law jurists' claim to make the law by interpretation. Nor did Harrington hold a "common-law" view of freehold property.[36]

The decisive difference between the legacy of Hobbes and Machiavelli lies in the conception of sovereignty. We can perceive this in the findings of *The Machiavellian Movement*. Writing of Giannotti's "primitive attempt at a theory of sovereignty," Pocock comments, "we may add that the linguisitic confusions which arose when one spoke of sovereignty in a context of mixed government, and vice versa, were to bedevil political discourse to the

American Revolution and beyond." (315) But it was not the confusion with the division of powers that was responsible here. Giannotti's "failure to develop a theory of sovereignty resting on the legislative power meant that he had not escaped from the world in which Contarian myth [the "myth of Venice" as the serene republic by grace or good fortune] and Machiavellian or Guicciardinian realism were the confining alternatives." (328) This brings Pocock to a very significant conclusion, "for all the tough-mindedness of Machiavelli and Guicciardini, the fact remains that the weakness of the Aristotelian and humanist tradition was the insufficiency of its means for discussing the positive, as opposed to the preservative, exercise of power." (329)

"If Machiavelli and Guicciardini did not, with all their brilliance, succeed in seeing political activity as creative, but only in showing just how difficult, or impossible, the maintenance of republican order really was," (328) this should have major consequences for any assessment of the continuity—or gulf—between them and Harrington. In the passage where he characterizes Harrington's understanding of the importance of freehold property as "common-law" Pocock refers to the "setting of Civil War England, where the conflict of Tudor monarchism with Puritan religious nationalism and sectarianism ensured the presence of many more competing styles and languages of thought than seems to have been the case in Florence." (ix) This way of describing the situation overlooks the crucial issue of the Civil War, sovereignty, just as the Hobbesian vocabulary of sovereignty is generally elided in Pocock's consideration of the profusion of styles and languages of thought in Civil War England.[37]

At one point Pocock writes that Hobbes's *Leviathan* "differed altogether in structure from the Machiavellian vision and may seem to have reduced the latter's role in English thinking to one of secondary importance." (380) Whether or not he means to question this apparent predominance of Hobbes, Pocock's understanding of his conception of sovereignty is clearly deficient. He sees Hobbes as belonging to a group of thinkers "prepared to isolate a timeless 'moment of nature,' and out of it to reconstitute authority as a rigorously natural phenomenon,"

(401) whereas sovereignty is emphatically artifical for Hobbes, man-made against the state of nature.

To return to Harrington, the idea of the indivisibility of sovereignty is fundamental to his own review of English history leading up to the Civil War and thus to his indictment of "the Gothic balance" or "modern prudence." Of this basically feudal order, which others (including later Pocock's "Neo-Harringtonians") revered as "the ancient constitution," Harrington writes,

> this government, being indeed the masterpiece of modern prudence, hath been cried up to the skies as the only invention whereby at once to maintain the sovereignty of a prince and the liberty of the people; whereas indeed it hath been no other than a wrestling match, wherein the nobility, as they have been stronger, have thrown the King, or the king, if he have been stronger, hath thrown the nobility . . . (H 196)

In his review of the recent history of that wrestling match he draws most significantly on Bacon, at the very outset on the essay, "Of the True Greatness of Kingdoms and Estates," and later, following the passage just quoted, on Bacon's *History of the Reign of King Henry VII*. In the essay Bacon argues that the greatness of the state depends on the quality of its people, as distinct from its "nobility and gentlemen." If the latter classes "multiply too fast, . . . that maketh the common subject grow to be a peasant and base swain, driven out of heart and in effect but a gentleman's labourer." (H157) Bacon therefore praises Henry VII for his "profound and admirable" device: "in making farms and houses of husbandry of a standard; that is, maintained with such a proportion of land unto them as may breed a subject to live in convenient plenty and no servile condition, and to keep the plough in the hand of the owners and not mere hirelings." (H 158)

Bacon is concerned with "the breed and disposition of the people" in regard to the kind of soldiers they make, and he draws on *The Prince* (chapters 12 and 13 and *The Discourses* (II, 10 and 20), where Machiavelli extols the militia and warns against mercenaries. It is Bacon who combines Machiavelli's theory of arms with an understanding, though again hardly "common-law," of the importance of freehold property. Harrington sees Bacon as having anticipated his own idea of "the balance of dominion or property," but says he "harps upon a string which he has not perfectly tuned." Bacon did not see that this trend must lead not to the greatness of the English monarch, but to a republic; and Henry VII did not deserve praise because he could not have intended the results of his legislation, which ultimately included the downfall of monarch.

When Harrington comes to draw upon the same point as made in Bacon's *History*, the emphasis on arms has shifted. The important consideration now seems to be that the independence of the commoners deprived the nobility of an army they could control. Henry VII reinforced the small land holdings by his "Statute of Population," "An Acte against the pulling down of towns," which—Harrington writes—encouraged the typical "dweller not to be a beggar or cottager, but a man of some substance that might keep friends [Toland's edition has "hinds" and Liljegren's has "Hiends"] and servants and set the plough on going." (H 197)

> This did mightily concern (saith the historian of that prince [i.e. Bacon] the might and manhood of the kingdom, and in effect amortize a great part of the lands unto the hold and possession of the yeomanry, or middle people, who, living not in servile or indigent fashion, were much unlinked from dependence upon their lords and, living in a free and plentiful manner, became a more excellent infantry, but such an one upon which the lords has so little power, that from henceforth they may be computed to have been disarmed. (H 197)

Harrington has already said it was the dangerous flaw of the English "monarchy by a nobility" "that the nobility had frequent interest and perpetual power by their retainers and tenants to raise sedition." (H 179) The commoners who now could fight for their own interests not only deprived the nobility of this perpetual power of raising sedition, but also presented a new and secure basis in "interest" for the stability of sovereignty.

But the shift in the distribution of property had only begun. The nobles were led to sell land becasue they gravitated from a Country to a Courtly way of life. (H 198) It should be noted that where Harrington contrasts Country and Court or City as ways of life, he emphasizes that husbandry provides a more stable base for a republic than the commotion of cities, explicitly following Aristotle (*Politics* vi, 4). Where a republic is based in the city and court, "ambition would be every man's trade," but where agriculture provides the foundation, "the plough in the hands of the owner findeth him a better calling, and produceth the most innocent and steady genius of a commonwealth, such as is that of [England]" (H 158-59) The Country way of life is associated, for Harrington, with industrious commoners, the people, insofar as a Country orientation is important to republicanism. Moreover, the connection of owning the land and wielding the plough is more important in this respect than that of owning land and bearing arms.

The shift of property continued as Henry VIII, "dissolving the abbeys, brought with the declining estate of the nobility so vast a prey unto the industry of the people, that the balance of the commonwealth was too apparently in the popular party to be unseen by the wise council of Queen [Elizabeth]." Her "love tricks" and "romance" with the people corresponded to a neglect of the nobility and the rise of the House of Commons to real power, so that nothing was "wanting unto the destruction of the throne but that the people, not apt to see their own strength, should be put to feel it." (H 198)

So it fell to the Stuarts to provoke the people into an awareness of their own power. And they discovered that "a monarch divested of her nobility hath no refuge under heaven but an army. *Wherefore the dissolution of this government caused the war, not the war the dissolution of this government.*" (H 198) This was only the completion of what Henry VII had started by watering the wine of the nobility, "for whereas a nobility striketh not at the throne, without which they cannot subsist, but at some king that they do not like, popular power striketh through the king at the throne, as that which is incompatible with it." (H 197) This is the setting in which Harrington, "raising such superstructures of government as are natural to the known foundations," (H 202) put forward his model of a republican constitution for England.

Pocock maintains that Harrington's historical analysis was "founded on the Machiavellian theory of the possessison of arms as necessary to political personality," that "the function of free proprietorship became the liberation of arms, and consequently of the personality," (386) but I can find no evidence of this either in Harrington's text or in Pocock's argument. The notion of personality seems dragged in without justification. And in the wake of such claims Pocock quietly makes what is in effect a sweeping concession:

> Harrington showed himself inclined to discount Machiavelli's emphasis on a strictly moral corruption, and actual disintegration of the civic personality, as a main cause of the decay of governments. When a government became "corrupt," he thought, it was less because the citizens had ceased to display the virtues appropriate to it than because the distribution of political authority was no longer properly related to the distribution of property that should determine it. (386-87)

What Harrington in fact does in the passage in question is quite deliberately to rid the concept "corruption" of all moral meaning. Playfully he takes the concept over from Machiavelli and, as if correcting him, turns it into a value-neutral notion of change, which can switch from negative to positive connotation through a shift of context or perspective.

> A people (saith Machiavel) that is corrupt is not capable of a commonwealth; but in showing what a corrupt people is, he hath either involved himself or me, nor can I otherwise come out of the labyrinth than by saying that, the balance altering, a people, as to the foregoing government, must of necessity be corrupt; but corruption in this sense signifieth no more than that the corruption of one government (as in natural bodies) is the generation of another; wherefore, if the balance alter from monarchy, the corruption of the people in this case is that which maketh them capable of a commonwealth. (202)

Unlike Machiavelli, Harrington does not propose the republic as a means of working a moral alteration, a change in manners or men's natures, but rather appeals to a change that has already been made, by a shift in the balance or a "natural revolution [which] happeneth from within, or by commerce." (H 405) Encouragement of the industry of the people begets its own sort of temperance, and this steadiness provides the fundament or material for a commonwealth.

The assertion that in Harrington, "as in Machiavelli, the bearing of arms is the essential medium through which the individual asserts both his social power and his participation in politics as a responsible moral being," (390)—true to Poccok's own diagnosis of the Machiavellian tradition—focuses on crisis, war or civil war, and ignores the peaceful life of the polity, the positive and creative use of power, which was Harrington's ultimate concern just as it was that of Hobbes. The idea that Harrington's "dominant purpose is the release of personal virtue through civic participation" (394) never is given textual support and flies in the face of Harrington's liberal conception of popular government in which political virtue, as recognized by the suffrage of the people, is meant to serve their welfare and happiness.

Harrington quotes from Bacon's essay, "Of Empire," a criticism of the Machiavellian approach which comes close to Pocock's remarks on the neglect of sovereignty and the positive (as opposed to preservative) use of power, "The wisdom of these later times in princes' affairs is rather fine deliveries and shiftings off dangers when they be near, than solid and grounded courses to keep them aloof." (H 258) He had echoed the same essay a bit earlier by referring to the Council of Trade in the republic of Oceana as the "*vena porta* of this nation," (H 251) which is what Bacon had said of the nation's merchants. The steady life of the commonwealth, which is presupposed by Harrington where he emphasizes the industry of the people, depends on the circulation of wealth through commerce.

Harrington was certain England would overtake the Dutch "in manufactures and merchandise [i.e. commerce]" because he saw their profitableness to be rooted in land. Holland had to import raw materials and provide carrying trade for others' products; "but at the long run it will be found that a people working on a foreign commodity doth but farm the manufacture, and that it is entailed upon them only where the growth of it is native; as also that it is one thing to have the carriage of other men's goods, and another for a man to bring his own unto the best market." (H 305)

Harrington's underlying assumptions about the economy of England are revealed in the Lord Archon's arguments in answer to the charge that an agrarian law would discourage industry:

> It tendeth not unto the improvement of merchandise [i.e. commerce] that there be some who have no need of their trading, and others that are not able to follow it. If confinement discourage industry, an estate in money is not confined; and lest industry should want whereupon to work, land is not engrossed nor entailed upon any man, but remains at her devotion. . . . The Spartan could have no trade; the Oceaner may have all. . . . The agrarian in Laconia banished money; this multiples it. (H 238)

The mandate for empire which is elaborated at the conclusion of *Oceana* is to be brought about not simply by war and conquest, but by colonization and commerce. If England was to show Machiavelli wrong and establish a republic that was both expansive and stable or peaceful (cf. H 272-74, 320-23), it was because it would be based in an agricultural-commercial economy that was itself expansive.

The possible colonization of Ireland is seen wholly in these terms in the Introduction to *Oceana*, "neither likely to yield men fit for arms, nor necessary it should," but "both rich in the nature of the soil and full of commodious ports for trade." The "advantage of the agriculture and trade" in such colonies should enable England to be "a commonwealth for increase, and upon the mightiest foundation that any hath been laid from the beginning of the world unto this day" (H 159-60). Pocock writes, "Harrington had been unspecific as to what kind of expansion he had in mind: possibly agrarian plantation beyond seas," (422) in connecting him with the "neo-Harringtonian" Charles Davenant who he suggests may have "thought of trade and naval power as a species of expansive *virtù*." England was a "trading commonwealth" already for Harrington, though he had seen no need to dress its commerce in incongruous Machiavellian garb.

It should be clear by now that Harrington projected a liberal, and not a rigoristic, republican model and that his importance for American independence had more to do with his affinities with the Hobbesian moment, which connects sovereignty and self-interest, than with any opposition of virtue to corruption or to commerce. Pocock's attempt to link Harrington to the American Revolution by way of "neo-Harringtonianism" that opposes virtue to "modernity" or "early modern capitalism" (e.g. ix, 330, 477, 506) breaks down not only because he is led to distort Harrington's thought so radically. The grounds offered for construing Shaftesbury, Bolingbroke, and the Country party as "neo-Harringtonian" are just as faulty.

The most direct support Pocock puts forward for the aptness of his coinage is a passage from a Shaftesbury speech to the House of Lords in October 1675:

> My Lords, 'tis not only your Interest, but the interest of the Nation, that you maintain your Rights, for let the House of Commons, and Gentry of England, think what they please, there is no Prince that ever Governed without Nobility or an Army. If you will not have one, you must have t'other, or the Monarchy cannot long support, or keep itself from tumbling into a Democraticall Republique. (415)

"The language is unmistakably Harringtonian, being a direct allusion to that passage in *Oceana* (quoted above, p. 54) where it is explained that the decay of the feudal aristocracy brought about the Civil War," Pocock remarks, "and yet the sense is strangely reversed." (415) In his essay, "Machiavelli, Harrington and English Political Ideologies in the Eighteenth Century," in which Pocock first proposed his thesis of "neo-Harringtonianism," he wrote, "The actual passage to which Shaftesbury seems to be alluding. . . ." and then, "But to regard this as a direct source for Shaftesbury's argument raises in acute form the question: what was Shaftesbury doing quoting Harrington to the House of Lords in 1675?"[38] This skirts the question: was he in fact quoting or alluding to Harrington? On Pocock's own showing it seems quite unlikely.

The term "neo-Harringtonian" was originally introduced to characterize a "transformation of Harrington," a development of his ideas "only after they had been so sharply modified . . . as almost to merit the use of the term 'stood on their head.'"[39] We must not be too liberal in allowing Pocock his paradox, for it is the key to his maintaining the continuity of his paradigm. He goes so far as to say that "the essence of neo-Harringtonianism lies in the drastic revision of Harrington's historical doctrine" which their use of his terms "necessitated." As Pocock sums it up in *The Machiavellian Moment*, "Harringtonian freedom was made to exist in the Gothic and English past instead of being founded on its ruins," (416) his "commonwealth of armed proprietors" relegated to the past, (420) while the House of Lords was reaffirmed on a basis he did not foresee.

It is important for Pocock to be able to construe the Country orientation as a continuation (however perverted or paradoxical) of Harrington's because this continuity supports his thesis of a close affinity between Bolingbroke and the eighteenth-century Commonwealthmen, such as Trenchard and Gordon. The opposition of virtue and commerce cannot be found in the latter, however, and they owe as much to Hobbes as to Harrington.[40] Similarly in a confrontation which Pocock arranges between his "neo-Harringtonian" and proto-Rousseauan, Andrew Fletcher, and Defoe, it seems Defoe is closer to Harrington. It seems, furthermore, that the neo-Harringtonian view of history is separated by a gulf from the Harringtonian, which ambiguously persists in its own right in Toland, (449) while Hume is said to have "adopted the perspective of Harrington . . . against that of the neo-Harringtonians." (493)

The pseudo-continuity from Harrington through Shaftesbury to Bolingbroke is the persistence of the paradigm of rigoristic republican virtue. Whether it is opposed to mercenaries or to a standing army, "Whether in 1656, 1675 or later, the idea of citizenship is the same. It is, as I have said, essentially Greek,"[41] This again means the Spartan or Stoic moral personality that owes more to Rousseau than to anything classical. "Politics must be reduced to ethics if it was not to reduce itself to corruption; the rhetoric of the classical style commanded this, irrespective of the sincerity with which Bolingbroke or any other employed it," (484) and so "Bolingbroke was driven to stake his intellectual and rhetorical all on the concept of virtue." (485)

In eighteenth-century England this Country ideology was opposed by that of the Court, "less eloquently rhetorical because less morally normative. . . . which accurately identified the forces making for historical change . . . but which supplied neither polity nor personality with a coherent moral structure." (467) In America, however, there was no Court ideology: "the ideology that presented virtue as ever threatened by corruption was little mitigated by any sense that it was possible to live with the forces of history and contain them." (467) This is truly a striking claim; Pocock says "the present state of research strongly suggests" it, meaning, above all, studies by Bernard Bailyn, Gerald Stourzh, and Gordon Wood. But do they subscribe, as he claims, to a Colonial American "dread of modernity itself?" (509)

Though "not all Americans were schooled in this tradition," namely "neo-Harringtonian civic humanism," "there was (it would almost appear) no alternative tradition in which to be schooled. In consequence, Bailyn and others have argued, the ideology of eighteenth century opposition acted as a restricting and compulsive force in the approaches to revolution." "Once Americans began to talk of corruption, the situation rapidly passed out of intellectual control." (507) Here we hear "that paranoiac note . . . when men are forced by the logic of mental restriction to conclude that malign agencies are conspiring against the inner citadels of their personalities." (508)

The opposition of virtue and corruption "formed a closed and compulsive scheme," but "could only operate as such when no other scheme was known." The association of commerce and corruption, which the Colonists alledgedly inherited from the Country party, would support the total dominance of Country ideology. This situation prevailed up to 1776 and beyond; that is what Pocock means by saying the Revolution was "an essay in Kuhnian 'normal science.'" (508) It was only later, he maintains, in the period of the making of the Constitution, that an alternative orientation arose, Madisonian republicanism (or representative democracy), and it arose only in the wake of the failure of the classical model, specifically, the failure of an elite "natural aristocracy" of leaders to emerge from the many. This latter contention I hope to take up elsewhere. Here it is a question simply of the original conception of American independence.

Pocock first developed these ideas in a review essay, devoted to Stourzh's *Alexander Hamilton and the Idea of Republican Government* and Wood's *The Creation of the American Republic 1776-*

1787, entitled, "Virtue and Commerce in the Eighteenth Century." There he included in the classicist legacy left to the Colonists by the Country ideology "a Renaissance pessimism concerning the direction and reversibility of social and historical change," and infers,

> The classical view of p-olitics was consequently a closed ideology. Bailyn—now followed by Wood—argued that its grip on the colonial mind was so absolute that the Americans of the 1760s and 1770s were compelled first, to identify as "corruption" what seemed to be threats to their polities and, second, to conclude that the degeneration not merely of their liberties but also of their moral personalities would soon pass beyond redemption unless they reaffirmed the first uncorrupt principles of civic virtue. Their revolution was thus primarily a *rivoluzione, ricorso*, or *ridurre ai principi*—the terminology is appropriately Machiavellian—rather than a transformation; only in its consequences did it become the latter.[42]

In a long chapter of *The Ideological Origins of the American Revolution* entitled "Transformation," Bailyn argues, much in the way Cecilia Kenyon had, that "the radicalism the Americans conveyed to the world in 1776 was a transformed as well as a transforming force."[43] And in his opening chapter, "'Resort to First Principles,'" Stourzh unmistakably argues rather for a Hobbesian right of self-preservation of the people as a whole, as the principle to which Hamilton and others had recourse. How Pocock could manage to overlook Stourzh's explicit and emphatic argument that Hamilton's republicanism was Hobbesian well before the Revolution, though his opposition to the rigorist principles of virtue of classical republicanism only emerged later, is a puzzle. The twin elements of what I have called the Hobbesian moment, self-interest, and the foundation of sovereignty, are nicely elucidated by Stourzh.

Pocock superimposes his Spartan-Stoic republican model, with its "neo-Harringtonian" antagonism to economic interdependence and appetite, onto Bailyn's and Stourzh's interpretations of the motivation and rationale of the Revolution and thereby turns them into something they were not intended to be. The American republic, like Oceana, was expansive yet stable because its basis was an expansive agrarian-commerical economy. The assertion and establishment of American independence undeniably drew on a rich background of republican thought, above all from seveteenth-century England, but this republicanism was rooted in the identification of private and public good through the fundamental role accorded to self-interest in attaining and maintaining political sovereignty.

NOTES

1. *The Life and Selected Writings of Thomas Jefferson*, ed. Adrienne Koch and William Peden (New York: Random House, 1944), p.296.

2. J. A. W. Gunn, *Politics and the Public Interest in the Seventeenth Century* (Toronto: University of Toronto Press, 1969), pp. 4-5. Cf. p. 7, Madison's *Federalist*, No. 10 anticipated in 1642.

3. *Ibid.*, pp. 16-21. C. B. Macpherson, *The Political Theory of Possessive Individualism* (Oxford: Oxford University Press, 1964), pp. 140-41, discusses Overton's Hobbesian derivation of rights from self-preservation as the first law of nature. The Levellers' "proprietarian" conception of freedom, based in the natural property one has in one's self, i.e. a right to the free use, improvement and enjoyment of one's capacities, led them to assert "the individual right to trade as a natural right." "The primary function of government was to secure precisely that property, that is, to make and enforce the rules within which men could make the most of their own energies and capacities." (p. 144)

4. Gerald Stourzh, *Alexander Hamilton and the Idea of Republican Government* (Stanford: Stanford University Press, 1970), p.22, quotes Hamilton from 1775, "When the first principles of civil society are violated, and the rights of a whole people are invaded, the common forms of municipal law are not to be regarded. Men may betake themselves to the law of nature. . . ."

5. *The William and Mary Quarterly*, 3rd ser., 19 (1962), 153-82. In the following paragraphs I quote from pp. 153, 166-69, 171, 173-74.

6. See Jeffrey Barnouw, "The 'Pursuit of Happiness' in Jefferson, and its Background in Bacon and Hobbes," *Interpretation. A Journal of Political Philosophy*, 11 (1983), 225-48.

7. Appleby, "Liberalism and the American Revolution," *The New England Quarterly*, 49 (1976), 3-26, p.25.

8. Appleby, "Economic Rationalism and the Rationale for the American Revolution," paper read to the 1975 Annual Meeting of the American Historical Association.

9. Appleby, "Ideology and Theory: The Tension between Political and Economic Liberalism in Seventeeth-Century England," *The American Historical Review*, 81 (1976), 499-515, p. 500. Cf. Appleby, *Economic Thought and Ide-*

ology in Seventeenth-Century England (Princeton: Princeton University Press, 1978), p.134.

10. Appleby, "Ideology and Theory," p. 505: *Economic Thought*, p.169.
11. *Ibid.*
12. See Appleby, "Locke, Liberalism and the Natural Law of Money," *Past and Present*, 71 (1976), 43-69, and *Economic Thought*, pp. 220-41, 250-54.
13. "Ideology and Theory," p.511.
14. "Economic Rationalism," pp.15-16
15. Cf. "Liberalism and the American Revolution," pp.17,24.
16. Cf. "Economic Rationalism" pp.22-23.
17. "Economic Rationalism," p. 23. Cf. p. 25, a pamphlet from the 1696 re-coinage controversy, *A discourse of money* "claimed that giving surety for good behavior created a stronger bond than conscience, religion or honor. 'In these we are sure there may be Hypocrisies, but in Interest we know there is none.'" For variations on the theme "Interest never lies," see Gunn, *Politics*, pp. 36-38, 43-45.
18. "Economic Rationalism," p. 26.
19. See Jeffrey Barnouw, "Johnson and Hume considered as the core of a new 'period concept' of the Enlightenment," *Transactions of the Fifth International Congress on the Enlightenment*, I (*Studies in Voltaire and the Eighteenth Century*, 190.) (Oxford: The Voltaire Foundation, 1980), 189-96.
20. See Jeffrey Barnouw, "Commerce and Commonwealth in *Cato's Letters*," paper for the session Liberty and Commonwealth: Studies in Honor or Caroline Robbins" at a meeting of the North American Conference on British Studies, October 1981. Being revised for publication.
21. J. G. A. Pocock, *The Machiavellian Moment. Florentine Political Thought and the Atlantic Republican Tradition* (Princeton, 1975), page references given in my text.
22. *Machiavellian Moment*, p. 518, "At the core of Hobbe's moral theory is indeed the statement that it is only when I become capable of owning another's actions as my own that I become capable of civic morality," representation which Pocock sees not only as the opposite of participation, but as a transfer or surrender "of one's plenitude of power and one's *persona* if not one's individuality." "Republican humanism, which was fundamentally concerned with the affirmation of moral personality in civic action, had cause to ask whether the concept of representation did not exclude that of virtue." In *Oceana* Harrington quotes Thucydides, VIII, 97, (in Hobbes's translation) "the Athenians seem to have ordered their state aright" by measures that Harrington calls "the first example that I find, or think is to be found, of a popular assembly by way of representative," *The Political Works of James Harrington*, ed. J. G. A. Pocock, (Cambridge: Cambridge University Press, 1977), p.279. Pocock's opposition of rotation to representation is forced; Harrington's republicanism presupposes representation of the people.
23. *The Spartan Tradition in European Thought* (Oxford: Oxford University Press, 1969), p.2.
24. *Ibid.*, pp.137-38.
25. *Ibid.*, pp.142, 151-55, cf. p. 199.

26. *Ibid.*, p.238.

27. Pocock considers two other approaches to the "universality" of the republic, but abandons both. A Renaissance humanist "conversation" across the
ages (63) tends too much towards Athenian emphasis on what is polite, civil,
urbane, as distinguished from what is political, civic, urban, and thus is
more apt, he says, for princely than for republican rule. (64) Salutati's
characterization of lawmaking in *On the Nobility of Law and Medicine* is then
identified with "Plato's architectonic art, the conduct of human activity at
the point where it attained universality." (65) Pocock overlooks that Salutati associates the law-making with the rule of kings and princes,
emphasizes its origin in the will that must be obeyed because it holds the
power to punish, and sees it as completing the laws of nature, which only
incline us, by making civil laws that bind us. In short, a remarkable anticipation of Hobbes.

28. Pocock, *Politics, Language, and Time. Essays on Political Thought and History*
(New York: Atheneum, 1971), pp. 80-103; see p.88.

29. *Ibid.*, p.96.

30. Pocock, *The Ancient Constitution and the Feudal Law. English Historical Thought
in the Seventeenth Century* ,(Cambridge: Cambridge University Press, 1957;
repr. New York: Norton, 1967), p.129.

31. *Ibid.*, pp.142-43.

32. *The Political Works of James Harrington*, p. 230. this edition will be cited in
parentheses within my text in the following way: (H 230).

33. *Political Works*, p. 171, "and 'as often as reason is against a man, so often
will a man be against reason.'" The probable reference is ch. 11 of *Leviathan*, ed. Macpherson, (Baltimore: Penguin, 1968), p. 166, "setting
themselves aginst reason, as oft as reason is against them."

34. *Leviathan*, p. 227. (ch. 17)

35. *Ibid.*, p. 223.

36. In his Introduction to *The Machiavellian Moment*, p. vii, Pocock writes that
Harrington brought about a synthesis "of Machiavelli's theory of arms with
a common-law understanding of the imporatnce of freehold property."
(cf. p. 17) Pocock also seems to attribute a common-law conception of
property to Ireton, p. 376, on the basis of a passage that rather suggests
Hobbes: "The Law of God doth not give me property, nor the Law of Nature, but property is of human constitution. I have property and this I shall
enjoy. Constitution founds property," p. 375. This hardly reflects a desire
"to anchor the individual in custom, in a law made by men indeed, but by
men who could not be identified."

37. If Pocock tends to neglect the importance of sovereignty, and its function
in and for peace, in Harrington, he also emphasizes local contexts of constitutional controversy at the expense of the general drastic situation of civil
war which made the issue of stability paramount. In *Oceana, Political Works*,
p. 241, Harrington contrasts his own time with "those ancient and heroical
ages when men thought that to be necessary which was virtuous."

> But now, when no man is desired to throw up a farthing of his
> money or a shovelful of his earth, and that all we can do is but to
> make a virtue of necessity, we are disputing whether we should have
> peace or war. For peace you cannot have without some govern-
> ment, nor any government without the proper balance; wherefore,

if you will not fix this [balance] which you have, the rest is blood, for without blood you can bring in no other.

38. Pocock, *Politics, Language and Time*, pp. 104-47; p. 117.

39. *Ibid.*, p. 115.

40. See the essay cited above in note 20.

41. *Politics, Langauge and Time*, p. 127.

42. *Journal of Interdisciplinary History*, 3 (1972), 119-34, p. 120.

43. *The Ideological Origins of the American Revolution* (Cambridge, Mass.: Harvard University Press, 1967), p.161.

Tommy Paine and the Idea of America

ISAAC KRAMNICK

An American finding himself in England, as I did in July 1976, had two alternatives if he wanted to pay his respects to Englishmen who played an important role in bringing about the American Revolution. He could visit the marble tomb of George III or the Norfolk village where Tom Paine was born. It should surprise no one, leaving even politics aside, that this American chose to spend a Sunday in the quiet market town of Thetford rather than battle the tourist queues of Windsor Castle.

The Paine memorabilia were hard to find even in little Thetford until some helpful local workmen were spotted passing their morning with a few pints in front of the village pub— a sacramental celebration of the Lord's day that would have appealed to Tom Paine in more ways than one. Asked for directions to the market place and the famed Paine statue, the three workmen came alive with enthusiasm and warmth for the visiting American interested in their native son. Directions were carefully given to what they described as the Tommy Paine statue; I was told not to miss the Tommy Paine hotel, where legend has it that Tommy Paine was born. I should also see, they added, the school house where Tommy Paine learned reading and writing. They spoke as if Tommy Paine were their living mate, as if his spirit breathed through the egalitarian comradeship of their working lives. There was something else, too, in their jovial and easy conversation with me. It was a sense that I as an American could particularly understand their affection for Tommy Paine. As it had been for Paine in 1776, so it was for these men in Thetford in 1976. America was matey, America was equality, America was a land not of privilege and natural guvnors, but of hardworking equals.

Being not of a mind to correct this reading of America 1976, I was, in fact, deeply moved by this chance encounter. Long after leaving Thetford I remembered these three workingmen and understood from our meeting ever more vividly what all those magisterial pages of E. P. Thompson's *Making of the English Working Class* had tried to convey—the place of Tom Paine in the hearts of the English common people. He was their Tommy, their own hero. I was also struck by their instinctive linkage of him with America and their unabashed affection for both. Tom Paine would have liked that; few Englishmen have so loved America as Paine did. It is impossible to understand the mind of their beloved mate Tommy Paine without realizing how critical America and its meaning were to this son of a Norfolk staymaker. This, then, is my theme—Tommy Paine and the idea of America. What I want to argue is that America had a specific idealized meaning for Paine. It symbolized the new age, the new bourgeois age, that Paine saw replacing the archaic and aristocratic world from which he personally had fled in 1774. And this would be the case throughout his life. The idea of America would be a critical component of his radical ideology. It provided tangible evidence of the future. America was the pattern for the new social, political, and economic ideals that would rise from the ashes of the *ancien régime*.

Let us begin this dicussion of what the idea of America meant to Paine by turning to his first important piece of work, his phenomenally successful *Common Sense*. Paine, a monumental failure at age thirty-seven, had been in America for only fourteen months when he wrote *Common Sense* in 1776. It was published anonymously, signed only "by an Englishman." This signature speaks volumes, however; *Common Sense*, so critical in turning American opinion to independence, was written very much with England's problems on Paine's mind. He was an Englishman and it is this which breathes through every page of this remarkable work. He brought to the burning issues of the American winter of 1776 the theoretical mind and raging anger of English radicalism.

While the intellectual roots of Paine's pamphlet were, of course, the late seventeeth-century liberal ideas of John Locke, he was himself the product of their radical restatement in the writings of the English dissenting ministers like Priestley, Price, and Burgh in the late eighteenth century. British government is attacked in Paine's pamphlet with all the savagery that one finds in the London defenders of John Wilkes and all the fiery passion that one finds among the Unitarian and Calvinist opponents of the Test and Corporation Acts which excluded dissenting Protestants from government and municipal positions from Oxford and Cambridge. Nowhere in *Common Sense* does Paine itemize the grievances of the American colonies. It is simply taken for granted that their treatment by the English government violates universal reason and natural rights. It is an "exceedingly complex" and exceptionally corrupt engine of oppression that hangs as a weight upon the energetic Americans as it does upon the virtuous English.[3]

We know now that Americans were keenly interested in English developments in the 1760s and 1770s and followed very closely the writings of English radicals the likes of Wilkes, Price, and Priestley. Their confrontations with Parliament and George III were eagerly followed in the colonies.[4] Indeed, the trials and tribulations of America after 1763 were seen in this larger perspective. There was a common battle against tyranny and corruption—the Eastern front saw English radicals fighting the good battle and the Western front saw the colonists manning the defenses of freedom.[5] Paine, then, in *Common Sense* could call upon issues that addressed grievances common to the discontented non-Anglican populations of both countries. We are justified, then in speaking of trans-Atlantic radicalism and Paine is its most distinguished theorist.

In England one particular group that sensed itself oppressed was the talented middle class. And it is their grievances that Paine and his radical colleagues in England articulated in the assault on the monarchic and aristocratic principle. Traditional society assumed certain natural distinctions which, as Paine noted, exalted certain ranks above others. Where one fit into this hierarchical order was determined by birth. In turn, prestige, power, and privilege were accorded individuals by dint of rank and distinction. Against this aristocratic ideal the English bourgeoisie, whose articulate ranks were being swelled by the successful entrepreneurs of the industrial revolution, offered a new ideal: that of careers and rewards open to the talented. Armed with a vision of "mankind being originally equal in the order of creation," as Paine put it, the middle class attacked the dominance of idle monarchs and useless aristocrats in society and politics and demanded in turn an end to all elements of traditional privileges which froze individuals into permanent inequality.[6] What mattered was not lineage but talent and merit. It is this ideological camp with Paine very much at its center that I want to call bourgeois radicalism—a radicalism that floursiehd in the colonies, in England, and of course in France.[7] It is symbolized dramatically, if you wish, in this period by the charge of Beaumarchais' Figaro to Count Almaviva.

> Just because you're a noble Lord, you think you're a genius. Nobility, fortune, rank, position—you're so proud of these things. What have you done to deserve so many rewards? You went to the trouble of being born, and no more.[8]

One is reminded that dissenting Protestantism was a critical component of the ideology of this talented bourgeoisie by the importance Paine gives in *Common Sense* to scriptural, primarily Old Testament, injunctions against monarchy and aristocratic distinctions in general. It provides a link with the levelling radicalism of the seventeenth-century civil-war sects, many of whose descendants had emigrated to the more egalitarian shores of America, and to the many English religious entrepreneurs of the late eighteenth century who threatened to leave for America if the religious exclusiveness of the Anglican establishment were not modified. The Quaker Tom Paine knew his audience well and knew that Biblical arguments against the British would move them. He also knew that hard-working, self-reliant Americans had no love for the hereditary principle by which a man has "a right to set up his own family in perpetual preference to all others forever."[9]

The attack on privilege and the privileged orders would be the continuous motif of Paine's life and career, and for this he became a symbol to his age. In one of his novels, Robert Bage, the late eighteenth-century English radical novelist, for example, indicated the passing of the old order by describing a change in the reading habits of his hero. "In my youth I also read tragedies, epic poems, romances, and divinity. Now I read *Common Sense*."[10] The author of *Common Sense* was no ordinary radical. His was perhaps the most devastating assault on the old order that could be found in the bourgeois camp. Burke wrote of Paine that he sought to destroy "in six or seven days" the feudal and chivalric world which "all the boasted wisdom of our ancestors has labored to bring to perfection for six or seven centuries."[11] Part of Paine's achievement was indeed to mock the past so venerated by Burke. For Paine it was "the Quixotic age of chivalric nonsense." He ridiculed the ancient principles of British society, beginning in *Common Sense* with the useless and unproductive monarchy. It is an anger that would please my friends in Thetford.

> In England a king hath little more to do than to make war and give away places; which in plain terms, is to impoverish the nation and set it together by the ears. A pretty business indeed for a man to be allowed eight hundred thousand sterling a year for, and worshipped into the bargain! Of mor worth is one honest man to society and the sight of God, than all the crowned ruffians that ever lived.[12]

This is England. America is something else, indeed, to Paine and his fellow radicals in the late eighteenth century. America is a beacon of hope. For Paine and for other spokesmen of English bourgeois radicalism, America is paradise. It is the vital and virtuous egalitarian ideal held up to corrupt and aristocratic England.

The irresistible attraction of America is an all-powerful theme in English life and letters in the last four decades of the eighteenth century. Paine is but an expression of a very general tendency in England, most particularly evident, of course, in radical circles. In English popular literature, for example, one of the books of the period most widely read and reprinted deals specifically with the paradise that is America—Robert Bage's *Hermsprong: or Man As He is Not. Hermsprong* depicts a noble savage raised by American Indians who is brought to England to show off his unadulterated virtue, and to heap scorn on the pretensions of birth and polished society. He is the simplicity and ingenuousness of America incarnate. He ridicules all the apparatus of aristocratic civilization, glittering coaches, ponies, palaces, gluttony, and war. His tastes are simple and ascetic. He drinks neither wine nor ale, only water. More significantly, he owes obedience and subordination to no one. "Nor can I," he proudly proclaims, "learn to suppress the sentiment of a free-born mind, from any fear, religious or political. Such uncourtly obduracy has my savage education produced."[13] Hermsprong refuses to defer to anyone, which leads to the inevitable confrontation with the symbolic representative of aristotcracy, in this case the arrogant Lord Grondale. Through his narrator, Bage indicates his feelings about such insolence and refusals to defer to betters.

> I, the son of nobody, felt myself raised, exalted by it. I almost began to think myself a man. But is a word of bad augury. Kings like it not. Parsons preach it down; and justices of the peace send out warrants to apprehend it.[14]

Hermsprong was not merely a wild savage, however, mindless, for example, of the rights of property. He was the very model of a bourgeois savage, appalled, to be sure, at the rule of unmerited and untalented privilege, but one whose egalitarian vision by no means involved absolute levelling. There are after all fundamental variations in talent and merit. So it is that we find our very bourgeois radical savage lecturing a mob of rioting miners: "My friends, we cannot all be rich; there is no possible equality of property which can last a day."[15]

Like Paine, many English radicals came to the paradise that was America. After they arrived one of the first things they often did was write back to their radical friends in England about America. Thomas Cooper was just such an English radical of these years who popularized America as an alternative to the corruption of Albion. Manchester cotton manufacturer and radical activist, he ultimately emigrated to Pennsylvania. Once there, he wrote a pamphlet encouraging other dissenters, religious and political, to follow him across the Atlantic. "The first and principal feature of America," he argued, was "the total absence of anxiety, respecting the future success of a family." In Great Britain, he wrote, "the middle class of moderate fortune, must work incessantly, deprive themselves of comfort, and pay anxious attention to minute frugality, with little probability of ultimate success," especially those with a large family. In America, he insisted, in language not uncharacteristically reminiscent of Bunyan, this "whole weight is taken off the father of a family." "Anxious industry deserves a better reward" than it receives in England. Social mobility is a reality in America, success is easy and a family quickly set up in land and wealth. Even God testifies to this land where bourgeois values have replaced aristocratic values. Cooper quotes with approval Ben Franklin's claim "that the people (in America) have a saying—that God Almighty is Himself a mechanic, the greatest in the universe, and He is respected and admired more for the variety, ingenuity and utility of His handiwork, than for the antiquity of His family."[15]

The two towering figures of English radicalism, the Reverends Richard Price and Joseph Priestley, were also dazzled by America. They saw it as part of God's divine plan, as evidence of the coming millennium. Americans were, Price preached, witness "to a progessive improvement in human affairs which will terminate in greater degrees of light and virtue and happiness than have yet been known."[17] For Priestley, America showed the way. Soon, he predicted, all the world would, like her, "be flourishing and happy." In America, he wrote, was proof "of a new era in the history of mankind . . . a change from darkness to light . . . from a most debasing servitude to a state of the most exalted freedom."[18] And so, in fact, Priestley came to America, the paradise of freedom, encouraged, to be sure, by the Birmingham mob that had burned his house and laboratory in 1791.

Price and Priestley nothwithstanding, no one of this period was able to approach Tommy Paine in singing of the millennial promise of America. In *Common Sense* America stands as the living repudiation of the old aristocratic and monarchic order. Her independence strikes the first blow in the battle to overthrow the *ancien régime*; it would usher in a new era in world history.

Paine's rhetoric in *Common Sense* reminds his readers, indeed flatters his fundamentalist readers, that the independent of the thirteen colonies was an event of momentuous importance, not unlike the dramatic events told of in the scriptures. Like the Hebrews, the Americans were invested with a messianic mission. "The cause of America is in a great measure the cause of all mankind," Paine points out in the introduction. The scriptural tone is repeated later in the pamphlet when he notes that "posterity are virtually involved in the contest, and will be more or less affected, even to the end of time, by the proceedings now."[19] American independence was a flood which would wipe clean the slate of history. America had it in her power, Paine writes, "to begin the world over again." A situation, similar to the present, "hath not happened since the days of Noah until now." Barred from the rest of the world, freedom, like Paine, had crossed the Atlantic.

> O ye that love mankind! Ye that dare oppose not only the tyranny, but the tyrant, stand forth! Every spot of the old world is overrun with oppression. Freedom hath been hunted round the globe. Asia, and Africa, have long expelled her—Europe regards her like a stranger, and England hath given her warning to depart. O! receive the fugitive, and prepare in time an asylum for mankind.[20]

America represented a millenial regeneration, an egalitarian humanity being literally twice born. In a letter to the Abbé Raynal, Paine described the events in America as those in which the very "style and manner of thinking have undergone a revolution." In America, he wrote, "we see with other eyes; we hear with other ears; and we think with other thoughts, than we formerly used."[21]

Paine had seen the future in America. It would be, he was convinced, the spark that set off the flame of bourgeois revolution in Europe. America was a new Athens, "the admiration and model for the present." America ushered in a new are in human history, what Paine described as the "birthday of a new world." The American Revolution introduced a world dominated by republican principles and bourgeois ideals, and these political principles would rapidly spread throughout the world, Paine assumed. This millennial mission or worldwide reform could even be rendered in mechanical terms. Paine, the engineer, likened America's destiny to Archimedes' famous quest. "Had we," said he, "a place to stand upon, we might raise the world. The Revolution in America presented in politics what was only theory in mechanics."[22]

What were these new political principles? American government was, first of all, inexpensive. The civil list for the support of one man, the King of England, Paine noted, "is eight times greater than the whole expense of the federal government in America."[23] American government was also simple and understandable. The Americans put into practice Paine's maxim that the "sum of necessary government is much less than is generally thought."[24] There was no room in the limited scope of American government for the craft and obfuscation of courts. Everyone understood the operation of government there; nothing was hidden in recesses of complexity and arcane knowledge. "There is no place for mystery; no where for it to begin." In *Common Sense* Paine praised the simplicity of American government as "less liable . . . to be disordered." By contrast, "the constitution of England is so exceedingly complex" that its ills endure for years while the source of the fault is hunted down. The advantages of government in America are all interrelated. It is only by getting men to believe "that government is some wonderful mysterious thing, that excessive revenues are obtained," Paine wrote.[25]

Finally, government in America, to which the world would soon turn, was representative government, firmly rooted in the consent of the governed. Here, too, Paine the bourgeois radical is evident. Describing the profound revolution that is popular government he reads like the often-parodied bourgeois liberal describing government as a joint stock company. Not only was his image of American government that of a business enterprise, but his description of consent and representation was rendered in the cost-accounting language of capitalism. He wrote of free America:

> Every man there is a proprietor in government, and considers it a necessary part of his business to understand. It concerns his interest, because it effects his property. He ex-

amines the cost, and compares it with the advantages; and
above all, he does not adopt the slavish custom of following
what in other governments are called LEADERS.[26]

Government was founded in America, Paine wrote, on "a
moral theory," on the "indefeasible, hereditary rights of man."[27]
And it was this spirit, Paine suggested, which was sweeping from
West to East. Government based on this moral theory had dramatic social and economic implications. In *The Rights of Man*
Paine's message was that these, too, would soon cross the Atlantic.

> There [America] the poor are not oppressed, the rich are
> not privileged. Industry is not mortified by the splendid ex-
> travagance of a court rioting at its expense. There taxes are
> few, because their government is just.[28]

Paine wrote his *Common Sense* in Philadelphia with English
radicalism very much in the back of his mind. In the 1790's he
wrote the *Rights of Man* in London with the ideal of America on
his mind. What is depicted as most damningly wrong with English politics and society in *The Rights of Man* is that neither is like
their American counterparts.

> I see in America, a government extending over a country ten
> times as large as England, and conducted with regularity, for
> a fortieth part of the expense which government costs in
> England. If I ask a man in America, if he wants a King? he
> retorted, and asks me if I take him for an idiot? How is it
> that this difference happens are we more or less wise than
> others? I see in America, the generality of people living in a
> style of plenty unknown in monarchical countries; and I see
> that the principle of its government, which is that of the equal
> Rights of Man, is making a rapid progress in the world . . .
> From the rapid progress which America makes in every
> species of improvement, it is rational to conclude, that if the
> governments of Asia, Africa, and Europe, had begun on a
> principle similar to that of America, or had not been very
> early corrupted therefrom, that those countries must, by this
> time, have been in a far superior condition to what they are.
> Age after age has passed away, for no other purpose than
> to behold their wretchedness.[29]

Paine, writing in 1791 his most famous book, describes England mired in corrupt wretchedness and America frolicking in virtuous happiness. In practical political terms what this means for Paine in *The Rights of Man* is that England still lives in Burke's beloved age of chivalry. On top of a harmonious self-regulating society there sits in England, according to Paine, an overblown unnecessary Government whose greedy hand "thrusts itself into every corner and crevice of industry, grasping the spoils of the multitude." This expensive tyrannical government taxes the industrious to finance vast armies, navies, and an even more costly and dispensable monarchy. It subsidizes an idle aristocracy for whom "useless posts, places and offices must be found."[30] Freedom in *The Rights of Man* is relief from taxation. Republican government, American government, is cheap and decentralized government. Tyranny is expensive taxing British government.

British government, unlike its American counterpart, fails even to provide the security essential for men to enjoy the fruits of their labor. As such it deserves to be overthrown, according to Paine. *The Rights of Man* justifies revolution, then, on these very practical bourgeois grounds.

> When we survey the wretched condition of man under the monarchical and hereditary systems of government, dragged from his home by one power, driven by another, and impoverished by taxes more than by enemies, it becomes evident that those systems are bad, and that a general revolution in the principle and construction of governments is necessary.[31]

After the Revolution in England which Paine called for in *The Rights of Man*, England, he assumed, would resemble his beloved America. All the accumulated absurdities of the ages so praised by Burke would be swept aside and the American egalitarian ideal would be found in England's green and pleasant land. Is there anything more absurd than the hereditary principle, Paine asked in *The Rights of Man*, "as absurd as an hereditary wise man and as ridiculous as an hereditary poet-laureate?"[32] What mattered was not a man's pedigree but his productivity. This was the message of Adam Smith, and Paine berates his arch-opponent Burke in *the Rights of Man* for his false reasoning which he would have recanted "had Mr. Burke possessed talents similar to the author of *On the Wealth of Nations*."[33] Government required "talents and abilities," yet its offices were filled by a nobility which, according to Paine, really meant "no ability."[34] The aristocracy were unproductive idlers, parasites who lived off the work of the industrious classes. No one missed them in America and they would be missed even less in postrevolutionary Britain.

> Why then does Mr. Burke talk of his house of Peers, as the pillar of the landed interest? Were that pillar to sink into the earth, the same landed property would continue, and the same ploughing, sowing, and reaping would go on. The aristocracy are not the farmers who work the land and raise the produce, but are mere consumers of the rent; and when compared with the active world are the drones . . . who neither collect the honey nor form the hive, but exist only for lazy enjoyment.[35]

There is really little contradiction between Paine's radical egalitarian views and his defense of property and business enterprise. Paine, even in America, was an English radical, nurtured in an aristocratic society. Bourgeois ideals were, in his mind, inextricably linked with an egalitarian vision of society. The stratified society of privilege and rank perpetuated by the hereditary principle would be leveled in a bourgeois world where political and social place would be determined by talent, merit, and hard work. To be a fierce egalitarian, to be acutely sensitive to injustice, was by no means incompatible in this era with being bourgeois; indeed, for some time in England the two would be by no means contradictory. Only in America and other societies which lacked an oppressive and hierarchical past was there a problem in being both a bourgeois ideologue and and egalitarian. But even here the two were by no means always mutually exclusive, for liberal egalitarianism does not insist on equality of conditions, but only equality of opportunity

Enterprising individuals left alone by government would not produce a completely egalitarian social structure. Good bourgeois liberal that he was, Paine saw the post-revolutionary order free of the aristocracy but still characterized by economic differentiation. "That property will ever be unequal is certain," in wrote in 1795. This was not unjust, but simply a result of "industry, superiority of talents, dexterity of management, extreme frugality, and fortunate opportunities."[35]

To emphasize the bourgeois Paine is not to discount the Paine who later would become a hero for the Chartists, early trade unionists, and for my friends in Thetford. It is simply to insist that his radicalism be seen as still within the bourgeois fold, a line of interpretation receiving little stress in recent discussions of his politics. There is no doubt that while other bourgeois radicals may have just as bitterly assailed the higher ranks of privilege few could match Paine in his sympathy for the lower ranks of the poor and destitute. This, however, was by no means the major emphasis in his writings. Nevertheless, it informed the brilliant series of policy reforms he advocated in *Rights of Man* Part Two, which anticipated so much of twentieth-century social welfare legislation. What is so fascinating in retrospect is the extent to which Paine's radicalism, his bourgeois radicalism, was given content by his sense that America, its reality as well as its ideals, represented the post-revolutionary order incarnate. He had come to Philadelphia and seen the future, to borrow a phrase from a later revolutionary era.

There is no doubt, then, that Paine pushed bourgeois radicalism to its outermost limits and that in doing this represented for conservatives of his era a dangerous influence. American conservatives hated Paine, too. Edmund Burke had good company. There is, for example, America's second president, the patriot John Adams. A leader of colonial protest against England, an advocate of independence, Adams had never lost his basic conservative ideals. The radical and egalitarian vision of Paine offended Adams' sense of the given and proper ranks that necessarily structure the social order. Paine's vision of an egalitarian America, albeit one where talent and merit were rewarded by differential status, and his vision of cheap virtually nonexistent government as an ideal were too much for Adams. Not all Americans shared the idealization of their revolutionary objectives that we have seen in Paine. Adams sensed the evil even in *Common Sense*, calling it "a poor, ignorant, malicious, short sighted, crapulous mass." In a letter of 1805 Adams wrote:

> I know not whether any man in the world has had more in-
> fluence on its inhabitants or affairs for the last thirty years
> than Tom Paine. There can be no severer satyr on the age.
> For such a mongrel between pig and puppy, begotten by a
> wild boar on a bitch wolf, never before in any age of the
> world was suffered by the poltroonery of mankind, to run
> through such a career of mischief. Call it then the Age of
> Paine.[37]

John Adams notwithstanding, Tommy Paine loved America. His sense of its symbolic mission and its anticipation of the
future provide a thread of continuity to his varied and brilliant
career. But Adams was a sign of the times. America failed to return the love that Paine gave it. In 1802 Paine returned to
America for the final and most tragic chapter of his career. The
America he found was very different from the Philadelphia he
had known in 1774 or even in 1783. *Common Sense* was a thing of
the distant past. Paine was no longer the celebrated author of the
pamphlet so influential in its day. He was not the notorious author of the godless *Age of Reason* with its assault on Christianity.
Jefferson was man enough to renew his old ties with Paine, but
most Americans ignored him.

The aging Paine, with no family and few close friends, became cantankerous and argumentative, turning more and more
to the solace of drink. His last years were spent in New York City,
in what is now Greenwich Village, or on his farm in New Rochelle outside the city. He died on 8 June 1809. Few people saw
the coffin from the city to the farm in New Rochelle. At the burial
site there were even fewer present, merely a handful of New Rochelle neighbors and friends. There were no dignitaries, no
eulogies, no official notices of his death. The staymaker from
Thetford who had shaped the world as few have ever done, who
had known and been known by the greats of America, France,
and England, was laid to rest in a quiet pasture with no cere-
mony, no fanfare, no appreciation. The irony of such a funeral
for such a man was too much for Madame de Bonneville, who
had acted for several years as Paine's housekeeper, and who was
one of the few present. She later wrote:

> This interment was a scene to affect and to wound any sensible heart. Contemplating who it was, what man it was, that we were committing to an obscure grave on an open and disregarded bit of land, I could not help feeling most acutely. Before the earth was thrown down upon the coffin, I, placing myself at the east end of the grave, said to my son Benjamin, "stand you there, at the other end as a witness for grateful America." Looking round me, and beholding the small group of spectators, I exclaimed, as the earth was tumbled into the grave, "Oh! Mr. Paine! My son stands here as testimony of the gratitude of America, and I, for France!" This was the funeral ceremony of this great politician and philosopher![38]

Such was the gratitude of America in 1809 for Tommy Paine. Times have now changed. In recent years, America has returned some of Paine's love. It has even put his face on a postage stamp. But it's a sobered-up Paine that thrives today, a deradicalized Paine. Times have changed and to quote Paine today is to rip him from the context which inspired his bourgeois rage. Two hundred years later, almost to the same January day, Americans paid their debt to Tommy Paine in the person of another president, who repeatedly invoked Paine's *Common Sense* in a "State of the Union Address." Gerald Ford's speech in January 1976 used Paine's ideas to defend the ranks of privilege. Bourgeois radicalism had been transformed in these two hundred years. As it shifted from expressing the interests of a rising class to the interests of a triumphant class, what was once a critical ideology became a status-quo ideology. The spirit of 1776, bourgeois radicalism has become the spirit of 1876 and 1976, bourgeois conservatism. How this happened is another story that goes beyond the limits of this paper. Our concern is with the eighteenth-century parents, not the nineteenth- and twentieth-century children. Still, we could safely predict that were Tommy Paine around today he would have had a good laugh at Gerald Ford's invocation of his ideas to defend the privileged of America. Were he sitting with my friends of Thetford that Sunday in July, Paine would probably have grunted something unprintable about the radicalism of one age becoming the conservatism of another, and then without doubt, he would have joined his mates in another pint, another and still another—until at least the church services were over.

NOTES

1. Some of the themes developed in this paper are further elaborated in my Pelican Classics edition of *Common Sense* (London, 1976).

2. For further discussions of the social and political attitudes of English dissent in these years, see my "Religion and Radicalism: English Political Thought in the Age of Revolution," in *the Journal of Political Theory*, 5 (1977).

3. Paine, *Common Sense* ed. I. Kramnick (New York, 1976), p. 68. Citations that follow are to this edition.

4. See Pauline Maier's *From Resistance to Revolution* (New York: Random House, 1974) for an interesting discussion of this English connection.

5. See Bernard Bailyn's *The Ideological Origins of the American Revolution* (Cambridge, Mass.: Harvard University Press, 1967) for the classic statement of this view.

6. Paine, *Common Sense*, p.71.

7. The notion of bourgeois radicalism is developed most completely in my "Religion and Radicalism" and in Chapter One of my book *The Rage of Edmund Burke* (New York: Basic Books, 1977).

8. Beaumarchais, *Marriage of Figaro*, Act V.

9. *Common Sense*, p. 76. For the biblical passages see pp. 72-76.

10. Robert Bage, *The Fair Syrian* (London, 1787), I, 43.

11. Edmund Burke, "Letters on A Regicide Peace," in *Works of the Right Honorable Edmund Burke* (London, 1883), V, 395.

12. *Common Sense*, p. 83.

13. Robert Bage, *Hermsprong: or Man As He is Not*, ed. O. Wilkins (New York: Library Publishers, 1951), p. 73.

14. Ibid., p. 99.

15. Ibid., p. 225.

16. Thomas Cooper, *Some Information Respecting America* (London, 1974), p. 53.

17. Richard Price, *Evidence for a Future Period of Improvement in the State of Mankind with the Mean and Duty of Promoting It* (London, 1787), p. 25.

18. Joseph Priestley, *Letters to the Rt. Honorable Edmund Burke* (Birmingham, 1791), Letter XIV, p. 251.

19. *Common Sense*, pp. 63, 82.

20. Ibid., p. 100.

21. Tom Paine, "Letter to Abbé Raynal on the Affairs of North America," in

Writings of Tom Paine, ed. Moncare D. Conway (New York: G. P. Putnam's Sons, 1894-96; repr. New York: AMS Press, 1967), II, 105.

22. Tom Paine's *Rights of Man*, Pelican Classics edition (Harmondsworth: Penguin, 1969), p. 181.

23. *Rights of Man*, pp. 205-06.

24. "Thomas Paine's Answer to Four Questions on the Legislative and Executive Powers" (Paris, 1791), in *Writings of Thomas Paine*, III, 245.

25. *Common Sense*, p. 68; *Rights of Man*, p. 206.

26. *Rights of Man*, p. 206. Capitalization is Paine's.

27. Ibid., pp. 183-84.

28. Ibid., p. 189.

29. Ibid. pp. 147, 182.

30. *Rights of Man*, p. 277.

31. Ibid., p. 183.

32. Ibid., p. 105.

33. Ibid., p. 97.

34. Ibid., p. 128.

35. Ibid., p. 249.

36. "Dissertation on First Principles of Government (Paris, 1795), in *Writings of Thomas Paine*, III, 268.

37. Cited in David Freeman Hawke's *Paine* (New York: Harper and Row, 1974), p. 7.

38. Cited in Audrey Williamson, *Thomas Paine* (New York: St. Martin's Press, 1973), p. 275.

The Pattern of British Abolitionism in the Eighteenth and Nineteenth Centuries

ROGER T. ANSTEY

THE THEME of this paper is the way in which an essentially eighteenth-century impulse in Britain—anti slavery—develops and mutates in the nineteenth. The process of ending this major denial of civil, personal, and often religious liberty is inherently important, and I hope not only to illuminate this process, but to contribute in a modest way to the analysis of the reform process, by relating British abolitionism to Oliver Macdonagh's model of administrative reform and then by tentatively suggesting a model of my own.

This is not an explicitly controversial paper—though I hope it is a challenging one—but it is nonetheless useful to mention the salient features of the movement we are talking about by reference to rival interpretations which often seem as far apart as the polar opposites. The late Professor Coupland,[1] F. J. Klingberg,[2] and others essentially amplified W. E. H. Lecky in his dictum that "the unweary, unostentatious and inglorious crusade of England against slavery may probably be regarded as among the three or four perfectly virtuous pages comprised in the history of nations."[3] They saw the abolition of the British slave trade in 1807, the emancipation of British West Indian slaves in 1833, and the sixty-year combat against the so-called foreign slave trade as the signal triumph of a mainly religiously inspired hu-

93

manitarianism. Dr. Eric Williams, on the other hand, in *Capitalism and Slavery*, first published in 1944,[4] argued that the role of the humanitarians had been "seriously misunderstood and grossly exaggerated by men who have sacrificed scholarship to sentimentality and, like the scholastics of old, placed faith before reason and evidence."[5] What we had to study was "the role of . . . mature industrial capitalism in destroying the slave system [in Britain]."[6]

It is not my purpose here to comment directly on either of these interpretations—especially as I offered a critique of Williams some years ago.[7] I am concerned only to outline a thesis on the origins and development of British anti-slavery in the eighteenth century, its two triumphs of 1807 and 1833, and not least interesting, the paradox that the yet later triumphs of British abolitionism took place precisely when popular enthusiasm for the cause had largely disappeared. It is that fourfold task which I wish to attempt.

First, then, the eighteenth-century intellectual and religious origins of anti-slavery in Britain (here I briefly trench on the ground of a recent book of my own). It would be foolish to assert that the major significance of all eighteenth-century British philosophers, still less of the French *philosophes*, was that they demanded the abolition of slavery. It would be no less foolish to claim that I have studied in depth the development of their individual thought and the interconnections between their philosophies. For that I refer you to David Brion Davis's outstanding *Problem of Slavery in Western Culture*[8] and, more generally, to studies of the Enlightenment. What I believe one can demonstrate is that, however much the thinkers of the century differed amongst themselves, there was mu[h common ground between them in what, in both a general and a particular sense, pertained to anti-slavery. It can be shown that they attached much importance to liberty and tended to extend the definition of it; that a belief in benevolence, in its eighteenth-century sense, was general among them; that happiness as the particular expression of the principle of utility was frequently invoked as a criterion; that in Britain there was much more often than not, or was felt to be, a compatibility between the teachings of moral philosophy and of revealed religion; and that the one believed in a moral order, the other in a compatible idea of a providential order. One signifcance of all this is that the more emphasis was given to liberty and happiness, the more condemned and isolated did the slave system appear. Moreover, slavery was specifically condemned with near unanimity by the leading moral philosophers of the day. At the risk almost of pedantry let us list those authorities: Hutcheson, Montesquieu (included in this British list because of his great influence in Britain), Burke, Ferguson, Beattie, Wallace, Blackstone, Paley, Adam Smith, James Foster, John Millar, and, on balance, David Hume. From France came specific condemnations from Jaucourt, Voltaire, Turgot, albeit a shade equivocally, Mercier, Condorcet, and, very importantly, the Abbé Raynal and Rousseau.

A further significance of eighteenth-century thought that is highly relevant to our theme is that the emphasis on benevolence and the invoking of the principles of nature and utility were themselves marks of a growing disposition to effect change in the area of natural, civil, and political liberty by legislative action—a noteworthy development. And the trend was furthered by the development of a dynamic out of a static concept of the Chain of Being.

The relevance of mainstream theological developments to anti-slavery reform lay in the theological origins and religious dimension of the powerful idea of benevolence; in the the reinforcement of belief in a providential moral order as a sanction on conduct, and in that important root of the idea of progress which consisted in the belief in revelation as progressive, with the necessary corollary that the Christian was called to new commitment as he received new revelation. Eighteenth-century literature, mainly through the anti-slavery implications of the noble savage theme and through its reflection—appropriation even—of ideas of liberty and benevolence, sharpened and extended awareness of the problem of slavery, and made its own contribution to the emergence of anti-slavery conviction.

In essence, little serious intellectual defense of slavery was being offered by about the end of the third quarter of the eighteenth century. Indeed, that prosaic journal the *Annual Register* in 1788 made a very wide claim, indeed, using the fact of a forthcoming abolition notion as ground for resolving the problem of whether or not humanity was making progress:

> This problem is hastening fast to a decision. Liberty, humanity and science are daily extending, and bid fair to render despotism, cruelty and ignorance subjects of historical memory, not of actual observation. A considerable part of the proof of this was exhibited in the English Parliament during its present session—when an abolition motion was first proposed.[9]

But if we follow the *Annual Register* all the way in its ingenuousness, we succumb to the danger of supposing changes in ideas necessarily bring changes in the realm of action. We should rather remember John Millar's reflection on "how little the conduct of men is at bottom directed by any philosophical principles."[10]

In the next stage of our argument we shall seek to demonstrate that it was mainly religious conviction, insight, and zeal which made it possible for anti-slavery feeling to be subsumed in a crusade against the slave trade and slavery. But there *was* nevertheless profound significance in the way in which intellectual attitudes to slavery and change had altered, both in itself and because abolitionists thereby had a complex of ideas to which to appeal, and because, being children of their age, it was part of their own thinking.

For the dynamic of change, in the eighteenth and earlier part of the nineteenth century at any rate, we have to look to Quakerism and Evangelicalism; to Quakerism because it was in the bosom of the Anglo-American Quaker community that ever hardening anti-slavery resolve was fashioned as a result of a transatlantic dialogue in which the pressure for action came first from one side of the Atlantic and then from the other. What this suggests is the important role of a denominational community in which sharpening conviction and growing consensus can develop side by side until commitment and action result. The contribution of Evangelicalism was rather different. In assessing the importance of the mainly evangelical abolitionist leadership one must keep in tension that they did share many of their age's assumptions *and* that they had an extraordinary and positive dynamic of their own. They accepted much of the moral philosophy of their day, the emphasis on liberty, benevolence, and happiness, but transposed it into a religious key; from the assurance that their sin was forgiven through the grace of God in the redemptive work of Christ, they knew not only that they could overcome the evil in their own hearts but also that they could conquer those evils in the world which they felt called to combat. They believed especially powerfully in Providence as the sustaining power in the moral order and this belief gave them a satisfactory and coherent, albeit disturbing, philosophy of history. Equally their lively sense of a particular Providence directing their own lives was also their inescapable summons to mold the world to a righteousness which would avert national catastrophe, relieve the earthly sufferings of men, and pave the way for the salvation of men's eternal souls. Finally, in the very warp and woof of Evangelical faith, slavery, of all social evils, stood particularly condemned. This was because Evangelicals apprehended salvation primarily through the concept of redemption and when they related the idea of redemption, in its existential, individual application, to God's great redemptive purpose as made known in the Old Testament they saw that, historically, redemption was not least a redemption from physical bondage. Moreover, two abolitionist Evangelicals, Granville Sharp and Rev. Thomas Scott, so interpreted scriptural passages on the treatment and emancipation of slaves owned by the Hebrews that the hesitancy and ambivalence of Scripture about slavery were cut through and virtually all forms of slavery condemned at the bar of the law of love. All in all, the Evangelical was likely to be a formidable force if he turned to political action against the slave trade.

In analyzing what happened when Evangelicals did turn to political action we must be even more summary than we have already been. Admittedly they were unsuccessful in their first great campaign for nigh on twenty years—explicable in terms of the limits on Pitt's abolitionism imposed by contemporary conventions of the narrowness of the claims on Cabinet unanimity, a generalized fear of *all* reform, stemming from the French Revolution, and a widely disseminated sense amongst the political nation that the West Indies, and hence the slave trade which

supplied them, were a vital Imperial interest with which one would tamper at the nation's peril. The decisive change came when a fortuitous combination of circumstances permitted abolitionists to present the supplying of enemy, other foreign and captured territories with slaves by British slave ships as simple foolishness on the grounds that those selfsame slaves were then used to grow sugar which undercut or would undercut British-grown sugar on the all-important Continental market—whether or not it was carried in neutral ships. In other words the abolitionists in 1806, inspired by James Stephen the elder, had the wit to see that abolition of about two-thirds of the British slave trade could be procured by disguising their own humanitarian motivation as elementary national interest in time of war, and were able to secure the vital support of the leading men in the Ministry of all the Talents, that of prime minister Grenville being especially important.

A commentator of 1806, probably Stephen himself, aptly put it "that moral reformation might reasonably be deferred, till the extent of the sacrifice involved in it, was first reduced to its true value by the application of a merely political retrenchment."[11] Appropriate though these comments are, and important as it is to see the vital role of the neglected 1806 Foreign Slave Trade bill in abolitionist strategy, it is no less important to see that the 1807 measure of abolition, whose actual effect, given the Foreign Slave Trade bill of the previous year, was to end the slave trade to the older British West Indian islands, and which was overtly based on justice and humanity, served no national interest but in fact ran starkly counter to it. The manifest interest of Britian by 1806-07 was to maintain and even augment her own slave trade and deny slaves to her rivals.[12] Seymour Drescher's recent work has shown that "over the whole period from 1783-1807, the British slave system enlarged its frontier, its supply of virgin soil, its relative proportion of British trade, its imports and exports, its share of world sugar and coffee production . . . and the slave trade was, of course, a major ingredient in the continuing expansion of the slave system. . . . Abolitionism came not on the heels of trends adverse to slavery but in the face of propitious ones."[13]

Thus far in our analysis British anti-slavery we have seen intellectual and theological change, religious dynamism, the political weight of ministers of the Talents Government, the brilliant stroke of taking advantage of a fortuitous politico-economic conjuncture in 1806 to "cheapen the cost of morality"[14] and abolish two-thirds of the British slave trade, and action manifestly against the national interest in the 1807 measure. To these one should add the establishment of a grass roots national anti-slavery organization and a considerable appeal to public opinion, especially in 1792.

The explanation of the emancipation measure of 1833 has many similarities. What, conspicuously, we see in the emancipation campaign of 1823-33 is, as before, a group of parliamentary abolitionists. This time the group is dominated by Fowell Buxton, Stephen Lushington, and Henry Brougham. All three were churchmen but only Buxton was an Evangelical. I am inclined to think that Brougham was relatively more important in all aspects of abolition at this time than he is usually given credit for. Perhaps his arrogance, his deviousness, and his eccentricities[15] have prevented this recognition. Certainly the other abolitionists both believed his services to their cause were immeasurable and stood in some awe of his intellect and sheer doggedness. As Zachary Macaulay put it, Brougham "is without doubt an engine of amazing power."[16] Lushington, too, as has been recently demonstrated by David Eltis, was of more importance than is usually believed. A member of parliament from 1806, he combined, until 1841, a political career with the attainment of great eminence as a civil lawyer. His particular contribution in the emancipation campaign was as Buxton's right hand man, and despite the fact of his own earlier radicalism, to help persuade the more radical anti-slavery men of the need to maintain unity, while putting the maximum practicable pressure on Government.[17]

The emancipation campaign still showed the mainly religious character of the earlier abolition campaign—with these differences. As Dr. Ian Rennie has argued, the old guard Evangelical abolitionists were increasingly isolated from the main body of Evangelicals by their association with Whigs and radicals in the anti-slavery cause,[18] while as David Davis has shown, there was a strong element of immediacy in the emancipation campaign[19] actualized most strikingly in the so-called Agency Committee, which acted as a powerful ginger group in the Anti-Slavery Society. And with this immediacy was a changed religious emphasis—less Evangelical and of a more generalized Christian appeal[20]—while to some extent religious support depended on the widespread sense of outrage occasioned by *causes célèbres* involving persecution of missionaries in the West Indies.[21]

"The Anti-Slavery Committee in London, the Committees through the Country and the whole body of Evangelicals and Dissenters look to Emancipation and nothing short of it," reported the abolitionist Lushington, himself disturbed at the difficulty in guiding his unruly cohorts.[22]

Or, as the diarist Greville noted: "It is astonishing the interest the people generally take in the slavery question, which is the work of the Methodists, and shows the enormous influence they have in the country."[23]

Indeed it may be that George Stephen, James Stephen the elder's fourth son, himself active in the Agency Committee, provided the essential text for the study of the politics and ideology of emancipation in his assertion that "Emancipation [was] the result of popular feeling excited by religious principle," while of the Agency Committee's important role he added, "We had excellent engineers but engineering was useless without a storming party."[24]

What is lacking, in 1833 as in 1806-07, is any convincing political expression of the capitalism which is supposed to have destroyed the slave system.[25] It is rather that the interest of the emerging capitalists in a campaign in which James Cropper and Zachary Macaulay tried to link emancipation with Free Trade[26] just could not be gained. After the impeccable observation, in February 1828, that "Ladies Associations . . . seem to form now the mainstay of our hopes," Macaulay, who was at the center of the whole abolitionist web, immediately added, "I wish I could also see our commercial and manufacturing bodies duly affected with the evil effects of monopoly, and with a sense of the extensive benefits which cannot fail to result from its complete extinction."[27] It is however the case, as Drescher does not deny, that the importance of the West Indies in the British Imperial economy was declining after about 1820.[28] To that extent emancipation may have been easier.

But if specific economic pressures retreat, on examination, into the realm of fantasy, much remains to be explored of the politics and ideology of emancipation. Although we know something, for instance, of the younger James Stephen's role from within the Colonial Office, and despite various scholarly contributions, such questions as the broadening of the anti-slavery movement into a popular campaign and the precise connections between the Reform Bill agitation and passage and the achievement of emancipation require further study.[29]

So far then, and though there were differences, we have seen that the late eighteenth-century agitation against the slave trade and the campaign from 1823 against slavery had certain important elements in common. Intellectual condemnation of slavery, religious dynamism, political agitation, the exertions of "great men" and of influential experts, and the taking advantage of fortuitous political conjunctures and the greater or lesser use of popular clamor were all there. I believe that this kind of picture will be strengthened when more work is done on the politics of emancipation. But, and I come to a pivotal point in my paper, how are we to explain the continuance, nay strengthening, of measures against the slave trade when popular support had fallen away, when political support was much diminished, and when the principal branch of the official anti-slavery movement opposed the Government in its policy of forcibly suppressing the continuing slave trade?

Everything seemed to go wrong for the abolition cause in the 1840s. As late as 1838 Greville comments that "the Anti-Slavery question . . . is a favorite topic in the country,[30] but the failure of the abolitionist-inspired and Government-supported Niger expedition in 1841-42 brought a dramatic change. This project of interior settlement, extension of legitimate commerce, and salvation of Africa by its own exertions had been held up to the British public as the sovereign remedy for the slave trade and the effect of the failure seems to have been as devastating on public opinion as it was on Buxton, its advocate, personally. Public support for the policy, begun in 1808, of diplomatic and naval action against foreigners who continued to trade in slaves[31]weakened sharply. As the *Spectator* put it in 1847, "the Anti-Slavery Asssociation went out of fashion, and the Anti-Corn Law League came in—Anti-Slavery sentiment gave place to Free Trade dogma."[32] Not only this, the British anti-slave-trade lobby was in disarray. From as early as 1839 the British and Foreign Anti-Slavery Society increasingly followed the pacifism of leading lights like Joseph Sturge;[33] secondly, the British anti-slavery movement both came to reflect the divisions in the American anti-slavery movement *and* to preoccupy itself at worst with the politics of that rivalry and at best with a problem—slavery in the United States—about which British anti-slavery men could do nothing effective;[34] thirdly, there was some division within the anti-slavery movement over the pressure in the 1840s to equalize the sugar duties, that is, progressively to end the preference on Imperial which since emancipation had been *free*-grown sugar, admit the cheaper Brazilian and Cuban slave-grown sugar, and thus encourage these two lusty, surviving brances of the slave trade;[35] fourthly, the abolitionists who remained true to the policy of coercion hardly had it in them to be as impressive a group as that which had been united under Wilberforce half a century earlier. Fifthly, Evangelicalism had now suffered internal division and the heirs of the old Claphamite group, from which earlier much abolitionist leadership had come, were now relatively weaker.[36] Finally, the Whig Government itself seemed to have fatally compromised with slavery by attempting sugar equalization in 1841 and achieving it in 1846, while the continued existence of the West African squadron and of the whole diplomatic campaign against the slave trade seemed seriously threatened by William Hutt's Commons Committee of enquiry into the effectiveness of the coercion policy.

Yet by 1851 the major branch of the Atlantic slave trade, that to Brazil, was substantially ended and, though the Cuban slave trade lasted another decade, imports, compared with the 34,000 a year to Brazil in the 1840s averaged only about 12,000 a year.[37] How is this seeming contradiction to be explained?

At first sight abolitionist leadership in the 1840s can hardly have been instrumental. Wilberforce had retired in 1823 and died in 1833; Buxton never really got over the failure of the Niger expedition and died in 1845; Clarkson lived until the ripe age of eighty-six but was naturally failing; and Zachary Macaulay had died in 1838. There seems at one time to have been a hope that Thomas Babington would eventually take over the leadership of the abolitionists. But Macaulay never shared his father's passion for abolition and opposed coercion.[38] Sir R. H. Inglis, a high Tory and Claphamite Evangelical, was loyal to the cause and did it signal service but such leadership as existed came more from a trio of lawyers—Brougham, Lushington, and Lord Denman. Curiously the three had been intimate since they acted together in Queen Caroline's defense in 1821 and earlier.

Lushington's contribution to abolition in the 1840s may at first sight seem unimportant, given his retirement from Parliament in 1841. In fact his prestige as a civil lawyer and, from 1828, as Judge of the High Court of Admiralty and member of the judicial committee of the Privy Council put him in a position where he could make a most important contribuion to the abolition cause. His seemingly unrivaled prestige in slave trade suppression matters was based particularly on his major role in drafting the 1826 suppression treaty with Brazil, when he had successfully urged the potentially most important step of defining the Brazilian slave trade as piracy, and on his involvement in the formulation of the tough 1839 policy against Portugal. Now, in the summer of 1845, Lushington was centrally involved in the drafting of the so-called Aberdeen Act, the need to enact which had arisen adventitiously following the expiry of a particular Anglo-Brazilian agreement, an act whereby the piracy clause of the 1826 treaty was so construed as to permit *British* warships to treat Brazilian slavers as pirates. Interestingly, both a memorandum of Lushington and an opinion of the Law officers make clear that they believed that such treatment must be confined to the High Seas. The fact remains that the Act as passed contained no such qualification,[40] and as we shall see, the blanket authority conferred on British warships had considerable importance within a few years. More than this, when the whole propriety of the bill received direct challenge in the Commons by an eminent opposition lawyer and future Lord Chancellor, Peel and—perhaps less surprisingly—Aberdeen were reduced to confusion, and their Attorney General was unable to rescue them. They could only agree to give serious consideration to the objections made. In such a situation the expert who also knows his own mind comes into his own. It was to Lushington that the matter was referred and, predictably, he provided the required stiffening of purpose in a meeting with Peel and Aberdeen held only hours before Peel had to report back to the Commons.[41] Thus Lushington had played a vital part in providing the Government with justification for potentially much more damaging action against the Brazilian slave trade. It only remained for political will to be generated.

Brougham, whose herculean parliamentary efforts against the slave trade and slavery we have already noted, continued to agitate in Parliament, but for much of the 1840s the third member of the trio, Lord Denman, was an equally if not more important parliamentary force. With all the prestige of Lord Chief Justice, an office which he filled from 1832-50, he first manifested a concern for abolition in 1839 by a speech in favor of the bill to take unilateral action against the Portuguese slave trade. Driven on, it would seem, by strong emotion, which may well have fed on the experiences of his son Captain Joseph Denman RN, one of the more distinguished officers of the African Squadron and a strong protagonist of coercion, it is even claimed that "from 1843 . . . his energies were . . . chiefly occupied with the extinction of the slave trade."[42] Certainly he saw the pro-slavery implication of the equalization of the Sugar Duties Bill in 1846, and opposed it—"Nothing is so preposterous as to talk of free trade in this matter," he wrote to Brougham.[43] He also made two notable speeches in 1848 in favor of retention of the naval squadron.[44]

But before we progress to the political struggle of the later 1840s centering on the continued use of naval power against the slave trade, it is important to draw out a further significance of parliamentary interventions of this kind.

What Denman's intervention on this occasion really was was a humble address to the Crown which Lord Palmerston, the Foreign Secretary, and Lord John Russell, the prime minister, took seriously as a virtual, if welcomed, instruction,[45] and which points to an important force which kept up the momentum of anti-slavery in the 1840s when the popular appeal of the cause had greatly diminished. We must remember that the intensifying process of diplomatic and naval action against slave-trading powers, which had begun as early as 1808, had *always* rested on humble addresses to the Crown, supported by other parliamentary representations. This procedure had first been adopted even before the completion of the British abolition in 1807 when, as a related move, taken both for its own sake and to reduce the domestic opposition to British abolition, a Humble Address had been voted requesting that steps be taken to persuade foreign powers to cease slave trading.

In the years that followed, abolitionists maintained the pressure. Between February 1808 and May 1814 there were eleven such addresses or kindred interventions[46] and, to take a subsequent random period, nineteen between 1816 and 1822, the object being both to keep up pressure on the ministry and to strengthen its hands, both aims being served by the virtually complete unanimity of parliamentary opinion. It is important in this context to remember that those who opposed British abolition in 1806-07, because of the advantage abolition would afford to foreign competitors, were consequently now as enthusiastic as convinced abolitionists for the suppression of the foreign slave trade. In short, one can confidently say that within a very few years of 1807 parliamentary opinion had crystalized as solidly behind the suppression of the foreign slave trade. Drawing out one of the implications of this brings us to an important truth. It is that parliamentary support for the diplomatic and naval action had become institutionalized, a part of received tradition, an attitude which scarcely needed to be argued from parliament to parliament. W. E. Gladstone saw this very clearly when in 1850, as Leslie Bethell points out, "he warned the House that the slave trade preventive system was in danger of being perpetuated unquestioningly on a permanent basis, thereby becoming 'one of the institutions of the country,' and beyond rational criticism."[47] Furthermore, Palmerston was a conspicuous case of a minister who was conscious of the need to keep the support of Parliament—over suppression as other matters—as numerous references in his private correspondence attest.[48]

If the institutionalization of suppression was important, so also was what I will term the bureaucratization of the preventive policy within the Foreign Office. This process began with the creation of a separate Slave Trade Department in 1819. As is the way with such agencies, its business steadily increased over the years and, although by 1850 its staff consisted only of a super-intendent and four clerks,[49] remember that the total Foreign Office strength in 1853, including the housekeeper, "Chamber keepers," porters, and doorkeeper was only fifty-three.[50] In short, two vital conditions for a policy to go rumbling on existed, namely the institutionalization of legislative backing and the bureaucratization of executive action. Together these are a striking exemplification of something akin to what Robinson and Gallagher in their study of imperialism call "the offical mind."[51]

Let me now interject a story about the man who was head of the Slave Trade Department until his retirement in 1841, James Bandinel, and who was often called in to advise thereafter. On 2 February 1843 he wrote the following to a superior, the Chief Clerk:

> Mr. Bandinel begs to report that he discovers this instant smoke issuing in considerable quantities from the inside of the Window Sash, and that there is a smell in the room like that proceeding from ignition of wood.[52]

Now to write a memo to one's superior when one's office is catching fire may betoken an enviable stoicism but, we may be justified in concluding, a certain lack of initiative! In fact there is other evidence that Bandinel did not welcome responsibility,[53] and even though he had a real horror of the slave trade he was not the man to initiate action. The tradition of the Department was thus that the machine was kept going, it executed estab-lished policies and fresh instructions, spelt out the options, but took few intitiatives itself.

Now these limitations notwithstanding, what we have been saying about institutionalization may still explain why the coer-cion policy continued through the 1840s; but it can not really explain why the policy prevailed against an attempt in the Com-mons to overset it, and why it had a signal triumph, resulting from a new initiative, in 1850-51.

The answer, in three words, is "Russell and Palmerston." Palmerston, particularly, had earlier been active against the slave trade. When he went out with the Whigs in 1841 he had had an almost unbroken decade at the Foreign Office, over a period which had seen some real triumphs against the slave trade, especially effective action against Portugal in 1839.[54] Moreover, this was at a moment when, in my view, the trade was on the point of virtual extinction by forceful action on the West African coast which Palmerston authorized.[55] But, as we have already seen, the atmosphere after 1841 was very different, and of this the attempts to equalize the sugar duties were both cause and consequence. The fact is, after all, that when the Whigs unsuccessfully attempted equalization in 1841, and successfully carried it in 1846, Palmerston and Russell were both in the Cabinet, the latter prime minister in 1846, and they both accepted equalization.

It is clear, and could usefully be demonstrated at much greater length, that the reasons why Palmerston and Russell accepted the need for equalization were a signficant shortage of Imperial-grown sugar, a revenue deficit which equalization, by increasing comsumption, would alleviate, Free Trade orthodoxy—and party unity. Russell's initial uneasiness is well seen in a memo to the Cabinet of February 1841 which includes the words "When it is proposed to favour the foreign slave trade to increase the revenue and obtain sugar cheap . . ."[56] There were complex reasons, of which abolitionist conviction was only one, why the measure was thrown out in 1841.[57] But at the turn of 1845 and 1846, when it looked as if the Whigs would resume office, Russell felt he "could not dispense with the assistance of Lord Grey who had taken so prominent a part in favour of free trade"[58] and then, when the Whigs actually did get back into office in July 1846 there was an implied bargain whereby acceptance of Grey's insistence on hurrying on with Free Trade was the return for Grey's withdrawing his objections to serving in the same ministry with Palmerston.[59] Russell, of course, felt he needed both men. And remembering that the traumatic episode in the victorious march of Free Trade, the Repeal of the Corn Laws by Peel, had taken place, one can almost see the final inducement to equalize in Cobden's exhortation to Russell in a private letter of 4 July, "Do not lose the Free Trade wind . . . sugar and coffee must be equalised. I would not give the sugar interest a longer respite than Peel has given the English agriculturalists."[60] In any event the Cabinet discussed qualization on the fourth and then on 18 July Hobhouse's diary had the laconic report of that day's Cabinet meeting: "Sugar bill settled—5 years gradual equalization—all agreed."[61]

And so, it would seem, principle had been abandoned, the pass had been sold. Slave-grown sugar, and consequently the slave trade, were encouraged, as abundant evidence testified.[62] That this was seen as a major departure from humanitarian principle is suggested by several comments. Not only did a man like Deman believe equalization "the most criminal act ever done by any Government,"[63] but a Whig less committed to abolition, Sir F. T. Baring, in reviewing anti-slavery policy in a private letter to Brougham, said of equalization, "Clarkson and Buxton are gone in good time . . . whether inevitable or not the whole story is little creditable to the Country."[64] Aberdeen freely confessed to Brougham that he was relieved at not having had to vote.[65]

Quite apart from the fact that Free Trade and an attack on monopolists were not least causes with moral appeal, had vital principle, in fact, been forsaken? Palmerston's parliamentary defense was "that if we had thought that this measure would give to the slave trade any encouragement, which we should not be able by other means amply to counterbalance, we would not have proposed the measure to Parliament, whatever might have been the advantages otherwise to be gained."[66] The fact is that his and Russell's actions over the five years after passage of equalization were exegesis of the words just quoted: "by other means amply to counterbalance." The "other means" were of course the Navy[67] and diplomatic pressure. But as the 1840s drew to a close, these "other means" were challenged, and the very maintenance of the traditional suppression policy put at issue. The session after equalization a radical M. P., Willliam Hutt, successfully moved for a parliamentary committee to investigate the success—or failure—of the existing policy on the slave trade, and recommend accordingly. Some thousands of paragraphs of evidence later the Committee, after being reappointed for the 1848 session, reported in a sense broadly hostile to the squadron.[68] The history of its deliberations has yet to be written, but it appears that Inglis fought the good fight for the old policy, that he received some help from Sir Edward Buxton, Fowell Buxton's son, but that more aid came from Monckton Milnes.[69] Milnes seems sometimes to have concerted strategy with Inglis and, interestingly, was "Palmerston's man" on the Committee, "his lacquey," as Greville disparagingly called him.[70]

Here in any event in the Commons Committee's clear tendency was a major threat to the suppression policy and one which the reports favorable to the squadron of a Lords Select Committee under Bishop Samuel Wilberforce,[71] William's famous son, could not entirely gainsay, for if the Commons at the end of the day voted in the way Hutt's Committee was pointing, coercion would be a lost cause.

In bold terms we have already seen why coercion remained British policy and why it had a major triumph in 1850-51—because of Palmerston and Russell. It is now appropriate to spell out that explanation a little more. One should rather say that Palmerston and Russell exercised the requiste political will and muscle in the face of serious constraints; that Palmerston felt his way to an effective means of ending the Brazilian slave trade, by seizing opportunities which he had the skill to discern and by operating at different but complementary political and diplomatic levels; and that both ministers positively used the major attack on the traditional policy of coercion to force that policy to yield up real triumphs and thus justify its re-endorsement and continuation. This will become apparent in the highlighting of the crucial developments in the campaign against the Brazilian slave trade.

When Palmerston turned to the matter of the Brazilian slave trade after returning to office in 1846 the basic constraint upon him was not that the Aberdeen Act was inadequate—"we should ourselves have proposed and passed it, if our predecessors had not done so for us"[72]—but that "the British Government had not determined to resort to active naval operations on the coast of Brazil in virtue of the Act of Parliament of 1845."[73] In this situation Palmerston, though not giving up hope of negotiating a treaty so effective as to render the 1845 Act unnecessary, could only give somewhat measured encouragement to the naval squadron in South American waters.[74] But right up into 1850 the Navy's primary task in South America was the British intervention in the River Plate, and an unreadiness to will the extra means meant that the Navy had few ships to spare for effective patrolling against the slave trade.[75] Palmerston first sought to frame a more positive policy in August 1848 as a specific response to intimations that the Commons Committee on the slave trade was going to recommend the Government to negoitiate with that of Brazil to induce the Brazilian Government to fulfill its engagements by suppressing the slave trade. How, he asked James Hudson, the chargé d'affaires in Rio, in a private letter, could Britain compel Brazil to effective action? We must take "vigorous steps between this and the next session."[76] When, however, Hudson reported in favor of a blockade of Rio and Bahia as the key sanction,[77] a tactic which Palmerston himself had favored in principle since 1844,[78] neither the Cabinet nor even Russell would agree.[79] Twelve months later, in the autumn of 1849, and again specifically on account of the continuing deliberations of the Slave Trade Committee, Russell sees need for "some further measures" and is himself prepared for a blockade of Brazil (and Cuba) but does not think the Cabinet or House of Commons would back such a course.[80] Through 1849 therefore, and well into 1850, Palmerston was unable to get the necessary political backing for tough action but from March 1849 onwards an alternative method of coercion was being fashioned.

This new approach began when Commander Skipwith of HMS *Hydra* seized an empty Brazilian slaver close to shore and repeated the tactic in August.[81] These are significant features of this action. Action close to shore seems to have been particularly serious for the slave dealers; the naval officers' reports were somewhat vague as to whether the various seizures were within territorial waters, and bear better the interpretation that they were not fully aware of the significance of acting within territorial waters than that the captains were being disingenuous in merely pretending not to see the distinction between the High Seas and territorial waters.[82] In any event, Palmerston was fully prepared to approve this new initiative and specifically to renew his approval when Brazilian protests made it unequivocally clear that the action complained of was within the three mile limit.[83] In some ways most significantly of all, it seems likely that Hudson may have been behind the new inshore tactics. When we know of Hudson's immense and sustained activity against the slave trade it is highly significant to learn on the authority of Baring, the First Lord of the Admiralty, that Skipwith was Hudson's "naval advisor."[84] We know further that Hudson was very much in Palmerston's confidence, that he shared his views on suppression, and that he owed much to the enjoyment and expectation of Palmerston's patronage.[85] It is therefore probable that Skipwith was encouraged by Hudson to interpret his instructions less rigidly than had his predecessors; or it may just possibly be that between them they had simply stumbled into a policy that was to prove highly effective.

Be that as it may and probably because Hudson had rightly read Palmerston's mind, Britain had hit on a new and effective tactic. Renewed by Captain Schomberg and Lt. Crofton of the *Cormorant* and *Rifleman* respectively in January,[86] the new pressure on Brazil was accompanied by strong recommendations from Hudson that the favorable posture of the Brazilian anti-slave-trade party, the need for Brazil not to alienate Britain while she had trouble with General Rosas on her southern border and incipient rebellion at home, the excellence of the information on slave traders' plans that the British Legation was receiving, and the growing tendency, much encouraged by Hudson, of Brazilians to identify the slave trade with wealthy resident Portuguese—all were such that this was the time for firm action.[87] Indeed, said Hudson in a private letter to Palmerston of 21 February 1850, "There is nothing you cannot do, at this moment with the Brazilian Government who with Revolution before and behind them, fear of Rosas, and hampered by the first Article of the Treaty of 1826 are entirely at you mercy."[88]

In short, the time was ripe and a highly effective tactic which had the beauty of being less than the blockade which had been such a stumbling block had been fashioned by the men on the spot.

This was essentially the state of affairs when a crucial test of strength came on in the Commons over the resolutions of Hutt's Slave Trade Committee, with their clear threat to the continuance of naval measures. In a flurry of private communications in the middle of March 1850 Palmerston, Russell, and Sir Charles Wood discuss the form of a placatory yet firm Humble Address on the Squadron. How should the case be presented to the rank and file of the Whigs? Should there be a meeting of the ministry's supporters to whip up a favorable vote? Yes, at any rate if Russell remains determined to make it a question of confidence.[89] To the surprise of many of the Whigs Russell was so determined. He summoned them to 10 Downing Street on 19 March and warned that if Hutt's motion were passed, "With the respect that I entertain for the authority of the House of Commons, I could not advise the Crown to reject the prayer of that address. With the consequences which appear to me to flow from it, I should be the basest of base men if I advised the Crown to comply with it. Neither could my noble friend the Secretary for Foreign Affairs write a despatch in pursuance of such an address."[90] It might be put melliflously but the message was clear and even in an age of looser party allegiance 176 out of 224 Whigs in the division voted for the Squadron, and that made it safe.[91] Clearly the same insistence had previously been displayed in the Cabinet, for Grey is known to have headed a group hostile to the Squadron.[92] In other words the threat led not only to the reassertion of the old policy but in effect to an advance upon it while Palmerston took advantage of the same political crisis and "succeeded in getting the consent of the Cabinet" for "vigorous operations on the Brazilian Coast," as he told Clarendon three years later.[93]

For all the importance of the initiatives of the men on the spot, the "signal triumph," as Pamerston termed it to Hudson,[94] of 19 March was a turning point. So overt had the threat to the traditional suppression policy been that Palmerston and Russell had been led to stake all on the Commons vote. Once taken two consequences ensued. Here was a renewed mandate for effective action but it was not a mandate in perpetuity. Therefore the old policy must be applied with such vigor that the House of Commons would continue the means for carrying it out. "The House of Commons have given us another years trial of the African Squadron, but if we are not able at the end of that time to show that we have made some considerable progress, they will be much tempted to withold the means which they at present afford us."[95] In other words, the Huttite threat led not only to the reassertion of the old policy but to a more intensive application of it. There was also the fortuitous help of Palmerston's great popularity at this time. "They (Ministers) are now all tried and bound to him in respect to the future as completely as to the present and the past," was Greville's rather sour comment.[96]

The principal fruit of the new resolution of the Whig ministers was further endorsement of the tactic Skipwith, Schomberg, and Hudson had fashioned, and specific extension of it. Palmerston took advantage of an intimation from the Commander in Chief of the South American station that he had urged caution on his captains to advise the Admiralty, on 22 April 1850, that the Foreign Office would find no greater difficulty in replying to Brazilian protests about captures in Brazilian "waters or ports" than on the High Seas.[97] The clarification would seem to be a very Palmerstonian touch. Doubltless Palmerston had long realized that the Aberdeen Act made no apparent distinction between the High Seas and territorial waters. Certainly there is no trace of a reference to the Law Officers on this point—just conceivably that might have upset the apple cart. What proven success in Brazilian waters and new found resolution at home now allowed were instructions in accord with the full vigor the Aberdeen Act, in the knowledge that the man on the spot, Hudson would read Palmerston's mind appropriately. In fact the South American squadron appears to have resumed active cruising before a copy of the letter of 22 April had been received, but when Hudson and Admiral Reynolds read that letter they initiated really draconian action, albeit with only one handful of ships.[98]

In the last week of June, HMS *Sharpshooter* and HMS *Cormorant* cut out half a dozen slavers within Brazilian anchorages and sometimes from under the guns of coastal batteries. In some intricate diplomacy during the summer Hudson played his cards with great skill and saw, as the consummation of his efforts, an effective law against the slave trade reach the statute book on 4 September.[99] It is interesting to observe that the response of the men on the spot had again served Palmerston's and Russell's ends perfectly. As Baring was honest enough to admit to Russell when commenting on the news of the successes of high summer, "All this is vy favourable and a great deal more than I have expected

[though?] yr. expectations were of an entirely different character."[100]

Baring might admit he had been wrong—and in ignorance
that victory had been won by 4 September agree to send as many
more ships as might be wanted—[101] but Sir Charles Wood, and
probably others, were averse to imposing a "Brazilian blockade,"[102] one of various more drastic actions which were evidently
being discussed by ministers from later September.[103] The beauty
of what Russell and Palmerston had done, either in persuading
ministers to go along with the instruction of 22 April or in simply encouraging yet more forceful naval action with the tacit
compliance of other ministers, was complete. Precisely because
the tactic was a total success there was no need to press the proposal for the blockade and thus risk splitting the ministry. And
one may conclude that Palmerston and Russell would only have
made such a calculation out of a conviction that the opportunity
which the men on the spot were being given was one they would
act upon. Well might Russell represent to Palmerston in March
1851 that "now [?] we [?] have all the benefit [of blockade] without the embarassment."[104] In Rio Hudson had been keeping up
the pressure, urging again on Palmerston that essentially the
same constraints as previously continued to operate on Brazil and
urging that firm action be maintained.

"I beg also to point out to your Lordship," he wrote in a private letter on 2 September 1850, "that another so favourable
opportunity for acting against Slave Trade may not occur again
for years to come. The relations of Brazil with Buenos Ayres are
assuming a very threatening attitude—this Government cannot
successfully resist our attempts against the slave dealers and their
ships here, and meet General Rosas and tribe in the field at the
same moment: they must, to save Rio Granda de Sul and Para-
guay, abandon the slave dealers to our tender mercies."[105]

There is significance in the fact that the whole of the second
sentence is scored, presumably by Palmerston.

In the event the naval pressure that Hudson long feared was
based on too few ships was sufficient and the Brazilian slave trade
died with a whimper during 1851. It was entirely fitting that Russell should point out his success to his parliamentary masters in
his draft of the Queen's speech of December 1851.[106]

British suppression of the slave trade had, then, at the end of a most unpropitious decade, secured a major triumph. The rise of Brazilian abolitionism, the embarrassments of the Brazilian politicians and others who supported the slave trade, the accidents of internal South American rivalries, had contributed. But of decisive importance was the exertion of political will by Palmerston and Russell and the complementary perceptions and initiatives of the men on the spot, especially in the adoption of more effective naval tactics and in Hudson's skill in playing on the Brazilian opposition's desire for office to advance the anti-slavery cause decisively, and on the difficulties of the Brazilian government.[107] Both the political will and the pursuit of energetic methods by the man on the spot depend ultimately on the warrant of that parliamentary support which had been a constant since the closing off of the British slave trade. Both had to bring forth a triumph sufficient to give the policy of coercion an extended parliamentary warrant. A notable omission from the ingredients of success in the 1840s was, we have seen, the popular abolitionist enthusiasm which had been so marked before abolition and emancipation. That enthusiasm might seem to have become totally embalmed in the institutionalization of the anti-slavery impulse. What was present was the anti-slavery enthusiasm of the influential expert—Lushington. Instigator of the important definition of Brazilian slavery as piracy in the 1826 treaty, he was the highly influential advisor in 1839 and 1845 and fashioned the instrument Britain was eventually to wield in 1850. Indeed, there is a nice element of the unintentional about Lushington's role for, as we have seen, he believed a distinction had to be made between action against Brazilian slavers on the High Seas and in territorial waters. In the event, this distinction was, from Britain's viewpoint, providentially absent from the 1845 Bill as enacted. Altogether Lushington fulfilled a role somewhat similar to that of James Stephen the younger in 1832-33 and of the elder Stephen in 1806-07.

All in all, the abolitionist triumph of the end of the forties was considerable on account of the serious weakening in parliamentary and public support for the suppression policy and the sophisticated compound of ingredients which brought success.

Before we ask whether any contribution to a model of the

reforming impluse and its development emerges, we ought to notice that, so far as suppression is concerned, coercion, used particularly against Portugal and Brazil, was neither the only method used nor the only one to succeed. There was in fact another strand of British anti-slavery endeavor. The fascinating tale has yet to be told of the "Evangelical International," of how the tender plant of French anti-slavery zeal was nurtured by British abolitionists for three decades from 1814—a relationship hard to disentangle from the reinforcement which British and French Evangelicalism offered each other, for Protestants, including some influenced by the French Evangelical Revival, were disproportionately active in the French anti-slavery movement.[108]

An unpredictable fruit of this close association was garnered in the early 1830s, for such was the importance of French abolitionists in the ranks of the men who wrought the July Revolution that the prized mutual right of search treaties was able to be negotiated in 1831 and 1833. These seem at least to have been successful in sealing the end of the French slave trade and even when internal political hostility to the exercise by Britain of the right of search forced prime minister—and abolitionist— Guizot to jettison these agreements, they were immediately replaced by a new Anglo-French treaty, negotiated by the ubiquitous Lushington and by the Duc de Brogli, minister, abolitionist, and correspondent of British Evangelicals and abolitionists, which was envisaged as a major joint effort to prevent slavers from clearing from the African coast.[109] Such a development wholly cohered with Aberdeen's strong desire for friendly relations with France as the cornerstone of his foreign policy and with his wish to emphasize cooperation between the powers in suppressing the slave trade rather than to rest only on the right of search. One might conclude that the few months remaining to Peel's ministry were insufficient for the system of joint cruising by a total of fifty-two warships to produce decisive results—Palmerston in 1846 reverted to a wary rivalry with France[110] and in any event the July Monarchy fell in 1848—but events could well have turned out otherwise.

In the same vein one can argue that since there was manifestly no possibility of Britain's successfully coercing the United States, the conciliatory policy enshrined in the Webster-Ashburton treaty of 1842, and misliked by Palmerston, should have been persisted in, despite the failure of the United States to fulfill its obligations under it. After all, the United States, paradoxically, accepted the practice of visits by British warships to check the identity of suspected slavers wearing the U. S. flag, once Malmesbury, in 1858, abandoned the principle of the right of visit.[111]

Finally, the manner in which United States participation in and condoning of the (Cuban) slave trade eventually came to an end aptly demonstrates the sheer unpredictability with which any study of abolition and reform must reckon. The Lincoln Administration's anti-slavery disposition allied with the need to stand well with Britain after the outbreak of the Civil War acted to induce the United States Government to accept the mutual right of search in 1862. With that the Atlantic slave trade was virtually at an end.

I believe that some contribution to a model of the reforming impulse does emerge, first, in that, despite his disclaimer, we can see *some* similarities to Oliver Macdonagh's model of the "legislative-*cum*-administrative process."[112] We may recognize his "intolerability" principle in the resolve to end the slave trade and slavery; we may see the same stages of legislation, the slow realization that it is insufficient, and consequent further legislation; we may observe (in the Slave Trade Department of the Foreign Office) the accumulation of "evidence of the extent and nature of the evils" (of the slave trade); and we may discern that same Department coming to see that suppression was indeed "a slow, uncertain process of closing loopholes and tightening the screw ring by ring." But the similarities, if real, are limited and in any event our concern—a model of the reforming impulse-is not the same as Macdonagh's. What seem to me to be the key ingredients of the former are the preparation of the ground by changes in philosophical and theological ideas; the slow germination of reform in the bosom of a denominational community; the impetus for reform coming from a new, or newly rediscovered, religious dynamism; the decisive seizure by the reformers of unpredictable opportunities (in 1806 and 1807, and 1833);[113] the institutionalization and bureaucratization of the reforming impulse in the legislature and executive respectively so that that impulse outlasts the weakening of the forces which gave it life;

and the periodic and sometimes complex interventions of the committed expert and of "great men," especially Fox and Grenville in 1806-07 and Palmerston and Russell four decades later.

How wide is the application of this very tentative model I will answer that, still tentatively, by quoting Bentham: "We have begun by attending to the condition of slaves, we shall finish by softening that of all the animals which assist our labours or supply our wants."[114] The establishment of the essential links between the initial and the later movement remains to be effected. That Bentham's predicton was good prophecy is not open to doubt.[115]

NOTES

1. R. Coupland, *The British Anti-Slavery Movement* (London: F. Cass, 1964), especially p. 251; and his *Wilberforce* (Oxford, 1923).
2. F. J. Klingberg, *The Anti-Slavery Movement in England* (New Haven: Yale Univ. Press, 1926). See also various works by W. L. Mathieson and C. M. MacInnes.
3. W. E. H. Lecky, *A History of European Morals*, 6th ed. (London, 1884), II, 153.
4. At Chapel Hill; reissues in 1961, 1964, and 1966. All references in this paper are to the New York ed. of 1961.
5. Williams, *Capitalism and Slavery*, (London, 1944) p. 178.
6. Ibid., p. vii.
7. Roger Anstey, "Capitalism and Slavery: A Critique," *Economic History Review*, 2nd ser., 21 (1968) 307-20.
8. Ithaca, 1966.
9. *Annual Register* (1788), pp. 108-09.
10. J. Millar, *The Origin of the Distinction of Ranks*, 3rd ed. (London, 1779), p. 360.
11. Memo, probably by Stephen, on abolitionist tactics, 19 May 1806, Grenville/W. B. Hamilton Micofilm Collection, Duke University, reel 17, f. 189.
12. Unless otherwise indicated the source for the foregoing paragraphs is Roger Anstey, *The Atlantic Slave Trade and British Abolition, 1760-1810* (New York: Humanities Press, 1975), *passim*.
13. This convenient quotation is a summary in English of Seymour Drescher, "Le Declin du systeme escloivagiste britannique et l'abolition de la traite," *Annales, E.S.C.*, March-April 1976, —pp. 414-35, contained in the same author's "Abolition and the Historians," in Roger Anstey and P. E. H. Hair, eds., *Liverpool, the African Slave Trade, and Abolition* (Liverpool: Historic Society of Lancashire and Cheshire, 1976). Drescher's major work

on the subject is *Econocide: British Slavery in the Age of Abolition* (Pittsburgh: Univ. of Pittsburgh Press, 1977.)

14. Stanley L. Engerman's phrase in "Quantitative and Economic Analysis of West Indian Societies: Research Problems," unpublished paper read at New York Conference on Comparative Perspectives on Slavery in New World Plantation Societies, May 1976.

15. One of the more engaging of these many stories about Brougham is the account of Brougham's great speech on the Reform Bill. In the sober words of the *D.N.B.*, "the peroration is studied and unnatural. Brougham ended with a prayer; he fell on his knees, and remained kneeling. He had kept up his energy with draughts of mulled port, and his friends, who thought that he was unable to rise, picked him up and sat him on the woolsack."

16. Z. Macaulay to "My dear Friend," 16 Feb. 1828, Brougham MSS, University College, London, 10275. Note also the warm tone of Wilberforce's letters to Brougham, 3 Feb, 1826, Brougham MSS, 10965, and 10 May 1827, ibid., 10316. In the latter Wilberforce observed that "we are in circumstances in which you, under Providence, are become our Main Stay."

17. D. Eltis, "Dr. Stephen Lushington and the Campaign to Abolish Slavery in the British Empire," *Journal of Caribbean History*, Nov. 1970, pp. 41-56; *D.N.B.*; Charles Buxton, ed., *The Memoirs of Sir Thomas Fowell Buxton*, 1849. (London: J.M. Dent & Sons, 1925).

18. Ian Rennie, "Evangelicalism and English Public Life, 1823-1850" (Ph. D. thesis, University of Toronto, 1962), chap. 4. A copy exists in Cambridge University library and I am grateful to my colleague Doreen Rosman for drawing my attention to it.

19. David Brion Davis, "The Emergence of Immediatism in British and American Anti-Slavery Thought," *The Mississippi Valley Historical Review*, 49 (1962), 209-30.

20. Aptly demonstrated in P. F. Dixon, "The Politics of Emancipation. The Movement for the Abolition of Slavery in the British West Indies 1807-1833" (D. Phil. thesis, Oxford 1970), p. 286, where there is a synopsis of George Thompson's Agency Committee lecture at Dover, in 1831.

21. Z. Macaulay to Brougham, 13 May 1833, private, Brougham MSS, 10544.

22. Lushington memo., n.d. (1832?), Brougham MSS, 10376.

23. P. W. Wilson, ed., *Greville Diary*, (London, 1927), II, 59-60.

24. George Stephen, *Anti-Slavery Recollections* (London, 1854; Cass reissue, 1971), pp. 238, 245.

25. See Williams, *Capitalism and Slavery*, pp. 135-36, 154-77.

26. Cropper to Z. Macaulay, 2 May 1822, B.M. Add MS 41267A, ff. 102-3; same to same, 10 May 1822, ibid., ff. 104-6; same to same, 12 Jul. 1822, ibid., ff. 108-9; same to same, Aug. 1822, ibid., ff. 112-13; Cropper to Thos. Clarkson, 5 Aug. 1822, ibid., ff. 110-11; Cropper to Broughham, 30 Jun. 1822, Brougham MSS, 30452; Dixon, pp. 171-72.

27. Z. Macaulay to "My dear Friend," 16 Feb. 1828, Brougham MSS 10275.

28. Drescher, *Case of Econocide*.

29. Amongst other contributions to the study of emancipation, and apart from those already mentioned, see B. W. Higman, "The London West India

Interest, 1807-1833," *Historical Studies*, 13, no. 49 (Oct. 1967); W. L. Mathieson, *British Slavery and Its Abolition, 1823-1838* (London: Longmans & Co., 1926); Mary Reckord, "The Jamaica Slave Rebellion of 1831," *Past and Present*, 16 (July 1968). Edith F. Hurwitz, *Politics and the Public Conscience: Slave Emancipation and the Abolitionist Movement in Britain* (London and New York, 1973) can be criticized in some respects but contains valuable insights and analyses. Michael Craton and James Walvin are working on a jointly authored study of emancipation, while the present writer hopes to add to our knowledge of this important episode in two chapters of a forthcoming book on British anti-slavery in the nineteenth century.

30. *Greville*, II, 60; 8 Mar. 1838.

31. Christopher Lloyd, *The Navy and the Slave Trade* (1949), *passim*.

32. *Spectator*, 11 Dec. 1847, quoted in Elsie I. Pilgrim, "Anti-Slavery Sentiment in Great Britain, 1841-1854, its Nature and Decline with Special Reference to Its Influence upon British Policy towards the Former Slave Colonies," (Ph. D. thesis, University of Cambridge, 1957), p. 14.

33. Howard Temperley, *British Anti-Slavery 1833-1870* (London: Longmans, 1972), pp. 168-83.

34. Ibid., pp. 184-220; Betty Fladeland, *Men and Brothers: Anglo-American Anti-Slavery Co-operation* (Urbana: Univ. of Illinois Press, 1972), pp. 257-301. For divisions amongst anti-slavery men and women in Scotland see C. Duncan Rice's forthcoming *The Scots Abolitionists, 1833-1861* (Baton Rouge: Louisiana State Univ. Press, 1981) kindly lent to me in typescript. For a helpful introduction as well as 493 letters, see Clare Taylor, *British and American Abolitionists* (Edinburgh: Univ. Press, 1974).

35. C. Duncan Rice, "Humanity sold for Sugar!: The Anti-Slavery Interest and the Sugar Duties," *Historical Journal*, 13 (1970), 402-18, has demonstrated that most British abolitionists, though for the most part free traders, believed that there should *not* be free trade in slave-grown sugar.

36. Rennie, *Evangelicalism and Public Life, passim*.

37. P. Curtin, *The Atlantic Slave Trade: A Census* (Madison: Univ. of Wisconsin Press, 1969), pp. 36-43, 234. Contemporaries mostly believed the Brazilian trade to be much larger.

38. *Hansard*, 3rd ser., 77, 1290-1302, 26 Feb. 1845, quoted in Williams, *Capitalism and Slavery*, pp. 193-94.

39. *D.N.B.*; Lushington, Memo on proposed Brazilian treaty and encl. Draft Treaty, 26 Jan. 1826, FO84/60; L. Bethell, *The Abolition of the Brazilian Slave Trade* (Cambridge: Cambridge Univ. Press, 1970), p. 156.

40. Law Officers to FO, 30 May 1845 and 2 Jul. 1845 with enclosures, FO83/235; Lushington, memo communicated to Peel, 24 Jul. 1845, FO97/430; *Statues at Large, United Kingdom*, vol. 31, 8-9 Victoria, C122. For Lushington's role generally in the drafting and passage of the Aberdeen Act, see Aberdeen MSS, BM Add MSS, 43060, ff. 380-81, Aberdeen to Duke of Wellington, 14 June 1845 (copy); ibid. ff. 382-83 Aberdeen to Duke of Wellington, 30 June 1845 (copy); ibid., Add MSS 43064, ff. 241-44, Peel to Aberdeen, 25 Jul. 1845; ibid., Add MSS 43244, ff. 272-83, Lushington to Aberdeen, 30 June 1845 and encl., memo; ff. 294-95, Lushington to Aberdeen, 25 Jul. 1845; ff. 301-2, Lushington to Aberdeen, 30 Jul. 1845;

and ff. 303-4, Lushington to Aberdeen, 31 Jul. 1845; Peel MSS, BM Add. MSS. 40455, ff. 73-74, memo "sent by Lord Aberdeen to Dr. Lushington," 20 Jul. 1845.

41. Bethell, *Abolition*, pp. 258-66, 325 ff. and n. 40 above. Lushington was also involved in other slave trade treaty negotiations, particularly the 1845 French treaty.

42. *D.N.B.* But we have the excellent authority of George Stephen for the assertion that Denman devoted himself without stint to the cause of emancipation, that is, in the years before 1833 (Stephen, *Recollections*, pp. vii-viii).

43. Denman to Brougham, postmarked 24 July 1846, Brougham MSS 39369. The Denman correspondence in this MS collection is an important source for the study of his activities.

44. *D.N.B.*

45. Palmerston to Russell, 22 Aug. 1848, PRO 30/22/7c (Russell Papers), ff. 381-82. Russell to Palmerston, 22 Aug. 1848, Broadlands MSS, GC/RU/220.

46. See for example, Humble Addresses of 15 June 1810 *[Parliamentary Debates*, 17, 658-89], 14 Jul. 1813 *[P.D.*, 26, 1211-15], and 5 May 1814 *[P.D.*, 27, 656-62].

47. Bethell, *Abolition*, p. 323, quoting *Hansard*, CIX, 1160-70.

48. For instance of Palmerston's keen awareness of the importance of Parliamentary backing for suppression see Broadlands MSS, GC/HO/827 and 828, Palmerston to Howard de Walden, 12 and 19 May 1838 (copies); National Maritime Museum, Minto MSS, ELL solidus 218, Palmerston to Minto, 13 Nov. 1838, 9 Sep., 26. Sep., 17 Oct., and 29 Dec. 1839. See also n. 95 below.

49. Memo on business of Slave Trade Dept., n.d. F084/818.

50. *Foreign Office List, 1853* (1853), 9 and 11. See also ibid., 1852, the first to be published. The Slave Trade Dept. was one of five geographical divisions, each with a strength of four or five.

51. R. E. Robinson and J. Gallagher, *Africa and the Victorians: The Official Mind of Imperialism* (London: Macmillan, 1960). Note that only the English edition has this subtitle.

52. Bandinel to Chief Clerk, 2 Feb. 1843, FO84/500. The historian must record that Bandinel *did* also report the matter verbally!

53. See for example, FO84/380, Bandinel to James Stephen, where he disclaims any responsibility for planning the Niger expedition. But cf. CO2/21, Bandinel, Memorandum on . . . . putting down the Slave Trade, 30 Mar. 1839, where he deferentially advocates policies some of which were later adopted.

54. Also agreements on suppression with France in 1831 and 1833 and the addition of the so-called Equipment clause to the Spanish slave trade treaty in 1835.

55. There is a voluminous debate on this and I hope to justify my conclusion in a forthcoming book. I should also like to acknowledge the help given by David Eltis and by a former Hons. History student, Capt. Alan Lewis, in disentangling this complex question.

56. Russell, memo to Cabinet, PRO 30/22/4A ff. 79-82 (also printed in Spencer Walpole, *The Life of Lord John Russell*, [London: Longmans, 1889], 368-69).

57. For the then Chancellor of the Excequer's view see PRO 30/22/4B, ff. 112-13, Baring to Russell, 11 Aug. 1841.

58. Russell to Sir Charles Wood, 3 Jan. 1846, PRO 30/22/5A, ff/ 34-35. See also Grey to Russell, 16 and 19 Dec. 1845, in PRO 30/22/4E, ff. 78-80 and 223.

59. Grey to Russell, n.d. ibid., ff. 219-21; Wood to Russell, 30 June 1846, *Walpole*, I, 426-28, PRO 30/22/sA, ff. 329-30.

60. Cobden to Russell, 4 July, 1846, PRO 30/22/5B, ff. 96-99. The letter went on: "By the way I heard Bright declare (and it was repeated by the member for Dundee) that he should vote against your 5 years grace to the sugar interest [the protection was to be reduced in steps], on the ground that better terms could be made at the hustings. I shall not be in the House, but should regret if you were to lose the support of the ardent men out of doors by stickling for a year or two."

61. Diary 4 July 1846, BM Add MSS (Broughton Papers), 43748; and diary 18 July 1846, ibid., 43749.

62. For example *A & P*, 1850 (590), 5, Report from the Select Committee of the House of Lords . . . to consider the best means for the final extinction of the African Slave Trade.

63. Denman to Brougham, 9 Sep. 1850, Brougham MSS, 10923.

64. Baring to Brougham, 29 Nov. 1846, ibid., 14891.

65. Aberdeen to Brougham, 31 Aug. 1846, ibid., 10221.

66. *Hansard*, 3rd ser., 57, 648. See also FO97/430, Cabinet Minute, 23 July 1846, quoted in Bethell, *Abolition*, p. 274.

67. It is noteworthy that when discussing significant reductions in the Navy in Aug. 1848, Russell specifically excluded the Africa Squadron (Russell to Auckland, 26 Aug. 1848, quoted in *Walpole*, II, 28-29).

68. There were four reports in the 1847-48 session and two more in 1849; (*A & P*), 1847-48, four reports from the Select Committee on Slave Trade with the minutes of Evidence (272, 366, 536, 623); ibid., 1849, First and Second Reports (308, 410).

69. Hutt to Brougham, 15 Sep. 1848, Brougham MSS, 3029.

70. *Greville*, II, 352; *D.N.B.*

71. *A & P*, 1850, Reports from the Select Committee of the House of Lords on he African Slave Trade; Session 1849 (53) and Session 1850 (590).

72. Palmerston to Hudson, 5 Jan. 1847 (copy), Broadlands MSS, GC/HU/43.

73. Palmerston to Russell, 19 Jan. 1853, PRO30/22/10G, ff. 174-78.

74. FO84/704, Palmerston, Minute, 27 June 1847 on Ad. to F. O., 14 June 1847, and Encls; FO84/745, Palmerston to Admiralty, 17 Oct. 1848 and Encls; FO84/767, Baring to Palmerston (copy), 21 May 1849.

75. The frequently expressed hope was that the River Plate intervention would soon be wound up and the warships concerned freed for cruising against the slave trade (see for example Broadlands MSS, GC/HU/145 solidus, Baring to Palmerston, 9 Sep. 1849; ibid., GC/HO/955, Palmer-

ston to Howden, 2 Oct. 1847 [copy]). Failing this, as Baring made known to Palmerston, the only other recourse was ten or so ships from the Africa Squadron. "Without some alteration of that kind, our estimates would not allow of any increase of force off Rio" (FO84/767, Dundas to Baring, 18 May 1849 [copy], Encl. in Baring to Palmerston, 21 May 1849 [copy]).

76. Palmerston to Hudson, 4 Aug. 1848 (copy), Broadlands MSS, GC/HU/45.

77. Hudson to Palmerston, 10 Oct. 1848, ibid., GC/HU/6.

78. Bethell, *Abolition*, p. 307.

79. Palmerston to Russell, 15 Mar. 1851, PRO30/22/9B, f. 252.

80. Russell to Palmerston, 24 Nov. 1849, Broadlands MSS, GC/RU/306.

81. FO84/765, Hudson to F. O., 24 Mar. 1849 and Encl., Cdr. Skipwith to Hudson, 5 Mar. 1849 (copy); Hudson to F. O., 13 Aug, 1849 and Encls.

82. Ibid., Palmerston, Minute, 17 May 1849 on Hudson to F. O., 24 Mar. 1849 and Encls; Palmerston, Minute, n.d. [Oct.] on Hudson to F. O. and Encls. 13 Aug. 1849 and Encls. FO84/781, F. O. to Ad., 20 Oct. 1849.

83. FO84/766, Palmerston, Minute, 9 Dec. 1849 on Hudson to F. O., 10 Oct. 1849, and F. O. to Hudson, 31 Dec. 1849.

84. Baring to Russell, 30 Mar. 1850, confidential, PRO30/22/8D, ff. 131-40.

85. See especially Broadlands MSS, GC/HU/39, Hudson to Palmerston, 10 Oct. 1851, written in reply to Palmerston's private intimation (ibid., GC/HU/52, Palmerston to Hudson, 8 Sep. 1851 [copy]) that Hudson was to have his success in Rio crowned by promotion to British minister to Tuscany and the Vatican. "Had I not been possessed with your ideas—certain of your support—encouraged by your example—and cheered by your approval, I had done nothing . . . and if I have arrived at the point you desired, I am happy if you approve of the mode in which I performed the journey." Hudson refers later in the letter to "you who have so constantly protected me and have loaded me with benefits and favours."

86. Hudson to F. O., 20 Feb. 1850, (nos. 8, 9, and 10), FO84/802.

87. See Broadlands MSS, GC/HU/14/4, Hudson to Palmerston, 10 Jul. 1849; ibid., GC/HU/15, Hudson to Palmerston, 15 Aug. 1849; ibid. GC/HU/18, Hudson to Palmerston, 10 Oct. 1849, ibid., GC/HU/20, Hudson to Palmerston, 17 Jan. 1850, rec'd. 23 Feb. 1850; and ibid., GC/HU/21, Hudson to Palmerston 21 Feb. 1850, rec'd. 5 Apr. 1850 (copy in FO84/801).

88. Hudson to Palmerston, 21 Fb. 1850, Broadlands MSS, GC/HU/21.

89. PRO30/22/8D, ff. 12-15, Draft of Humble Address in Palmerston's hand, n.d.; ibid., ff. 16-19, Wood to Russell, Private, "Sunday afternoon" [17 Mar. 1850]; ibid., ff. 75-76, Palmerston to Russell, 17 Mar. 1850; ibid., ff. 77-78, Wood to Russell, 17 Mar. 1850; ibid., ff. 83-88, Russell to Palmerston, 17 Mar. 1850.

90. Printed text of Russell's Downing Street speech, 19 Mar. 1850, ibid.

91. Bethell, *Abolition*, pp. 323-24.

92. Grey to Russell, 1 Sep, 1846, PRO30/22/5C, ff. 6-7; see also Brougham MSS, 10911, Denman to Brougham, 17 Aug. [1848 or 1849]: "J. Campbell [Chancellor of the Duchy of Lancaster] let out to me that he was of the Grey faction against the Squadron."

93. Palmerston to Clarendon, 19 May 1853, Clarendon MSS (Bodleian), C3, ff. 23-26.

94. Palmerston to Hudson, 31 Mar. 1850 (copy), Broadlands MSS, GC/HU/48.

95. Palmerston to Hudson, 4 Jun. 1850 (copy), Broadlands MSS, GC/HU/49. There is an almost equally explicit awareness of the parliamentary sanction in Palmerston's earlier letter to Hudson of 31 March: "If we could by this time next year make a serious impression on the Brazilian slave trade, we should carry public opinion with us for the continuance of our maritime Police" (Ibid., GC/HU/48). See also ibid., GC/HU/50, Palmerston to Hudson, 6 Nov. 1850 (copy). Hudson was likewise conscious of the parliamentary sanction. As he reminded Palmerston in September 1850, "The Ides of March . . . are rapidly approaching: [ibid., GC/HU/26, Hudson to Palmerston, 2 Sep. 1850].

96. *Greville*, II, 353-56, 29 Jun. 1850. See also ibid., p. 349, 10 Feb. 1850; p. 352, 8 Aug. 1849; and p. 356, 1 Jul. 1850.

97. FO84/825, Palmerston, Minute, 12 Apr. 1850 on Ad. to F. O., 6 Apr. 1850 and Encls. *FO84/823*, F. O. to Ad., 22 Apr. 1850.

98. FO84/805, Hudson to F. O. 27 Jul. 1850 (secret). For laments about the shortage of ships see, for example, Broadlands MSS, GC/HU/15, Hudson to Palmerston, 15 Aug. 1849; ibid., GC/HU/22, Hudson to Palmerston, 27 Jul. 1850; and ibid., GC/HU/26, Hudson to Palmerston, 2 Sep. 1850.

99. Bethell, *Abolition*, pp. 327-41. In making this last acknowledgment of Bethell's work I would only add that I have no radical disagreements with his excellent account but have, rather, been concerned to ask certain different questions and to approach events from certain different perspectives.

100. Baring to Russell, 20 Sep. 1850, PRO30/22/8E, ff. 335-36.

101. Ibid., ff. 331-32, Baring to Russell, 18 Sep. 1850 (private); ibid., ff. 335-36, Baring to Russell, 20 Sep. 1850; and ibid., f. 75, Baring to Russell, 19 Oct. 1850 (private).

102. PRO30/22/8F, f. 7, Wood to Russell, 1 Oct, 1850.

103. Ibid., and Broadlands MSS, GC/RU/363, Russell, Memo, 24 Sep. 1850.

104. Broadlands MSS, GC/RU/406, Russell to Palmerston, 19 Mar. 1851 (clearly in reply to PRO 30/22/9B, f. 252, Palmerston to Russell, 15 Mar. 1851.

105. Broadlands MSS, GC/HU/26, Hudson to Palmerston, 2 Sep. 1850.

106. PRO 30/22/9K, ff. 17-19, Draft of Queen's speech on the prorogation of Parliament, n.d.

107. FO 84/805, Hudson to F. O., 27 Jul. 1850 (secret), and n. 98 above.

108. Serge Daget, "L'Abolition de la traite des noirs en France de 1814 a 1831," *Cahiers d'Etudes Africaines*, vol. 11, no. 41 (1971).

109. See especially Aberdeen MSS, BM Add MSS 43357, Confidential Print of minutes of evidence taken before de Broglie and Lushington, 31 Mar.-4 Apr. 1845; and ibid., 43215, ff. 319-39, Lushington's commentary on the Anglo-French treaty of 29 May 1845, n.d.

110. Roger Anstey, *Britain and the Congo in the Nineteenth Century* (Oxford: Clarendon Press, 1962), pp. 38-39.

111. See H. G. Soulsby, *The Right of Search and the Slave Trade in Anglo-American Relations, 1814-1862* (Baltimore: John Hopkins Univ. Press, *passim*, and A. Taylor Milne, "The Slave Trade and Anglo-American Relations, 1807-1862" (M.A. thesis, University of London, 1930), *passim*.

112. See Oliver Macdonagh, *A Pattern of Government Growth, 1800-1860* (London: Macgibbon & Kee, 1961) especially pp. 320-36, and Oliver Macdonagh, "The Nineteenth-Century Revolution in Government: A Re-Appraisal," *The Historical Journal*, 1 (1958), no. 1, 52-67 and especially 58-61.

113. Cf. Cobden's comment on the anti-Corn-Law campaign, "Ultimate victory would depend upon accident or upon further political changes. But our only chance is the enlightenmment of the public mind, so as to prepare it to take advantage of such an accident when it arises" (quoted in Donald Read, *Cobden and Bright* [London: Edward Arnold, 1967], p. 45).

114. Quoted by Brian Harrison in Patricia Hollis, ed., *Pressure from Without in Early Victorian England* (London: Edward Arnold, 1974) pp. 292-93.

115. I am grateful for comments on the original version of this paper made in general discussion at the 1976 Conference, and at a seminar at the University of Pittsburgh, as well as for comments on subsequent drafts, especially those of Mr. David Eltis, Dr. Stanley Engerman, and Dr. Oliver Macdonagh.

"Sweet Land of Liberty": Libertarian Rhetoric and Practice in Eighteenth-Century Britain

DONALD GREENE

WHEN I was growing up in western Canada, there was still a good deal of the British imperial mystique around. On occasions such as the anniversary of Canadian Confederation or the Silver Jubilee of King George V and Queen Mary we sang, loudly and enthusiastically, James Thomson's and Thomas Arne's "Rule, Britannia! Britannia, rule the waves! Britons never, never, never will be slaves," or, to Elgar's *Pomp and Circumstance*, "Land of hope and glory! Mother of the free!," or a rollicking ditty beginning "Britannia, the pride of the ocean, The home of the brave and the free!"

When the composer of the last, one David Taylor Shaw, performed before audiences in the United States, it is said that he merely changed the first line to "Columbia, the gem of the ocean," and, to great applause, continued with "The home of the brave and the free." Most of us also knew that denizens of the republic to the south of us devoutly sang Samuel Francis Smith's words, "My country, 'tis of thee, Sweet land of liberty . . . Let freedom ring," to the tune of *our* National Anthem, composed about the time of Thomson's insistence that we would never be slaves, to express devoted loyalty to King George II and his successors on the throne. This struck us as somewhat odd, but we were used to viewing the bizarreries of our neighbors across the

49th Parallel with amused tolerance. If, however, I sometimes wondered, both sets of people had been so raucously proclaiming, for so many generations, their fierce dedication to liberty and devoutly hymning their unalienable condition as freemen, what in the world was all the fuss about in 1776? And what, I puzzled my young head from time to time, precisely was meant by my loudly sung freedom?

These self-congratulatory ditties are not heard as often in Great Britain and the Commonwealth as they used to be; they tend to be associated with elderly members of the British and Canadian Conservative parties, and to be laughed at by younger, more enlightened generations. Yet south of the border, at such rituals as the Republican and Democratic presidential nominating conventions or the opening of the World Series, they still seem to be received with complete solemnity. Possibly this is the sort of thing John Brooke had in mind when he wrote, in his biography of George III, "Perhaps the only true Tories in the world today are to be found in the United States."[1]

My youthful question, what is meant by "freedom" in these contexts, is not easy to answer. "Abstract liberty," as Burke said, "like other mere abstractions, is not to be found. Liberty inheres in some sensible object."[2] But there seems no limit to the number of concrete situations to which the word has been applied. The oldest historical meaning, perhaps, is freedom of the individual as opposed to servitude. The oldest symbol of liberty is the pointed Phrygian or liberty cap, which, along with a rod, was given to a Roman slave when he was manumitted. There is the theological meaning of freedom from the bondage of sin ("Ye shall know the truth, and the truth shall make you free").[3] There is the nationalistic sense of freedom of one country from the overlordship of another. There is freedom from excessive governmental supervision and regulation of the individual's life. There is freedom of the individual's movements from one country to another, or from one part to another part of the same country. There is "due process"—freedom from arbitrary punishment or imprisonment without adherence to legal forms intended to protect the individual's right to defend himself. There is freedom from injury, robbery, or similar aggression by other individuals. There is, very importantly, economic liberty—liberty to buy, sell, trade, to make and spend money, to acquire or dispose of property without restriction.[4] Denial of this last freedom can be highly irritating. I have sometimes wondered whether George Orwell's immediate impulse for his nightmarish description of an unfree society in *Nineteen Eighty-Four* was the strict rationing of food and clothing that obtained in Britain for several years after the end of the Second World War. I lived there at that time, and like others highly resented walking past a shop window containing a piece of cheese or a candy bar, with adequate funds in my pocket to purchase it, but unable, by government decree, to do so until some date in the future when a coupon became valid. There was something intensely humiliating in being told over the BBC by an offical voice that next month I would be permitted to buy a few ounces more or less of some commodity than in last month, as though I were a naughty child whose allowance was dependant on his behavior. (Orwell is good on the grandiose reasons of state alleged by authority for such variations in one's ration.) I have seldom sensed a stronger feeling of incipient public rebellion than in California a few years ago, when the government of that state decreed that one could purchase gasoline only on stipulated days, depending on whether the last figure on one's automobile license plate was even or odd. Not even the widespread protests which had earlier taken place over the Vietnam affair seemed to carry with them an atmosphere of such imminent general mutiny.

The origins of both the Germanic word *free* and the Greek and Roman *eleutheros* and *liber* are curious. According to etymological dictionaries, *free* derives from an Indo-Germanic root meaning "to love," the same root from which come *friend*, German *Friede*, "peace," and the Norse goddess of love after whom Friday is named. ("Thank God It's Friday," or "T.G.I.F.," a popular American slogan, salutes the freedom of the following weekend, including, of course, freedom to make love on one's own time.) The *American Heritage Dictionary* lists an interesting sequence of semantic developments from this root: first, "beloved;" then "one of the loved ones;" then "not in bondage, free." *Eleutheros* and *liber* apparently come from the same root as German *Leute*, "we, the people," as opposed to the root of *Welsh*,

Wallachia, Vlach, "foreigners, outsiders." The semantic development of *liber,* "free," from this root, the *AHD* says, "is obscure." But a note in the *Oxford English Dictionary* throws light on it:

> The primary sense of the adj. [*free*] is "dear": the Germanic and Celtic sense comes of its having been applied as the distinctive epithet of those members of the household who were connected by ties of kindred with the head, as opposed to the slaves. The converse process of sense-development appears in Lat. *liberi,* children, literally the "free" members of the household.

In short, to be "free" or "liberated" means to belong to the exclusive, privileged, ruling class—to be one of "the loved ones," not one of the unprivileged, unloved lesser breeds. "Invested with the rights and privileges, admitted to the privileges of" is still one of the meanings of *free,* as in "Free and Accepted Masons," "to be given the freedom of the city," "to be made free of something."

This sense of elitist privilege may account for the fact that much seventeenth- and eighteenth-century libertarian rhetoric can hail the great slave-based societies of Greece and Rome as "cradles of liberty." When Samuel Johnson caustically observed of such patriots of the American Revolution as Thomas Jefferson and Patrick Henry, "How is it that we hear the loudest yelps for liberty among the drivers of Negroes?," he missed the point. Burke is closer to the usage of the day: "The spirit of liberty is more high and haughty" in the southern American colonies "than in those to the northward." Why so? "It is, that in Virginia and the Carolinas they have a vast multitude of slaves. Where this is the case in any part of the world, those who are free are by far the most proud and jealous of their freedom. Freedom to them is not only an enjoyment, but a kind of rank and privilege."[6] Burke sees nothing paradoxical in this. Johnson, ahead of his time as usual, does. Yet some decades later the great libertarian Shelley can write, "Let there be light! said Liberty, / And like sunrise from the sea, / Athens arose"[7]—Athens, one of the greatest slave markets in the ancient world.

One can think of many more such paradoxes, still much debated. Does freedom from violence at the hands of others entail

unrestricted freedom to possess and use firearms?[8] Does freedom of communication authorize Hitlerian rabble-rousing? Does
freedom of combination legitimize the closed shop? Does the
principle of nationalistic freedom, which authorizes the secession of a group of people from the rule of another group, in turn
authorize the secession of a subgroup from the rule of *that*
group?[9] Does freedom of travel and of trade authorize the pol-
lution of the atmosphere and the extravagant consumption of
limited supplies of energy? The practical difficulties of John
Stuart Mill's grand principle, that the only justification for in-
terference with anyone's actions is self-protection, have often
been canvassed.

What I want to do in this paper is to look at some British
expressions of libertarian sentiment of the first half of the eighteenth century in their historical context—more particularly in
the context of the long struggle to force Sir Robert Walpole from
office, when, as A. S. Foord says, "Opposition writers ham-
mered away for seventeen years with deadly and often hysterical
insistence upon the same points,"[10] one of them being the men-
ace to liberty presented by Walpole's regime. There had of course
been earlier such rhetoric in England. Caroline Robbins and
others have sketched much of it, from the original "Commonwealth men," Harrington, Algernon Sidney, Milton—Cromwell's
Latin secretary, who, after hymning "the mountain nymph, sweet
Liberty," was later to denounce his opponents as "hogs / That
bawl for freedom in their senseless mood, / And still revolt when
truth would set them free. / License they mean when they cry
liberty: / For who loves that must first be wise and good."[11] It must
have given Johnson pleasure to use this passage as the epigraph
for one of his political pamphlets, in which he satirizes the
American patriots who in 1774 were denouncing the North administration's grant of civil liberty to the Roman Catholics of
Quebec. "In an age where every mouth is open for 'liberty of
conscience,'" Johnson writes, "it is equitable to shew some regard to the conscience of a Papist."[12] A little later he was to write
of Milton's tyranny over his family, "It has been observed"—no
doubt by Samuel Johnson, in his earlier dictum about yelps for
liberty among drivers of Negroes—"that they who most loudly
clamour for liberty do not most liberally grant it."[13]

And, most importantly, there was Locke, who laid it down that the only reason for governmental intervention in the life of the people of a country is to protect the individual's life, liberty, and property—an inseparable trio on both sides of the Atlantic, found in the resolutions of the first Continental Congress in 1774 and the early form of the Declaration of Independence, until Jefferson tactfully emended "property" to the presumably synonymous "the pursuit of happiness." Much was made by political propagandists like John Trenchard and Thomas Gordon of the Lockean nexus. In *Cato's Letters* "liberty" is defined as "the power which every man has over his own actions, and his right to enjoy the fruit of his labor, art, and industry." Titles of some of the letters are "Trade and naval power the offspring of civil liberty only, and cannot subsist without it"; "Property and commerce secure in a free government only"; "Property the first principle of power."[14] However, instead of such political theorists, I should like to look at some expressions of similar views by other widely read writers of the time, chiefly poets, not so often studied from this point of view.

As good a place as any to start is with Joseph Addison, whose highly popular play *Cato* no doubt inspired Trenchard and Gordon to use the name of the Roman patriot for their *Letters*. Addison died prematurely, before Walpole fully consolidated his power, but he was politically active while Walpole was, and, though like Walpole a steadfast Whig, not a Whig of exactly the same stamp. In his and Steele's vastly popular *Spectator*, one of the leading members of the Spectator club is the London merchant, Sir Andrew Freeport—the name is significant—"a person of indefatigable industry, strong reason, and great experience. His notions of trade are noble and generous . . . He calls the sea the British Common . . . True power is to be got from arts and industry . . . He abounds in several frugal maxims, among which the greatest is 'A penny saved is a penny got'"[15]—it is easy to see that Franklin was an assiduous reader of *The Spectator*. Himself an impecunious scholar, Addison was taken up by Whig leaders like Somers and Halifax, who realized his usefulness as a party writer. They subsidized his early tour of France and Italy, which moved him to write, apropos of England,

O Liberty! thou goodess heavenly bright,
Profuse of bliss and pregnant with delight!
Eternal pleasures in thy presence reign,
And smiling plenty leads thy wanton train.

....

'Tis Liberty that crowns Britannia's isle,
And makes her barren rocks and her bleak mountains smile[16]

with the help of international trade, protected, of course, by a powerful navy. "There is no place [in London] which I so much love to frequent," he confesses in another *Spectator*, "as"—what? Westminster Abbey? St. Paul's? St. James's Park? No—"as the Royal Exchange. It gives me a secret satisfaction, and, in some measure, gratifies my vanity, as I am an Englishman, to see so rich an assembly of countrymen and foreigners consulting together upon the private business of mankind."[17] What has been said about his fellow government publicist, Defoe, perhaps applies also to Addison: "He comes nearest to being a poet when he writes in impassioned prose about the expansion of English commerce."[18]

In one of the *Tatlers*, Addison describes a dream vision of a "happy region" among the Alps—one recalls Milton's "mountain nymph"—"inhabited by the Goddess of Liberty, whose presence softened the rigours of the climate, enriched the barrenness of the soil, and more than supplied the absence of the sun. . . . On the left hand of the goddess sat the Genius of a Commonwealth, with the cap of liberty on her head." "Liberty" however is by no means a republican: "On the right hand of the goddess was the Genius of Monarchy," whose appearance "equally inspired love and veneration into the hearts of all that beheld her." There are two dependent goddesses; "The name of the first was Plenty, of the second, Commerce." The first is surrounded with the produce of native agriculture, the second "with groves of spices, olives, and orange trees; and in a word with the products of every foreign clime." But encamped outside Liberty's domain are "two formidable enemies," who have to be constantly guarded against. "Tyranny was at the head of one of these armies, dressed in an Eastern habit." One of her attendants is "Persecution, holding up a bloody flag, embroidered with flower-de-luces," the symbol of Louis XIV's France. She is followed by Oppression, Poverty, Famine, and Torture. Leading the other army is Licentiousness, "dressed in a garment not unlike the Polish cassock."[19] Like Milton, Addison is not one to confuse liberty with Polish licentiousness. It has often been noted that Montesquieu's later formulation was the one most frequently quoted during the century: "Political liberty does not consist in an unlimited freedom . . . . Liberty is a right of doing whatever the laws permit."[20] "Other nations," Montesquieu observes, "have made the interests of commerce yield to those of politics: the English, on the contrary, have ever made their political interests give way to those of commerce. They know better than any other people upon earth how to value at the same time, these three great advantages—religion, commerce, and liberty."[21]

Before Queen Anne's death in 1714, Addison, Walpole, and other Whigs had worked harmoniously in opposition to the Tory administration of Oxford and Bolingbroke, which concluded the War of the Spanish Succession on terms too lenient to France, the great rival of British trade and naval power, to suit the Whigs. But when, at George I's accession, Tories ceased to be a serious political force, strains developed in the Whig monopoly of power and led to the "Whig split" of 1717.[22] On one side were those who, like the new king, favored an aggressive foreign policy. They were led by General Lord Stanhope, formerly British commander-in-chief in Spain, and Marlborough's son-in-law, Lord Sunderland, Addison's patron, who got him appointments on the Board of Trade and Plantations, and as under-secretary of state and for Ireland. An important aspect of this policy was the expansion of British overseas commerce. George's acquisition of the Swedish territories of Bremen and Verden was intended to provide an opening to the lucrative trade of the Baltic, and access to the timber needed to build British naval and merchant ships. The "little Englander" Whig faction, on the other hand, distrusted such overextension, and its leaders, Walpole and his brother-in-law Townshend, resigned office in 1717, leaving the Stanhope-Sunderland group in control for four years. Then the South Sea Company scandal discredited them, and Walpole emerged as head of the government for twenty-one years. The short ascendancy of Sunderland and Stanhope, however, enabled Addison to attain his moment of glory, and for a year, until ill health forced him to resign, he held the great office of Secretary of State for the southern region, a post which gave him direction of overseas trade and colonial affairs, as well as the bulk of European diplomacy.

Walpole's pacific and cautious policies did not satisfy the vaulting imaginations of those who believed that entrepreneurship should be given a free hand to make Britain a great world power, with trade following the flag. The political animosity that pursued Walpole during the later part of his administration has seldom been equaled in virulence, not even in the McCarthy and Watergate years in the United States.[23] The inevitable charges of corruption and tyranny were heard; but running under them like a continuo bass was the cry, heard so often in the parliamentary debates of the years before Walpole's downfall, of "enemy of commerce."[24] What finally brought him down, of course, was his weakly allowing himself to be trapped into making war with Spain over the Spanish monopoly of trade in South American and Pacific waters, and then pursuing the war half-heartedly. It is against this background that the libertarian rhetoric of the 1730s and '40s needs to be read.

Let us take a closer look at James Thomson's "Rule, Britannia." Like many clever young Scots after the Union of 1707, Thomson migrated to London, to earn a precarious living as a writer, and, like a number of other ambitious young writers of the time, gravitated into the circle of Frederick, Prince of Wales, a nucleus of opposition to his father, George II, and Walpole. The song was first sung in 1740, as the finale of a masque entitled *Alfred*, performed before the Prince at his country residence, Cliveden (famous again, two centuries later, as a center of political intrigue). The masque was one of several eighteenth-century dramatic productions purporting to be based on earlier British history. Boadicea, Alfred, Edward III, and Elizabeth I were among the favored protagonists. They were heavily charged with propaganda—allegories showing how much happier and "freer" the English had been under these earlier "patriotic" monarchs, by comparison with their lamentable state under Walpole. The song may have been composed as a deliberate challenge to the "Establishment" anthem, "God Save Great George, Our King."

Thomson's use of the term "Britain" is significant: it includes Scotland, merged with England thirty years before, and feeling, as usual, slighted by the more powerful partner.[25] Several important Scottish politicians, notably the Duke of Argyll, chief of the Clan Campbell, were active in the opposition to Walpole. The text runs

> When Britain first, at Heav'n's command,
> Across from out the azure main,
> This was the charter of the land,
> And guardian angels sung this strain:
>
> "Rule, Britannia! rule the waves!
> Britons never will be slaves."
>
> The nations not so blest as thee
> Must in their turn to tyrants fall,
> While thou shalt flourish, great and free,
> The dread and envy of them all.
>
> "Rule, Britannia! rule the waves!
> Britons never will be slaves."
>
> Still more majestic shalt thou rise,
> More dreadful, from each foreign stroke;
> As the loud blast that tears the skies
> Serves but to root thy native oak.
>
> "Rule, Britannia! rule the waves!
> Britons never will be slaves."
>
> Thee haughty tyrants ne'er shall tame;
> All their attempts to bend thee down
> Will but arouse thy generous flame,
> But work their woe, and thy renown.
>
> "Rule, Britannia! rule the waves!
> Britons never will be slaves."
>
> To thee belongs the rural reign,
> Thy cities shall with commerce shine;
> All thine shall be the subject main,
> And ev'ry shore it circles thine.
>
> "Rule, Britannia! rule the waves!
> Britons never will be slaves."

> The Muses, still with freedom found,
> Shall to thy happy coast repair;
> Blest isle! with matchless beauty crowned,
> And manly hearts to guard the fair.[26]

Do these propositions have a familiar ring? Britain is a unique creation of Providence, under special protection from on high, and with a special manifest destiny; all other nations are inferior and doomed to tyranny; all foreigners envy it (and presumably would like to be British, if they could); its military and naval power is feared throughout the world; it enjoys unique economic prosperity; because of its freedom, the arts flourish in it; physically, it is unmatched for beauty—or does Thomson merely mean that its women are? At any rate, its men are ready to protect them with *macho* gallantry. Is not this all somehow reminiscent of "Only in America," "America the Beautiful," "It all began in 1776," "Novus ordo seclorum," and so on?

Thomson wrote much else in the same vein. In "On His Royal Highness the Prince of Wales," he laments that "Britannia, drooping, grows an empty form, / While on our vitals selfish parties prey, / And deep corruption eats our soul away." But the progeny of Frederick, "the friend of liberty"—headed by his oldest son, the future George III—will cause "the rekindling eyes" of "the Goddess of the Main" to "resume their fire, / The Virtues smile, the Muses tune their lyre . . . when France insults and Spain shall rob no more."[27] In the long poem he entitles simply "Britannia," that goddess laments that Walpole, in 1727, had not declared war on Spain when a British fleet under Admiral Hosier unsuccessfuly blockaded the Central American port of Portobello, suffering heavy casualties from disease: "War . . . yet mourns his fetter'd hands . . . Th'insulting Spaniard dares/ Infest the trading flood . . . Whence this unwonted patience? this weak doubt? . . . This meek forbearance? This unnative fear?"[28]

Thomson's most ambitious performance was a five-part, 3,500-line poem, *Liberty*. Liberty of course is born in ancient Greece, is transmitted to republican Rome, passes to the northern European nations, and at last to Britain. Part Four "concludes with an abstract of English history, marking the several advances of Liberty, down to her complete establishment at the Revolution"—that of 1688, of course; one wonders whether its tercentenary in a few years time will be celebrated with as much fervor and rhetoric as the bicentenary of that of 1776. Part Five gives us a prospect of the future, concluding with a lush description of facilities for trade and commerce—"see long canals and deepen'd rivers join . . . Lo, ports expand . . . On ev'ry pointed coast the lighthouse tow'rs, / And by the broad imperious mole repell'd, / Hark, how the baffled storm indignant roars!"[29]

Another product of Hosier's ill-fated expedition in 1727 was a ballad, *Admiral Hosier's Ghost*, by Richard Glover, written in 1739 to prod Walpole to more vigorous measures against the Spanish. The ghost of Hosier, accompanied by an entourage of three thousand other naval ghosts, confronts Admiral Vernon, now naval commander in the Caribbean, congratulates him on having taken Portobello with a smaller force than his own (which the ministry had not let him send against the place), and, with ingenious attention to rhyme, laments the orders that bound his hands:

> I by twenty sail attended
>   Did this Spanish town affright,
> Nothing then its wealth defended
>   But my orders not to fight.
>
> O, that in this rolling ocean
>   I had cast them with disdain,
> And obeyed my heart's warm motion
>   To have quelled the pride of Spain.
>
> For resistance I could fear none,
>   But with twenty ships had done
> What thou, brave and happy Vernon,
>   Hast achieved with six alone.
>
> Then the Bastimentos never
>   Had our foul dishonour seen,
> Nor the sea the sad receiver
>   Of this gallant train had been.[30]

Thus exhorted, Vernon went on to invest Cartagena, in what is now Colombia, producing a far greater disaster and many more thousand British casualties than had Hosier, gruesomely described in Smollett's *Roderick Random.*

Glover was a well-to-do member of the London business community, a "Hamburg and Bremen merchant," concerned to protect existing trade routes and open new ones. Another of his 1739 productions was a long poem, *London; or the Progress of Commerce.* It celebrates the Olympian birth of Commerce, child of Neptune, endowed with gifts from Ceres, Bacchus, and Minerva, whose mission is to bring the affluent society to the denizens of the earth. Her successive progress from Egypt to Phoenicia, Carthage, Rome, Venice, and Spain is described. Spain however proves unworthy of its guest—"Insatiate race! the shame of polish'd lands! / Disgrace of Europe! for inhuman deeds / And insolence renown'd." Spain's bad record in America is condemned—"And com'st thou, strengthened with the shining stores / Of that gold-teeming hemisphere, to waste / The smiling fields of Europe, and extend / Thy bloody shackles o'er these happy seats / Of Liberty?"[31] No way, declares Commerce; first Holland, finally Britain will be her residence, and a long, lush picture of an affluent and powerful Britain is given—"Albion, sea embrac'd, / The joy of freedom, dread of treacherous kings, / The destin'd mistress of the subject main / And arbitress of Europe . . . Thou nurse of arts, and thy industrious race, / Pleas'd with their candid manners, with their free/ Sagacious discourse, to inquiry led, / And zeal for knowledge . . ." and so on.[32] If American patriotic rhetoric contains a fair amount of self-congratulation, it can be seen that it had precedent.

Glover's masterpiece was *Leonidas*, a turgid blank-verse epic in twelve books, which was the best seller of 1737. "It has since been unaccountably neglected," a later editor complains.

> But its favorable reception was not entirely owing to its intrinsic merits. At the time of its publication, a zeal, or rather rage, for liberty prevailed in England; a constellation of great men, distinguished by their virtue, as well as their talents, set themselves in opposition to the Court; every species of composition that bore the sacred name of freedom recommended itself to their protection and soon obtained possession of the public favour. Hence a poem founded on the noblest principles of liberty, and displaying the most

brilliant examples of patriotism, soon found its way into the world.[33]

The "great man" to whom Glover dedicates the work was old Lord Cobham, the "godfather" of the Pitt-Grenville-Temple-Lyttelton clan, with William Pitt the elder preeminently representing the interests of the trading community, and the man who, in the 1750's, finally realized the ambition of the "patriots" and brought the first British Empire into being. The poem tells in tedious detail how the heroic Spartans, led by King Leonidas, fell at Thermopylae. The poem, "founded," as Glover says, "on a character eminent for military glory, and love of liberty," does not mention the wretched helots whose toil made it possible for the "free" Spartans to devote themselves exclusively to the pursuit of military glory.

There is much more such rhetoric that could be quoted. Pope's and Swift's anti-Walpolian jeremiads are well known—Pope declaiming, in *1738*, "Yes, the last pen for freedom let me draw"; Swift leaving an epitaph declaring that above all he strove strenuously for liberty. But they are only the tip of the iceberg. Lord Lyttelton, himself a "boy patriot," published a congratulatory poem to "Leonidas" Glover—"Thou, great poet, in whose nervous lines / The native majesty of freedom shines;"[34] an epigram on Walpole's depriving Pitt of his commission as an ensign in the army, "The servile standard from thy freeborn hand, / He took, and bade thee lead the patriot band;"[35] and similar squibs. There is Mark Akenside, whose *Pleasures of Imagination*, 1744, contains libertarian rhetoric which was much toned down in the revised form, *The Pleasures of the Imagination*, 1757-61. In 1744, for instance, we find "Majestic Truth, and where Truth deigns to come, / Her sister Liberty will not be far." In the revision this becomes "Wise Order; and where Order deigns to come, / Her sister Liberty will not be far."[36] There has been some puzzlement over these transformations. "It is evident," one student explains, "Akenside developed a sense of man's weakness, of the limits as well as the power of his reason."[37] What is rather more evident is that "the reversionary interest" of Prince Fred, inherited in 1751 by his son, later George III, had attained, or was on the point of attaining, power. Soon after George's accession, Akenside was given the court appointment of physician to Queen Charlotte. The "unnecessary and outrageous zeal for what he called and thought liberty"[38] which Johnson attributed to the earlier Akenside had become indeed unnecessary; for the liberty-loving patriots, and a patriot king, now governed the country, so that liberty was no longer in the slightest danger. Nothing is more familiar in politics than such transformations when the outs become the ins; "liberty" now having been achieved, "order" becomes necessary to preserve it from danger from counter revolutionaries (the former ins, who are now the outs, and, in their own eyes, the new "libertarians").

One last sample is perhaps worth quoting. The poet is John Gilbert Cooper, the inheritor of a comfortable family estate. The poem is addressed to William Pitt. The year is now 1756; the Seven Years' War has begun and is going badly. Pitt is still out of office. The Genius of Britain is upset to learn that Newcastle's administration has arranged to hire 6,000 Hessian troops to help defend British and Hanoverian possessions. The Genius expresses Pittite indignation at the humiliation of calling for aid on these slavish foreign mercenaries (though when Pitt eventually took over the conduct of the war, he subsidized foreign military assistance on an even greater scale):

> O, how can vassals born to bear
> The galling weight of slav'ry's chain
> A Patriot's noble ardour share
> Or Freedom's sacred cause maintain?
> Britons, exert your own unconquer'd might,
> A freeman best defends a freeman's right.

In particular, the war in America has gone badly; Braddock, and before him Washington, have suffered defeats by the French in the Ohio Valley. The Genius mourns the condition of his young American relative:

> But see, upon his utmost shores
> America's sad Genius lies,
> Each wasted province he deplores
> And casts on me his languid eyes.
> Bless'd with Heav'n's fav'rite ordinance I fly,
> To raise th' oppress'd, and humble tyranny.

> Thus said, the vision westward fled,
> His wrinkled brow denouncing war;
> The way fire-mantled Vengeance led,
> And Justice drove his airy car;
> Behind, firm-footed Peace her olive bore,
> And Plenty's horn pour'd blessings on the shore.

It is a not inappropriate allegorical representation of the descent of American patriotic libertarian (and "propertarian") rhetoric from British.[39]

Much study has been done, by Caroline Robbins, Bernard Bailyn, Laurence Leder,[40] and others, on the ideological origins of the American Revolution, as found in the writings of such political pamphleteers and journalists as Molesworth, Trenchard and Gordon, and Bolingbroke. Yet if, as John Brooke has remarked, "The fathers of the American republic were the heirs of the Tory tradition in British politics"[41]—Tories such as Paul Whitehead and Samuel Johnson did for a time add their denunciations of Walpolian tyranny to those of the Whig "patriots"— possibly such popular versifiers as Thomson and Glover had at least as large a circulation and influence across the Atlantic as prose writers of political theory. Certainly, two hundred and more years later, the rhetoric of the opposition to Walpole is still heard on American television and in the American press. One is tempted to quote Sir Lewis Namier's comment that the United States is "in certain ways, a refrigerator in which British ideas and institutions are preserved long after they have been forgotten in this country."[42]

Did that clamor of nearly two decades for "freedom" in fact result in striking increases in the amount of "liberty" available in Britain? So far as I can discover, not an iota. The average Briton was quite as "free," or alternatively as much a "slave," after, as before, Walpole fell from power, and was replaced by a coalition of his own former supporters and opponents, who, once they obtained power, conducted the government of the country in a way indistinguishable from his. The reforms they—like all other opposition groups of the century—had clamored for, annual parliamentary elections, the exclusion from Parliament of holders of government appointments (a trans-Atlantic legacy, for better or worse, to the United States), the abolition of the standing (regular) army, they made no gesture at implementing.[43] Their rhetoric fell into disrepute. A few years later "The name of patriot had become a by-word of derision," Macaulay, no anti-Whig, wrote. "Horace Walpole scarely exaggerated when he said that, in those times, the most popular declaration which a candidate could make on the hustings was that he had never been and would never be a patriot."[44] Johnson, who in his early anti-Walpolian writings had used the libertarian rhetoric as passionately as Thomson or Akenside, coined his immortal definition of patriotism as the last refuge of a scoundrel. At elections the cry of *"No* 'Liberty and Property' men!" was heard.[45]

Some effective derision of the Lockean slogan was written. There is Goldsmith's fine story of the life of "a poor fellow," whom he had met "begging at one of the outlets of London, with a wooden leg."[46] Born to poverty, brought up in the workhouse, jailed for accidentally killing a hare, transported to the colonies to work as a serf, impressed into the army, wounded fighting the French and imprisoned in France, at last discharged penniless from the army, no one could be a more dedicated patriot: "When my time [in the colonies] was expired, I worked my passage home, and glad I was to see Old England again, because I loved my country. O liberty, liberty, liberty! that is the property of every Englishman, and I will die in its defence . . . I hate the French because they are all slaves, and wear wooden shoes . . . I will for ever love liberty and Old England, liberty, property, and Old England, for ever, huzza!" Johnson marvels at the bravery of the English common soldiers: "There are some, perhaps, who would imagine that every Englishman fights better than the subjects of absolute government. But what has the English more than the French soldier? Property they are both commonly without. Liberty is, to the lowest rank of every nation, little more than the choice of working or starving"—later a familiar Marxist apothegm. "The English soldier seldom has his head very full of the constitution; nor has there been for more than a century"—that is, since the Civil War—"any war that put the property or liberty of a single Englishman in danger."[47] William Whitehead, for twenty-five years Poet Laureate to George III, in his burlesque heroic tragedy *Fatal Constancy, or Love in Tears*, advises the budding author, "In his dedication, if to a lord, the proper topics are his lordship's public spirit; the noble stand which he made in the cause of liberty; but more particularly his heroic disinterestedness in hiding from the world his own spirited [poetic] performances, that those of inferior authors might have a chance for success."[48]

And yet, in their birthday and New Year odes to George III, in the latter half of the eighteenth century, Whitehead and his successor Thomas Warton extol His Majesty's "noble stand in the cause of liberty"—and commerce: "Sacred to thee, / O Commerce, daughter of sweet Liberty, / Shall flow the annual strain. / Beneath a monarch's softer care, / Thy sails unnumbered swell in air / And darken half the main" (Whitehead in 1765).[49] Here is Whitehead in 1777 on American democracy: "Let cool reason clear the mental eye; / On Britain's well-mixed state alone, / True Liberty has fix'd her throne, / Where law, not man, an equal rule maintains. / Can freedom e'er be found where many a tyrant reigns?"[50] Soame Jenyns, in 1786, begins a poem "On a Late Execrable Attempt on His Majesty's Life," "Long had our gracious George, with gentle hand, / And love paternal, Britain's sceptre sway'd. / To render this a free and happy land / Was all for which he wished to be obeyed."[51] In the Preface to his *Dictionary*, Johnson fires up at Swift's suggestion of an English Academy, like the French, to rule authoritatively on what is correct English—"an institution which I, who can never wish to see dependence multiplied, hope the spirit of British liberty will hinder or destroy."[52]

Among the libertarian clichés of the time, there was one whose truth seems undeniable—that the inhabitants of no other European country possessed more civil liberty than those of Britain. Voltaire, visting England in the late 1720's, is amazed at the Parliamentary system of government, the nobility's lack of privilege, the equitable system of taxation, the freedom of religious worship ("An Englishman, as a free man, goes to heaven by whatever road pleases him"). English civil liberty, he believes, induces a liberation of the mind which results in brilliant discoveries in science like those of Newton, in medicine like that of Lady Mary Wortley Montagu, in a brilliant literature (though, to be sure, Shakespeare pushed dramatic libertarianism *too* far). And, of course, "Commerce, which has enriched the citizen in England, has contributed to make them free, and that freedom, in turn, has extended commerce."[53] During his visit Voltaire associated with oppositionists like Pope and Bolingbroke. But though he picked up some of their clichés, like the one about commerce, he is genuinely astonished by the quantity of liberty about, and certainly finds it in no danger. From time to time, English writers had expressed the same opinion. Dryden had written of his countrymen, "Those Adam-wits, too fortunately free, / Began to dream they wanted liberty"[54]—that is, lacked it. And Johnson, answering the Philadelphia congress of 1774, declares, "An Englishman in the common course of life and action feels no restraint. An English colony has very liberal powers of regulating its own manners and adjusting its own affairs."[55] At the same time he points out that, then as now, under every government, individuals are always subject to being deprived of life, liberty, or property, without their consent, by criminal or tax legislation.

It seems safe to assert that as much civil liberty as exists today in English-speaking countries existed in Britain in the eighteenth century—possibly more.[56] The Habeas Corpus Act, "An Act for the Better Securing the Liberty of the Subject," was passed in 1679, and its provisions, then as now, were generally observed, except in times of unusual national danger. Legislation outlawing Roman Catholicism and limiting the civil rights of Protestant Dissenters was still on the books, but after 1700 it was seldom enforced. When one reads the uninhibited satire of the century—or views it in the ferocious caricatures of Rowlandson and Gillray—much of it directed against the administration, the established church, and the royal family, it is hard to argue that freedom of speech and the press was greatly restricted. The legislation authorizing censorship of the press had lapsed in 1695. Printers were occasionally brought before the courts when they went too far, but none seems to have suffered any conspicuous martyrdom. The libel laws were complex and it was difficult to get a conviction under them.[57] What most seemed to concern Parliament was to prevent its own debates from being reported—no doubt from similar motives to those which now cause it and Congress to object to their being televised. But its fulminations did not prevent the *London Magazine* and *Gentleman's Magazine* from printing them, under transparent disguises, for several years at the height of the opposition to Walpole.

Censorship of the London stage, to be sure, was imposed in 1737, when Walpole felt its attacks on him were becoming too outrageous. But governments of later times were equally reluctant to give this up, and plays as late as those of Bernard Shaw and Tennessee Williams were banned from public production in London; such censorship was not abolished until, incredibly, 1968. Yet it was never hard to subvert its intent: in Walpole's time by printing the banned play, Gay's *Polly* or Henry Brooke's *Gustavus Vasa*, by subscription, with an indignant preface—a practice which may often have brought the author more publicity and income than if it had been produced; in the twentieth century by production by a "private" dramatic society, in which membership could be obtained for a nominal fee at the same time the ticket for the performance was purchased. Some relics of sumptuary legislation survived, like that requiring all Englishmen to be buried clad in wool, to help the trade—"Odious! in woolen! 'twould a saint provoke,' / Were the last words that poor Narcissa spoke."[58] The violence which Walpole's unsuccessful attempt to extend excise duties provoked, and the detestation in which excisemen were held, testify to the Englishman's love of privacy and hatred of snooping government inspectors. General warrants were ruled illegal in 1765 by Lord Chief Justice Camden. Travel was unrestricted; change of employment was unrestricted; the right of petitioning and public protest was very little restricted, as the Porteous, Wilkes, Gordon, and many other riots demonstrated. Perhaps the status of "Liberty and Property" in eighteenth-century Britain is best summed up by, of all people, George II's consort, the highly intelligent Queen Caroline, who like Voltaire had come to Britain from the Continent. Hervey reports her, in 1735, exclaiming in her downright way,

> My God! What a figure this poor island would make in Europe if it were not for its government. It is its excellent free government that makes all its inhabitants industrious, as they know that what they get nobody can take from them; it is its free government, too, that makes foreigners send their money hither, because they know it is secure, and that the prince cannot touch it; and since it is its freedom to which

> this kingdom owes everything that makes it great, what prince who had his sense and knew that his own greatness depended on the greatness of the country over which he reigned, would wish to take away what made both him and them considerable?[59]

Some recent historical work on the American colonies in the early eighteenth century suggests that, on the whole, the generalization applies: colonies tend to lag behind the mother country in the rate of change of their institutions.[60] One gets the impression that in, say, eighteenth-century Massachusetts and Connecticut, the individual lived under closer scrutiny from on high, reminiscent of the sixteenth and seventeenth centuries, than in eighteenth century England. And in the southern colonies, of course, there was slavery, which Lord Chief Justice Mansfield in 1772 had ruled could not legally exist in England. However that may be, if there is any validity in my thesis that the spate of libertarian rhetoric by the opponents of Walpole may have contributed to the libertarian rhetoric of the Revolution and later in America, it is ironic that the anti-Walpolian campaign concluded with one important advance in civil liberty in England, an advance which the United States has not yet apparently caught up with, and an advance for which Walpole's defenders were responsible and which his libertarian attackers opposed.

During 1976 the *New Yorker* magazine published a three-part article[61] about recent efforts of United States law enforcement officials to compel two young women to testify before a grand jury—an institution abolished in England some decades ago—concerning their acquaintance with two others, then fugitives, charged with bank robbery. Despite the Fifth Amendment to the Constitution of the United States, part of its "Bill of Rights"—"nor shall [any person] be compelled in any criminal case to be a witness against himself, nor be deprived of life, liberty, or property[62] without due process of law"—the article cites a long array of precedents, from the last hundred years of United States history, in which witnesses have been compelled so to testify, by the simple process of a court's granting them "immunity," sometimes a strictly limited immunity, from prosecution for what might emerge from that evidence. The article draws heavily on Leonard Levy's account, in his *Origins of the Fifth Amendment*,[63] of the long resistance of John Lilburne, in the early seventeenth century, to being forced to testify against himself. As Levy says, "From his time on, the right against self-incrimination was an established, respected rule of the common law, or, more broadly, of English law generally,"[64] and that right was eventually written into the Fifth Amendment. What the article fails to record, however, is that the method of subverting that right by granting "immunity" or "indemnity" from prosecution, still apparently practiced in the United States, was the subject of an important test case in England in 1742, which effectually ended its use in that country.[65]

The circumstances of the affair are remarkable. When the Prime Minister Walpole's "power-base" at last became so eroded in 1742 that he was forced to resign his office, his enemies set about securing their revenge. In the past, when an English political leader had been forced out of office, retribution had often been severe. For Charles I's minister, Strafford, it had been execution; for Charles II's Clarendon, permanent exile, both imposed by Parliamentary Acts of Attainder. More recently the terms had become somewhat more lenient. When Robert Harley, Earl of Oxford, was displaced by a Whig administration in 1714, he was imprisoned in the Tower for two years, awaiting trial by the House of Lords on his impeachment by the House of Commons. That trial, however, was sabotaged by, as it happened, Walpole, then in opposition to the ruling Stanhope-Sunderland Whig faction, and the Lords dismissed the impeachment. This operation was to pay off: when Walpole in turn was in danger of his political life in 1741, Oxford's nephew, later the third Earl, defended him, or at least refused to join the attack on him in Parliament.[66]

Immediately after Walpole's resignation, his enemies introduced a motion in the House of Commons for an investigation "into the conduct of affairs at home and abroad, during the last twenty years"—that is, during the whole of Walpole's tenure of office. It was designed to furnish the evidence for Walpole's impeachment, or perhaps even attainder. After much bitter debate, in which Walpole's friends strenuously defended him, the motion was defeated by two votes—244 to 242. Then another motion was introduced, calling for an inquiry "into the conduct of Robert, Earl of Orford, during the last *ten* years in which he was first Commissioner of the Treasury and Chancellor of the Exchequer." This more sharply focused motion, directed at Walpole's administration of the Treasury, was based on the strong suspicion that Walpole had been converting public funds to his own use. He had begun his political career a poor man; he ended it rich, with a magnificent country house and one of the world's greatest private collections of paintings. Even his modern biographer, J. H. Plumb, is unable to identify the source of his capital for these, which Walpole's official salary could not have provided. It was also charged that Walpole had permitted public funds to be used to assist the election to Parliament of his supporters (it all sounds quite modern). The House passed this motion by a majority of seven, and Walpole's enemies closed in for the kill.[67]

The investigating committee of the House of Commons called witnesses and heard testimony to some small peccadilloes. But when it summoned the man who was expected to be the chief source of damning evidence against Walpole, Nicholas Paxton, Secretary to the Treasury, the day-to-day administrator of the department, it found itself resolutely stonewalled. Paxton steadfastly refused to testify, on the grounds that his answers might incriminate him, and other witnesses followed his example.

Walpole's enemies now resorted to their last weapon. In order to compel Paxton to testify, they introduced a bill "for indemnifying [from criminal prosecution] such persons as shall upon examination make discoveries touching the disposition of public money, or concerning the disposition of public offices, or any payments or agreements in respects thereof, or concerning other matters relating to the conduct of Robert, Earl of Orford." The bill was passed by the House of Commons. But in the House of Lords, on 25 May 1742, it "produced a debate in which the greatest men of each party exerted the utmost force of their reason and eloquence."[68] The description is that of the debate's reporter in the *Gentleman's Magazine*, young Samuel Johnson. With its style no doubt polished by Johnson, the report is a superb piece of both English prose and trenchant legal argument. Most of the arguments for and against immunity discussed in the *New Yorker* article and Levy's book are there. To the argument that Walpole's alleged crimes were so great that extraordinary measures were needed to convict him of them, it was replied that a license to engage in such a fishing expedition would set a precedent endangering everyone's right to a fair trial; that the language of the bill, "matters relating to the conduct" of Walpole, was so vague that it could be twisted to mean anything; that the precedent of resorting to "extraordinary measures" could lead to a return to "foreign methods of justice," torture and the rack. What, asked Lord Ilay, was to exclude from pardon a murderer or traitor in imminent danger of conviction, if he perjured himself and swore "that in a plot for setting the Pretender on the throne, he was assisted by the counsels of the Earl of Orford"?

The argument of Justice Henry B. Brown, delivering the United States Supreme Court's majority ruling, which upheld the constitutionality of an 1896 Act of Congress providing that no witness before the Interstate Commerce Commission "shall be prosecuted or subjected to any penalty or forfeiture for or on account of any transaction, matter, or thing which he may testify," so that he can thus be compelled to testify, was "Every good citizen is bound to aid in the enforcement of the law" by testifying.[69] In 1742 the Duke of Argyll, one of Walpole's most formidable opponents, had used the same argument in the House of Lords. "The public has a claim to every man's evidence," he affirmed, "and no man can plead exemption from this duty to his country."

It seems fitting to conclude this paper with the words of that great lawyer, Lord Chancellor Hardwicke (assisted by Samuel Johnson), replying to that argument:

> The noble lords who have defended [this bill] appear to reason more upon maxims of policy than rules of law or principles of justice, and seem to imagine that if they can prove it to be expedient, it is not necessary to show that it is equitable. . . . It has, my Lords, I own, been asserted by the noble Duke that the public has a right to every man's evidence, a maxim which in its proper sense cannot be denied. For it is undoubtedly true that the public has a right to all the assistance of every individual; but it is, my Lords, upon such terms as have been established for the general advantage of all; on such terms as the majority of each society has prescribed. But, my Lords, the majority of a society, which

is the true definition of "the public," are equally obliged with the smaller number, or with individuals, to the observation of justice, and cannot therefore prescribe to different individuals different conditions. They cannot decree that treatment to be just with regard to one, which they allow to be cruel with respect to another. The claims of the public are founded, first upon right, which is invariable; and next upon the law, which, though mutable in its own nature, is however, to be so far fixed as that every man may know his own condition, his own property, and his own privileges; or it ceases in effect to be law, it ceases to be the rule of government, or the measure of conduct.[70]

Hardwicke had much more to say on the matter at hand, as did other members of the House; and no doubt he, Newcastle, and Carteret had their reasons, connected with their own political aims, for not wishing Walpole to be crucified. But the quotation above is the heart of the matter: an anticipation of Mill's insistence that the rights of the individual be protected against the tyranny of the majority; a restatement of Locke's insistence that the rule of *known* law is the only possible foundation for a civilized society; a restatement even of the hackneyed phraseology of Magna Carta, "To no man"—that is, to no single human being, however insignificant, or angrily opposed by however many millions—"To no man will we sell, to no man deny, to no man delay justice or right," or of the self-evident truth that all men are born equal in the sight of the law.

The bill was defeated in an unusually full House by the overwhelming vote of 109 to 57. Since that time, little has been heard in Great Britain of compulsion to testify by a grant of immunity from prosecution.

NOTES

1. *King George III* (New York: McGraw-Hill, 1972), p. 173.
2. *The Works and Correspondence of the Rt. Hon. Edmund Burke* (London: Rivington, 1852), III, 253; "Speech on Conciliation with the American Colonies."
3. John 8:32

4. It still causes confusion for modern American students when they fail to realize that the term "liberal," as applied to nineteenth-century British figures such as Macaulay and Gladstone, is used in this sense. The current American "liberal" creed holds precisely the opposite: it insists on the need for a strong central government strictly regulating private enterprise so as to prevent it from exploiting the poor. In this latter sense, the eighteenth-century English Tories Samuel Johnson and Oliver Goldsmith were thoroughgoing liberals—see, for instance, Chapter 19 of *The Vicar of Wakefield*—whereas a modern American "conservative" such as Senator Barry Goldwater follows the Victorian liberal line. From an etymological point of view the Victorian usage seems the more correct. Recently (1984) the term "neo-liberal" has begun to be used, with historical accuracy, to describe the economic philosophy of Prime Minister Margaret Thatcher, some of her British supporters, and even some American politicians whose economic views seem close to hers.

5. Johnson, *Political Writings*, ed. Donald Greene (New Haven: Yale Univ. Press, 1977), p. 454 ("Taxation No Tyranny") (*The Yale Edition of the Works of Samuel Johnson*, Vol. X).

6. Burke, III, 255.

7. *Hellas*, ll. 682-84.

8. This right, asserted in the American Bill of Rights (Second Amendment to the Constitution) and much cited by opponents of gun-control legislation, was stated, if less forceably, in the English Bill of Rights, 1689: "The Lords Spiritual and Temporal and Commons in Parliament assembled . . . for the vindication and asserting their earliest rights and liberties declare . . . That the subjects which are Protestants may have arms for their defence suitable to their conditions and as allowed by law." This was by way of riposte to the deposed King James II, who was accused of "causing several good subjects being Protestants to be disarmed at the same time when papists were both armed and employed contrary to law."

   Richard Harris (see n. 61 below), following Tom Paine, absurdly states that "the English Bill of Rights was largely a fraud, for it contained little to assure rights to the common man." Among rights so asserted, and repeated in the American Bill of Rights, were those of petitioning and of freedom from prosecution for petitioning, of bearing arms (under the conditions stated), of freedom from excessive bail, excessive fines, and cruel and unusual punishments. A much more detailed list, however, is given in the parallel Scottish Claim of Right. Of particular interest is its assertion, not mentioned in Leonard Levy's *Origins of the Fifth Amendment* (see n. 63 below), "That the forcing the lieges to depone against themselves in capital crimes, however the punishment be restricted, is contrary to law" (*English Historical Documents, 1660-1714*, ed. Andrew Browning [London: Eyre & Spottiswoode, 1966], p. 637).

9. The issue, of course, on which the American Civil War was fought.

10. *His Majesty's Opposition, 1714-1830* (Oxford: Clarendon Press, 1964), p. 170.

11. "L'Allegro," l. 36; Sonnet XII, "On the Detraction Which Followed upon My Writing Certain Treatises," ll. 8-12.

12. *Samuel Johnson*, ed. Donald Greene (Oxford: Oxford Univ. Press, 1984), p. 582 (*The Patriot*). (The Oxford Authors.)

13. Johnson, *Lives of the Poets*, ed. G. B. Hill (Oxford: Clarendon Press, 1905), I, 157 ("Life of Milton," par. 170).

14. *The English Libertarian Heritage*, ed. David L. Jacobson (Indianapolis: Bobbs, Merrill, 1965), pp. 137 (Letter 64), 172 (Letter 68), 205 (Letter 84), and 127-28 (Letter 62). For a hostile analysis of the position from a Marxist point of view, see C. B. Macpherson, *The Political Theory of Possessive Individualism: Hobbes to Locke* (Oxford: Clarendon Press, 1962).

15. *Spectator* No. 2 (2 March 1711).

16. Addison, *Works*, ed. Richard Hurd (London: Cadell and Davies, 1811), I, 41-42 ("A Letter from Italy to the Rt. Hon. Charles, Lord Halifax, in the year MDCCI"). Halifax was famous as the Whig Chancellor of the Exchequer who, among other financial innovations, founded the Bank of England, and thus modern governmental financial practice.

17. *Spectator* No. 69 (19 May 1711). For a description of this great "shopping center," see *Spectator*, ed. Donald F. Bond (Oxford: Clarendon Press, 1965), I, 293, n. 3.

18. James R. Sutherland, *Defoe*, 2nd ed. (London: Methuen, 1950), p. 47.

19. *Tatler* No. 161 (20 April 1710).

20. *The Spirit of the Laws*, tr. Thomas Nugent [1749] (New York: Hafner, 1949), I, 150 (Book XI, Sec. 3).

21. Ibid., I.321 (Book XX, Sec. 7).

22. Studies of the political situation at this time include John J. Murray, *George I, the Baltic, and the Whig Split* (London: Routledge and Kegan Paul, 1969), and Paul S. Fritz, *The English Ministers and Jacobitism between the Rebellions of 1715 and 1745* (Toronto: Univ. of Toronto Press, 1975).

23. A useful study is Bertrand A. Goldgar, *Walpole and the Wits: The Relations between Politics and Literature, 1722-1742* (Lincoln: Univ. of Nebraska Press, 1976).

24. See e.g., Donald J. Greene, *The Politics of Samuel Johnson* (New Haven: Yale Univ. Press, 1960), p. 125.

25. George III, heir to his father Prince Frederick's "patriotism," pointedly affirmed in his accession speech, "I glory in the name of Briton."

26. James Thomson, *The Castle of Indolence and Other Poems*, ed. Henry D. Roberts (London: Routledge, [1906]), pp. 241-42.

27. *The Works of the British Poets, with Prefaces Biographical and Critical*, ed. Robert Anderson (London: Arch, and Edinburgh: Bell and Bradfute, 1795). IX, 278-79.

28. Anderson, IX, 239.

29. Anderson, IX, 272.

30. Anderson, XI, 553.

31. Anderson, XI, 550.

32. Anderson, XI, 551.

33. Anderson, XI, 468.

34. Anderson, X, 270.

35. Anderson, X, 270.

36. Anderson, IX, 735, 757.

37. Jeffrey Hart, "Akenside's Revision of *The Pleasures of Imagination*," *PMLA*, 74 (March, 1959), 67-74.

38. Johnson, *Lives*, III, 411 ("Life of Akenside," par. 3).

39. Anderson, X, 781.

40. Robbins, *The Eighteenth Century Commonwealthman* (Cambridge, Mass.: Harvard Univ. Press, 1959); Bailyn, *The Ideological Origins of the American Revolution* (Cambridge, Mass.: Harvard Univ. Press, 1967); Leder, *Liberty and Authority: Early American Political Ideology* (Chicago: Quadrangle Books, 1968).

41. Brooke, p. 173.

42. *Crossroads of Power: Essays on Eighteenth-Century England* (New York: Macmillan, 1962), p. 78.

43. See Betty Kemp, "Frederick, Prince of Wales," in *Silver Renaissance: Essays in Eighteenth-Century English History*, ed. Alex Natan (London: Macmillan, 1961), p. 53.

44. *Critical and Historical Essays* (London: Longman, 1843), II, 458, 465.

45. John Carswell, *The Old Cause* (London: Cresset, 1954), p. 120.

46. Goldsmith, *Collected Works*, ed. Arthur Friedman (Oxford: Clarendon Press, 1966), II, 458-65 (*Citizen of the World*, Letter CXIX: "On the Distresses of the Poor, as Exemplified in the Life of a Private Centinel").

47. *Samuel Johnson*, ed. Greene, p. 550. ("The Bravery of the English Common Soldiers").

48. Anderson, XI, 954.

49. Anderson, XI, 961.

50. Anderson, XI, 968.

51. Anderson, XI, 1024.

52. *Samuel Johnson*, ed. Greene, p. 326 ("Preface to the *Dictionary*").

53. Voltaire, *Letters sur les Anglais*, ed. Arthur Wilson-Green (Cambridge: Cambridge Univ. Press, 1937), p. 32. My translation.

54. *Absalom and Achitophel*, ll. 51-52.

55. *Political Writings*, p. 423 (*Taxation No Tyranny*).

56. "Until August 1914 a sensible, law-abiding Englishman could pass through life and hardly notice the existence of the state, beyond the post office and the policeman": the opening sentence of A. J. P. Taylor, *English History, 1914-1945* (Oxford: Clarendon Press, 1965). *The Oxford History of England*, Vol. XV.

57. See C. R. Kropf, "Libel and Satire in the Eighteenth Century," *Eighteenth-Century Studies*, 8 (1974-75), 153-68.

58. Pope, *Moral Essays*, I, ll. 246-47.

59. John, Lord Hervey, *Lord Hervey's Memoirs*, ed. Romney Sedgwick (abridged) (London: William Kimber, 1962), p. 151.

60. Cf. Lord Hailsham (Lord Chancellor of Great Britain), "How Britain Lays Down the Law," *Saturday Review*, 11 June 1977, p. 26: "In many ways the American legal system resembles to the eye of a contemporary English lawyer nothing so much as a gigantic historical museum of olde Englishe

practices that, rightly or wrongly, in the 200 years since independence, we have cast aside or forgotten."

61. Richard Harris, "Taking the Fifth," *The New Yorker*, 5 April, pp. 44-95, 12 April, pp. 43-100, and 19 April, pp. 42-97. Later published in book form as *Freedom Spent* (Boston: Little, Brown, 1976).

62. It is interesting that Jefferson's "life, liberty, and the pursuit of happiness" of 1776 should have reverted in 1791 to its Lockean original. See also the quotation from the Scottish Claim of Rights, 1689, in note 8 above.

63. New York: Oxford, 1968.

64. P. 313.

65. Levy mentions it briefly in passing (pp. 328-29), but, strangely, fails to note its context, the narrow escape from impeachment of the ex-Prime Minister, Sir Robert Walpole. The effect is a little like that of a description of *Hamlet* without the Prince of Denmark, or of the exercise of the pardoning power of the President of the United States without mentioning Richard Nixon.

66. See *Parliamentary History of England* (London: Longman, Hansard, et al., 1812), XI, cols. 1268-69. An excerpt from the debate is given in *Samuel Johnson*, ed. Greene, pp. 103-12.

67. *Parliamentary History*, XII, 448-586.

68. *Parliamentary History*, XII, 627-714.

69. *New Yorker*, 12 April 1976, p. 70.

70. *Parliamentary History*, XII, 691-94.

Ethics and Aesthetics in Eighteenth-Century American Art

IRMA B. JAFFE

"As FOR *Ethics* . . . I will venture to say it is a *Vile Thing.* . . ." Cotton Mather wrote early in the eighteenth century. "It pretends to give you a Religion without Christ," he went on, "and a *Life* of Piety without a *Living Principle*; a Good Life with no other than *Dead Works* filling of it."[1] Although few today, if any, could share Mather's attitude to ethics, many might applaud his perception: ethics is the secular society's true religion. With the development, several decades after Mather wrote, of neo-classical art, we find ethics—particularly that aspect which celebrates noble character and courageous actions in secular terms—and aesthetics fused as the generating force inspiring much of art theory and pictorial imagery and thus substituting for religion and myth which had played that role from time immemorial.

Sir Joshua Reynolds in his Third Discourse refers to the principle of correcting nature's defects in order to create ideal forms—the supreme principle of art—as a "divine" idea: "It may be said to preside," he writes in imagery derived from the sacred tradition, "like a supreme judge, over all the productions of nature; appearing to be possessed of the will and intention of the Creator."[2] The aspiring artist must possess this idea "in its perfection" in order to achieve the highest purpose of art—the improvement of mankind.

Benjamin West was also animated by the notion of art as a

noble and virtuous activity. "The art of painting has powers to dignify man," he wrote, "by transmitting to posterity his noble actions, and his mental prowess, to be viewed in those invaluable lessons of religion, love of country, and morality."[3] Always the practical American even after decades of living in England, West saw the value of uniting what he called "philosophic science," meaning ethics, to art, to create works of noble character, in its pleasant effect on patronage, the end effect of which was patriotic: the accumulation of great works redounded to the greater glory of the nation.[4]

When John Trumbull was commissioned in 1817 to paint the four heroic scenes from the American Revolution for the United States Capitol Rotunda, he wrote John Adams of his hope that "the Example thus set will be hereafter followed, in employing the Arts in the Service of Religion, Morality and Freedom."[5] It was in this light that he saw his American history paintings.

In the first half of the eighteenth century, when Americans began to be virtually obsessed with the requirements of virtue, there is no record of anyone in the colonies supposing that virtue could be exercised on the field of a painted canvas, although there are fragmentary hints that some early American painters were well aware of the tradition of nobility associated with the arts. We know very little about early American artists—often not even their names—and consequently very little about what they thought: is it not curious that John Smibert, traveling in the entourage of Bishop Berkeley, should have been so literal-minded about what his eyes could see and his hands could touch (Fig. 1)? Or did he intend, by particularizing, to emphasize the merely sensational character of our perceptions that could be generated by acknowledged illusions (paintings) as well as by things ordinarily assumed to have substance.

There was little that could be called aesthetic theory in colonial America, and it has always seemed appealingly strange to the present writer that the most powerful aesthetic expression in eighteenth-century America is found in the writings of Jonathan Edwards—an artist manqué, one feels. Who but an artist could write,

There are beauties that are more palpable and explicable, and there are hidden and secret beauties. The former pleases, and we can tell why; we can explain the particular point for the agreement that renders the thing pleasing. Such are all artificial regularities; we can tell wherein the regularity lies that affects us. [The] latter sort are those beauties that delight us and we cannot tell why. Thus we find ourselves pleased in beholding the colour of the violets, but we know not what secret regularity or harmony it is that creates that pleasure in our minds. These hidden beauties are commonly by far the greatest, because the more complex a beauty is, the more hidden is it. In this latter fact consists principally the beauty of the world, and very much in light and colours.[6]

Edwards distinguished between judgment and taste, perceiving that "judgement reaches conclusions after reflection," while "Good Taste . . . ere it hashed time to consult . . . has taken its side; as soon as ever the object is presented it the impression is made, the sentiment is formed"[7] Leibniz had called this perception the "je ne sais quoi"; today we call it "gut reaction." How strange to find it in the last of the great captains of the American Calvinist ship as it foundered on the reefs of Arminianism and the good life afforded by prosperous trade.

Calvin doesn't seem to have stopped anyone from painting, but he does seem to have influenced Puritan taste for a time. While frugality was a fact of life in New England, the taste for simplicity prevailed, and the habits of simplicity persisted even beyond necessity well into the eighteenth century. There can be little doubt that this taste was rooted in ethics, in the sense that luxury was a vice, that the things of this world were but vanities. Near the end of the seventeenth century, Thomas Smith painted his self-portrait in a style characterized by simplified contrasts of light against dark, and a rectangular framework (Fig. 2). The rhyme between the folds of his face and the folds of his jabot is as simple as the rhymes of the verse he wrote on the sheet of paper beneath the skull, symbol of Vanity:

Why why should I the World be minding
therein a World of Evils Finding
Then Farwell World: Farwell thy Jarres
thy Joies thy toies thy Wiles thy Warrs

Truth sounds Retreat: I am not sorye
The Eternal Drawes to him my heart
By Faith (which can thy Force Subvert
To Crowne me (after Grace) with Glory.

Simplification remained characteristic of American painting through the first half of the eighteenth century. That this was
a conscious preference seems evident when we consider that so
much of colonial painting was based on engravings imported
from England. Since the American artist had the engraving from
which he copied before his eyes, he could have copied it line for
line. Comparing a few of these paintings with their sources we
can see that in each instance, changes were made that resulted
in a plainer image.

If we compare, for example, the portrait of the Duchess of
Marborough engraved after Sir Godfrey Kneller (1646-1723)
with that of Mrs. Kiliaen Van Rensselaer III by an anonymous
American artist (Figs. 3, 4), we observe the looser folds and forms
of the figure, the drapery, and the landscape in the British work.
The tree in the background is united with the arm of the Duchess, creating a unified, flowing space. In the American portrait,
light and dark contrasts are sharp, so there is no flow of forms:
Mrs. Van Renssalaer's left arm seems almost separated from its
surroundings. The effect of Kneller's composition is one of el-
egance and easy comfort; that of the American is of propriety
and uprightness. The sitter is like the unbending trees glimpsed
beyond the drapery.

Most of these observations apply to a comparison between
the portrait, also engraved after Kneller, of the Right Honourable Charles Montague and that of Andrew Oliver, by Nathaniel
Emmons (1728) (Figs. 5, 6). We may also note that Montague is
portrayed in terms of who he *is*, while Oliver is portrayed in the
context of what he *does*: the ship in the background proclaims
him as a successful merchant.

Portraits of children show the same kind of difference in
treatment by the English and American artist. Among several we
can consider the *Lord Buckhurst and Sister Mary*, engraved after
Kneller, compared to *John Van Cortlandt* (anonymous, ca. 1725)
(Figs. 7, 8). Again, in the British work, the shapes are integrated,

and the motifs are rendered in loose, flowing forms, creating a highly decorative image. The American portrait gives us silhouetted shapes, tight trees, and even omits the ornamental touch of the flowering branch at the step in the foreground.

Even the great John Singleton Copley simplified his source, on occasion. His portrait of *Mrs. Joseph Mann* is a reverse image of a portrait by W. Wissing of *Princess Ann* (Figs. 9, 10). Copley's contours are sharper, his light and dark contrasts tend to force a surface pattern on our view, and although far more sophisticated than Joseph Smith's self-portrait, one sees similar tendencies at work in both paintings.[8]

In addition to formal plainness and simplification, American paintings from engraved prototypes differed in other ways that reveal taste influenced by the Puritan ethic. In Copley's *Galatea*, for example, copied from a print after Gregorio Lazarini, the issue of nudity arises[9] (Figs. 11, 12). Copley's Galatea would surely drown, weighted down in her drapery. The female figure behind Galatea is also decently covered. Neptune has considerably more drapery around the crucial area, the putti at the center is well covered, although completely nude in the engraving, and the female figure at left, three-quarters out of the water in the engraving, is almost up to the waist in Copley's version.

Copley's reading had made him aware of the great tradition of history painting, painting, that is, based on subject matter from biblical history or mythology, and this early attempt, with other similar subjects, reveals his youthful hopes, doomed to disappointment in the colonies. It is well known that his decision to leave America, where he was highly successful as a portraitist, was dictated by his frustration at being unable to paint anything but faces. "Americans," he wrote, were "people entirely destitute of all just ideas of the Arts. . . . A taste of painting is too much wanting [at Boston] to afford any kind of helps; and was it not for preserving the resembla[n]ce of particular persons, painting would not be known in the plac[e]. The people generally regard it as no more than any other useful trade, as they sometimes term it, like that of a carpenter tailor or shew maker, not as one of the most noble arts in the World."[10] Art was his life, Copley said, and he was determined to go abroad where he could find not only the instruction he needed by seeing the great works of the Masters, but an audience for whom he could paint "sublime" subjects. In Rome in 1775 his first original history painting was *The Ascension*, drawn from Raphael, the prime source for the Sublime. Settled in London later that year, and with a family to support, he began to paint portraits, but by early 1778 he had finished the painting destined to become one of his most famous works, *Watson and the Shark* (Fig. 13).

It is particularly interesting to see how the religio-ethical mentality of an American artist found expression in a painting that, for all the admiration it has received, has never been fully understood. In discussing *Watson and the Shark*, writers have overlooked this religio-ethical mind-set of the painter. Professor Roger Stein recognizes certain "unearthly" and "iconic" elements in the painting, which, however, he attributes to the aesthetic influence at that time, of the Burkean Sublime.[11] While the aesthetics of the Sublime doubtlessly affected Copley, one must go beyond the aesthetic theory itself to see it absorbed into the religio-ethical mind-set of the painter in order to account for the specific imagery in *Watson*. Copley, be it remembered, was a Bostonian and an Anglican, a member of Trinity Church. Church attendance on Sundays, in eighteenth-century Boston, was an obligation few would dare fail to meet, and we can safely assume that Copley attended with fair regularity and that he was perfectly familiar with the Scriptures, particularly those passages dealing with resurrection and salvation, the central themes of Christian theology.

That the Christian religion held an important place in Copley's view of himself as a man and an artist is clear from his letter to his stepbrother, Henry Pelham, urging him to be diligent in his study of art. "It is an admasing [sic] advantage to the pursuit of any study to know what is right, and one-half is in a confidence that one can do what they wish. A Man in this [study of art] must have as much faith that he can do what he undertakes as a Christian must have in the truth of his religion."[12]

We must also keep in mind that Copley, like all artists of the period, not only in America but in Europe as well, turned to engravings from the Masters for lessons in composition, and in how properly to handle certain subject matter. Finally we should remember that Copley was exceedingly ambitious not only to rival the Masters in accomplishment, but also in reputation. With these considerations before us we may take another look at *Watson and the Shark*.

It has been said by the leading authority on Copley, Jules D. Prown, in a book that rightly commands the highest respect of the American art historical community, that

> Copley was not representing a significant or heroic event, but merely the unusual maiming of a quite ordinary individual. Such subjects were customarily the province of cheap sensational pictorial journalism rather than of history painting. This was novel. . . . In fact, however, fascination with the distant, the exotic, and the horrible was an integral part of eighteenth-century classicism, and Copley's depiction of these reflects a normal eighteenth-century interest in such matters. [The painting] was unusual only in that it was here accorded full history-painting honors. Copley does not seem to have provided new insights into the struggle between man and nature. . . .[13]

With all respect for Professor Prown's authority, I do not agree with his conclusion that "Copley was not representing a significant heroic event."[14] The painting is very large—71¾ × 90½—too large to be considered anything but a major effort. Surely Copley had in mind something more than "the unusual maiming of a quite ordinary individual"—Brook Watson, a London merchant who, years after the painting, became briefly lord mayor of London. In 1749, at the age of fourteen, he had been attacked by a shark while swimming in Havana Harbor. Fortunately, he was rescued (although not undamaged—he lost a leg to the shark) by men in a boat who managed to drive the monster away. It was Watson who commissioned the painting.

Copley had left America in 1774 for one reason: he wanted to establish himself as a painter in the first rank of his profession, that is, as a history painter—for which there was no audience in America. Looking for an appropriately "Sublime" subject for a history painting, it would not have been difficult for Copley to have seen in Watson's story of a man in the sea saved from a sea monster familiar symbols out of which he could create a secular reinterpretation of salvation. Benjamin West, seven years earlier, had painted with enormous public success a secularized Deposition-Lamentation in his *Death of Wolfe* (Fig. 14), with Wolfe, a modern hero in modern dress—contrary to contemporary theory and practice—slumped on the ground and supported by his comrades ("saints") as he lay dying on the battlefield of Quebec. The new realist direction in history painting had thus been signaled by West, and Copley, newly arrived in England, determined to follow suit.

He was well prepared. Realism, after all, had been a primary demand of his American sitters, a demand inculcated by the Puritan Ethic, founded on the laws of nature, which was God's law. As Perry Miller observes, "phenomena had significance because they were intentional," that is, ordered by God. Miller's comment on Puritan writing is equally and exquisitely applicable to Puritan-influenced painting:

> In the face of every experience [the Puritan] was obliged to ask himself, what does this signify? What is God saying to me at this moment? . . . The result . . . was an insistent literalness that sometimes . . . achieves a realism that is at the same time an implicit symbolism, because the plain statement of fact vibrates with spiritual overtones. . . . Concreteness . . . where a great wealth of observation is employed for thematic assertion, is the supreme achievement of the Puritan esthetic.[15]

Realism vibrating with spiritual overtones has been characteristic of much of American art throughout its history. In Copley's *Paul Revere* (Fig. 15) the sense of intense, motionless quiet and the unnatural airlessness seem to negate time and space even while we see movement and space represented. The disjunctive character of the forms, each within its own firm contours, separated by voids rather than related through space, creates in the objects as depicted a heightened effect of presence, a superior, or even a super, presence. In Copley's New England the tradition was strong that "profane work is sacred when done with a religious heart."[16]

It is illuminating to compare Copley's interpretation of Revere, a fellow artist, with his representation of a wealthy patron, Jeremiah Lee (Fig. 16). Colonial hierarchical notions were based on ministerial interpretations of Scripture. Though William

Hubbard had been dead since 1704, the conception of society that he articulated was very little changed in Copley's time. "Just as the angels in heaven are not all of one rank," he wrote, "it is not the result of time or chance, that some are mounted on horseback, while others are left to travel on foot."[17] It was not reasonable to conclude, Hubbard said, that "because we were all once equal at our birth, and shall be again at our death, therefore we should be so in the whole course of our lives." There was no dearth of rationale for the accumulation of wealth, since property was founded, as William Ames said, "not onely on human, but also on naturall and divine right."[18] In fact, to work and be successful at one's work was a warrant of virtue. Among the outward signs of success, wealth, and rank was clothing—and by extension, the furnishings that "clothed" a man's home. "Graduation in costume according to rank was the visible sign of a social philosophy based upon the law of nature and further sanctioned by revelation," Miller observes.[19]

In Copley's *Jeremiah Lee* we see the New England virtuous gentlemen *par excellence*, in his richly trimmed velvet suit, environed by his ornate furnishings, set off by gleaming satin drapery against a deep background of what we may take to be private property. In his hand and on the table are the attributes of the merchant: letters and ledger books, inkstand and plumed pen. John Hill Morgan wrote of Copley that he had two styles during his American period, "Realist" and "London Style," without attempting to account for Copley's choice in one portrait as against another.[20] Possibly the two styles should be seen as the working out in aesthetics of the Protestant Ethic which laid emphasis on the Scriptural view that assigned a proper image to each man and woman according to rank.

Understanding that Copley's mind was trained by Scripture and his eye by the habits of painstaking observation, we may see this artist undertake to portray the real-life drama of Watson's near death and rescue in the sea in terms of history painting's most sublime subject—resurrection and salvation. Against a background of an authentically represented Havana Harbor,[21] a naked youth is lying helplessly on his back in the water, with one arm raised. An enormous shark, its mouth gapingly opened in a frontal view, *as if to swallow the viewer*, has swirled around for another attack, having already torn off the lower part of the youth's right leg. A boat with ten men has drawn near. Two men reach out to grab the victim, one man has thrown out a rope, while another uses a boat-hook to stab at the monster and drive him away. How are these pictorial elements to be translated so as to give *Watson and the Shark* the significance its author must have intended it to have?

Let us consider first the Scriptures, as we suppose Copley to have done. In Job (7:12) we read, "Am I the Sea, or a whale that thou settest a watch over me?" In Isaiah (27) the Leviathan was a monster of primeval chaos, symbolized by the formless sea. Imaged as a "piercing," "crooked" "serpent," the Leviathan is a sea-dragon associated with the day of salvation when the sea dragon will be killed. Jonah, swallowed by the great Leviathan, prayed to God (Jonah 2:2ff):

> Out of the belly of hell cried I . . .
> For Thou hadst cast me into the deep . . .
> The water compassed me about, even to the soul;
> The depth closed me round about
> The weeds were wrapped about my head . . .
> Yet hast Thou brought up my life from corruption, O Lord
> my God . . .
> My prayer came in unto Thee . . .
> They that observe lying vanities forsake their own mercy;
> But I will sacrifice unto Thee with the voice of thanksgiving
>   . . .
> Salvation is of the Lord.
> And the Lord spake unto the fish, and it vomited out Jonah
> upon the dry land.

In Revelation (12:7ff) the Archangel Michael with his angels attacks the dragon: "And the great dragon was cast out, that old serpent, called the Devil, and Satan, which deceiveth the whole world: he was cast out into the earth, and his angels were cast out with him. And I heard a loud voice saying in heaven, now is come Salvation." Dragon imagery is also associated with St. George, who slew a terrible monster in the name of Jesus Christ and by this act brought about the conversion of all those who had witnessed the struggle.

1. Nathaniel Byfield (1653–1733), by John Smibert. Reproduced by permission of The Metropolitan Museum of Art, Bequest of Charles Allen Munn, 1924.

2. Self Portrait, by Thomas Smith. Reproduced by permission of the Worcester Art Museum.

3.   The Duchess of Marlborough, after Sir Godfrey Kneller. Reproduced by permission of the National Portrait Gallery.

4. Mrs. Kiliaen Van Rensselaer (1674–c 1730), attributed to Van Rensselaer limner. Courtesy of the New-York Historical Society, New York City.

5. The Right Honourable Charles Montague, after Sir Godfrey Kneller. Reproduced by permission of the National Portrait Gallery.

6.　Andrew Oliver, by Nathaniel Emmons. Reproduced by permission of the Frick Art Reference Library.

7.   Lord Backhurst and Lady Mary Sackvil his Sister. Reproduced by permission of the National Portrait Gallery.

8. John Van Cortlandt, by an unknown American artist. Courtesy of The Brooklyn Museum: Dick S. Ramsan Fund.

9. Mrs. Joseph Mann, by John Singleton Copley. Courtesy, Museum of Fine Arts, Boston. Gift of Frederick H. Metcalf, Holbrook R. Metcalf Fund.

The Princess Ann

10. The Princess Ann, by W. Wissing. Reproduced by permission of the National Portrait Gallery.

11. Galatea, by J. S. Copley. Courtesy, Museum of Fine Arts, Boston.

12. Galatée Triomphe sur l'Onde. Engraving by Augustinus, after Gregorio Lazarini.

13. Watson and the Shark, by J. S. Copley. Reproduced by permission of the National Portrait Gallery.

14. The Death of Wolfe, by Benjamin West. Reproduced by permission of The National Gallery of Canada, Ottawa. Gift of the Duke of Westminster, 1918.

15.   Portrait of Paul Revere, by J. S. Copley. Courtesy, Museum of Fine Arts, Boston.

16. Portrait of Jeremiah Lee, by J. S. Copley. Courtesy Wadsworth Atheneum, Hartford.

17. The Borghese Warrior, by Agasias of Ephesus.

18.   The Laocoön, by Agesandros, Athenodoros, and Polydoros, 1st Century B.C.

19.   St. Michael and the Dragon, by Raphael. Reproduced by
permission of the Louvre, Paris.

20. The Miraculous Draught of Fishes, by Raphael. Courtesy of the Victoria & Albert Museum, London.

21. The Miraculous Draught of Fishes, by Peter Paul Rubens. Detail of central panel of triptych, the Church of Notre-Dame, Malines, Belgium.

22.   The Miraculous Draught of Fishes, by Rubens or Van Dyke.

23.   Descent from the Cross, Visitation, and Presentation, by Rubens. Central panel, altarpiece, Antwerp Cathedral. (Scala New York/Florence.)

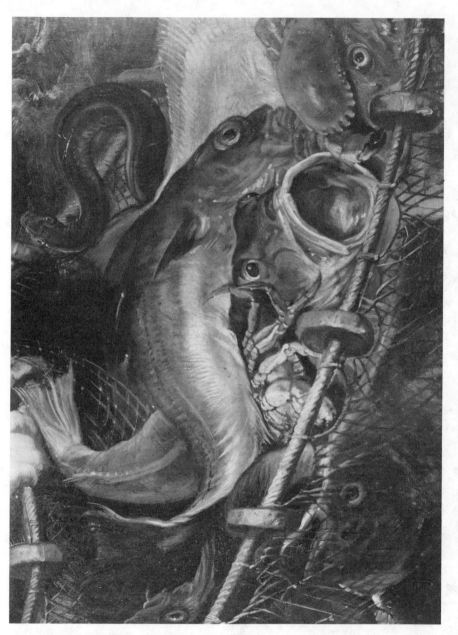

24. The Miraculous Draught of Fishes, by Rubens. Detail, Church of Notre-Dame, Malines, Belgium.

25. Portrait of Elkanah Watson, by Copley. Reproduced by permission of The Art Museum, Princeton University.

The symbolism of water, both as life giving and as trial, pervades Scripture. "Save me, O God," sings the Psalmist (69:1-2) for the waters are come into my soul. . . . I am come into deep waters, where the floods overflow me." The narratives of Noah and the great flood and the passing of Israel through the sea are archetypal images of salvation.[22]

The nudity of Brook Watson, in this context, takes on heightened interest. Almost always a viewer seeing this painting for the first time is curious about the youth being nude, and the usual explanation is the naturalistic one—that he was swimming nude in the early dawn. But such a simple view ignores the extensive iconography of nudity in the history of western art. Among its many meanings, it sometimes represents the man who "though engaged in the activities of life, nevertheless [is] not overcome by the evil and temptation which surrounds [him]. It represents the high and desirable quality of the virtuous life."[23] In Scripture we read, "For we brought nothing into the world, and it is certain we can carry nothing out." (I Timothy 6:76). Watson's pose also captures our attention. It has been claimed that his figure is based on the *Borghese Warrior*, placed on its side (Fig. 17)[24], but to the present writer it appears considerably closer to the famous Hellenistic Laocoön, also on its side (Fig. 18), a cast of which like the *Borghese Warrior* was in the Royal Academy in Copley's time, and the iconography of which was more suitable for Copley's imagery—the Trojan priest struggling in the coils of a monster emerged from the sea.[25] Special notice is due the upraised arm, not grasping for the rope, or the hands of the reaching men, but raised beseechingly to heaven as the true hope of deliverance. Watson's head, too, is turned upward, his eyes wide open as he prays for his salvation. His hair and the water swirl around his head like weeds recalling the verse in Jonah's prayer, "The weeds were wrapped around my head."

The boat is a widely recognized symbol of the Church. Standing with one foot on the edge, a modern-day St. Michael (Fig. 19) wields his boat hook as if it were a lance, which, because it was used to pierce the side of Christ on the Cross, is a symbol of the Passion. The rope, too, plays its role in this narrative of death and resurrection: it symbolizes the betrayal of Jesus by Judas as derived from the gospel according to John (18:13). A reviewer in the *General Advertiser*, 28 April 1778, criticized the futile way that the rope was handled, but we may suspect that this reviewer missed the point, and that the useless rope was meant to signify Watson's dependence on God for his salvation. We shall have occasion to refer again to this rope.

Prominent in the background are the towers of a convent, with crosses raised over the cupolas, echoing the cross bars of the masts that are repeated many times around the mouth of the harbor, enclosing it (itself cited as a symbol of eternal life) with the prime symbol of salvation.[26] The time of day, suggested by the rose-tinted sky above the horizon, appears to be dawn, signifying the Blood of Christ, for "Through the shedding of his Blood, the darkness of sin was overcome, and the dawn of eternal salvation made the world light.[27] The color of the sky heralding the sun reminds us that the sun is a symbol of Christ. As foretold by Malachi (4:2), "But unto you that fear my name shall the Sun of Righteousness arise with healing in his wings." Thus, Copley's painting seems to suggest, are we made whole again in the light of a new day.

Where, we may ask, would Copley have turned for inspiration, for clues as to how to handle his great theme? Most probably he would have thought immediately of Raphael and Rubens, two of the most revered masters of his time. Both had executed major works precisely on the subject of salvation in a watery setting, works that Copley, and every artist of his time, knew well. Seven of Raphael's cartoons for the famous set of tapestries commissioned by Pope Leo X in 1515, including *The Miraculous Draught of Fishes* (Fig. 20) were in London, at Buckingham House, when Copley was working on this painting. Sir Joshua Reynolds in his *Discourses* referred to the cartoons, along with the fresco works in the Vatican, as "the most considerable and the most esteemed works" of this Master,[28] and there can be no doubt that Copley studied them attentively. Furthermore, they had been engraved and Copley owned a set of engravings.[29] He could well have had Raphael's design for *The Miraculous Draught of Fishes* before his eyes as he worked.

Rubens had also painted *The Miraculous Draught of Fishes*. This is the subject of the central panel of the altarpiece at the Church of Notre-Dame at Malines (Fig. 21). He may have known that the Raphael cartoons which had remained in the weaver's studio in Brussels where the tapestries were executed, or he may have drawn his inspiration from the tapestries themselves, which he could have seen in several versions, since they had already been copied (Fig. 22) a number of times. This Notre-Dame composition was copied either by Rubens himself, or, possibly, by Van Dyke, who worked in the studio of Rubens, and was engraved by Schelte à Bolswert, who also engraved the original altarpiece composition. Copley at some time acquired a print of what was probably the Notre-Dame triptych, since it was on three sheets,[30] and could have had both versions of the Rubens work to draw on, together with the Raphael which had, it seems, inspired Rubens.

Comparing Copley's work with that of Raphael, we note that the Italian Master had set the scene in the harbor-like bay, enclosed by a hill town at the right and a bare hill at the left. We observe how the two boats in the *Miraculous Draught of Fishes* are arranged so that the effect is almost that of one boat. A reviewer in the *Morning Chronicle* for 25 April 1778 criticized *Watson* because the boat was not represented as tilting even though all the figures were on one side.[31] Copley was probably following his models, Raphael and Rubens, in designing his boat. Note that the boat, cut by the figures of the overreaching rescuers, has much of the effect of the two boats in Raphael's composition. Very dramatic is the motif of the two disciples who reach over the edge of the boat to hold the net. According to St. Luke, Christ has said to Simon, "Launch out into the deep and let down your nets for a draught." "Master," Simon replied, "We have toiled all the night and have taken nothing: Nevertheless at thy word, I will let down the net." When they had done this they netted a huge number of fish. Simon, James, John, and the others were overcome by the great catch, but Jesus said, "Fear not; from henceforth thou shall catch men" (Luke 5:1-11).

Rubens, in the Notre-Dame altarpiece, has transformed the classical Renaissance calm of the scene into a dynamic composition, bursting with the energy characteristic of Baroque art. But in the National Gallery work, that forceful movement is even more intensified. Christ, instead of standing quietly in the bow, has one foot on the prow, with the other in the floor of the boat, his flying drapery reinforcing the tension and excitement of his pose. Copley seems to have derived his boat-hook wielder from this figure, which he turned in the opposite direction. Again we observe the effective motif of arms reaching over the boat, and are reminded of another great Rubens, the *Deposition* in the Antwerp Cathedral (Fig. 23). Here, too, arms reach out toward the victim, one hand clasping the shroud drapery. If we turn the *Deposition* on its side, the similarity of the relationships in both paintings between the reaching arms and male figure with one arm stretched upward is quite striking.

It is also of the keenest interest that in both *Watson* and the National Gallery *Miraculous Draught*, a figure standing near the center of the composition is represented as a Negro, and has thrown a rope which lies in the foreground coiled around, like a snake, but also something like the mathematical sign for infinity. Then, too, we may observe the rower in the stern who, in both paintings, has his head turned outward with the direction of his gaze shifted to the far right corner of his eyes, imparting an expression of anxiety and strain that accords with the entire sense of strain in the pose. Finally, it is with some suprise that we may realize that the great shark attacking Watson may well have its genesis in the small fish with gaping mouth in the Rubens-Van Dyke *Miraculous Draught* (Fig. 24).

There is a further context in which we may place the meaning of Copley's *Watson*. In addition to the painting's religious iconography, it can be seen to have political connotations as well. Copley, we know, stressed his desire to be neutral in the conflict between Great Britain and the American colonies, "political contests being neither pleasing to an artist or advantageous to the Art itself."[32] Nevertheless, his self-identification as an American was explicitly, although privately, expressed, as was his early-formed confidence in an eventual American victory. In March 1775, he wrote from Rome to his stepbrother Henry Pelham, still in America, that he was certain that America

> will Imerge from he[r] present Callamity and become a Mighty Empire, and it is a pleasing reflection that I shall stand amongst the first of the Artists that shall have led that Country to the knowledge and cultivation of the fine Arts, happy in the pleasing reflection that they will one Day

shine with a luster not inferior to what they have done in
Greece or Rome in my Native Country.[33]

In July 1775, still in Italy, he had heard about Lexington and
Concord, and wrote his wife that it was his "settled conviction that
all the power of Great Britain will not reduce [Americans] to
obedience."[34] He realized, he wrote, that "it may seem strange to
some men of great understanding that I should hold such an
opinion, but it is very evident to me that America will have the
power of resistance until grown strong [enough] to conquer, and
that victory and independence will go hand in hand."[35]

While it is true that the scene of *Watson* is set in Havana, not
the colonies, and that the ships in the background as well as the
men coming to Watson's rescue are British, still, Havana is the
New World. The rosy-tinted dawn sky heralding the rising sun
is not only a symbol of the new light of Christ; it was also, for
Copley, a symbol of the rising of the new "Mighty Empire" which
he envisioned in his letter to Pelham, quoted above. Evidence for
this interpretation of dawn in Copley's work is found in the journal of Elkanah Watson, whose portrait Copley painted in 1782
(Fig. 25). Elkanah Watson wrote:

> The [portrait] was finished in most exquisite style, in every
> part except the background, in which Copley and I de-
> signed to represent a ship, bearing to America the
> acknowledgment of our independence. *The sun was just ris-*
> *ing upon the stripes of the Union* streaming from her gaff [my
> italics]. All was complete save the flag, which Copley did not
> deem proper to hoist under the present circumstances, as
> his gallery was the constant resort of the royal family and of
> the nobility. I dined with the artist on the glorious 5th of De-
> cember, 1782. After listening with [me] to the speech of the
> king, formally recognizing the United States of America . . .
> he invited me into his studio; and then with a bold hand, a
> master's touch, and I believe, an American heart, he at-
> tached to the ship [in the background of my portrait] the
> Stars and Stripes.[36]

So it seems we may also read *Watson and the Shark* as an al-
legory of the struggle between the Old World and the New, with
monstrous power on the side of the former, bare-handed, invin-
cible courage on the side of the latter. Neither interpretation

given here excludes the other, and, in fact, they merge on the religio-cultural level where man's virtue is a warrant of his salvation.

Cotton Mather's view of ethics had long ago gone down with the Puritan theocracy. He would have taken no comfort in this persistence of the sacred tradition, transformed into ethical terms. It was exactly what he foresaw, and heartily detested.

NOTES

1. Claude M. Newlin, *Philosophy and Religion in Colonial America* (New York: Philosophical Library, 1962), p. 35.

2. Sir Joshua Reynolds, *Discourses on Art*, ed. Stephen O. Mitchell (Indianapolis: Bobbs-Merrill, 1965), p. 30.

3. William Dunlap, *A History of the Rise and the Progress of the Arts of Design in the United States*, 3 vols. (Boston: C. E. Goodspeed, 1918), I, 93.

4. John Galt, *The Life of Benjamin West*, facsimile reproduction, introd. by Nathalia Wright, (Gainesville, Fla.: Scholars' Facsimile Reprints, 1960), II, 127; pp. 123-24.

5. Irma B. Jaffe, *John Trumbull: Patriot-Artist of the American Revolution* (Boston: New York Graphic Society, 1975), p. 237.

6. Jonathan Edwards, *Images or Shadows of Divine Things*, ed. Perry Miller (New Haven: Yale Univ. Press, 1948), p. 136.

7. Quoted in Newlin, *Philosophy and Religion*, pp. 99-100.

8. *The Waldron Phoenix Belknap, Jr. Collection of Portraits and Silver* (Cambridge, Mass.: Harvard Univ. Press, 1955), illustrates these and other examples of American copying from British engraved sources.

9. Jules David Prown, *John Singleton Copley*, 2 vols. (Cambridge, Mass.: Harvard Univ. Press, 1966), I, 17.

10. Guernsey Jones, ed., *Letters and Papers of John Singleton Copley and Henry Pelham, 1739-1776*, vol. LXXI, Massachusetts Historical Society Collections (Boston, 1914), pp. 64, 65.

11. This paper was delivered at the Bicentennial Conference of the American Society for Eighteenth-Century Studies on November 1976. I was unaware of Prof. Roger Stein's paper published about that time, "Copley's 'Watson and the Shark' and Aesthetics in the 1770s," in a festschrift, *Discoveries and Considerations: Essays on Early American Literature and Aesthetics Presented to Harold Janz*, (Albany, N.Y.: State University of New York Press, 1976). Prof. Stein wrote to me in Spring 1977 drawing my attention to his paper, upon hearing about mine from a colleague who attended the Conference.

12. Jones, *Letters*, p. 339.

13. Prown, *Copley*, II, 273 (text and n. 24).

14. Stein, "Copley's 'Watson,'" also rejects this view. However, he sees Watson as the "ordinary man" in terms that seem more appropriate to the twentieth century's notion of the heroic common man. This modern idea had hardly emerged in the eighteenth century, and it is my view that Copley, in 1778, and with upper-class social tendencies, could only have seen the ordinary man in Christian terms, that is, as "Everyman."

15. Edwards, *Images or Shadows of Divine Things*, p. 4.

16. Perry Miller, *The New England Mind From Colony to Province* (Boston: Beacon Press, 1961), p. 396.

17. Ibid., p. 48.

18. Ibid., p. 41.

19. Ibid., p. 48.

20. John Hill Morgan, *John Singleton Copley* (Windham, Conn.: Walpole Society, 1939.)

21. Prown, *Copley*, II, 271.

22. Stein, "Copley's 'Watson'" very usefully considers the relevance for Watson of the typological habit of thought that pervaded much seventeenth- and eighteenth-century literature; his comments (pp. 107-10) complement the discussion developed here below.

23. George Ferguson, *Signs and Symbols in Christian Art* (London: Oxford Univ. Press, 1975), p. 49.

24. Prown, *Copley*, II, 273.

25. Stein, "Copley's 'Watson,'" p. 103, points out also the relevance of the figure of the deranged child in Raphael's *Transfiguration*.

26. Ferguson, *Signs and Symbols*, p. 42.

27. Ibid., p. 41.

28. Reynolds, *Discourses*, Discourses 5 (p. 61) and 11 (p. 163).

29. Prown, *Copley*, II, Appendix, "The Copley Print Sale," item 131. It is not certain that Copley owned the engravings at the time he painted *Watson*, but it is likely that he did.

30. Ibid., item 73.

31. Prown, *Copley*, II, 267, n. 17.

32. Jones, *Letters*, p. 98.

33. Ibid., p. 301.

34. Martha Babcock Amory, *The Domestic and Artistic Life of John Singleton Copley* (New York: Kennedy Galleries, 1969), p. 62.

35. Ibid., p. 58.

36. Ibid., p. 463.

Scriptural quotations are taken from the King James Version of The Holy Bible.

Literary Excess
as Indigenous Aesthetic
in Eighteenth-Century America

KARL KELLER

I fear only lest my expression may not be extravagant
enough. . . . I desire to speak somewhere without bounds.
. . . And I am convinced that I cannot exaggerate enough
even to lay the foundations of a true expression.
HENRY THOREAU, Journal, 1854.

THOREAU'S INTEREST in hyperbolic reach, extravagant expectations, and exhilarating excess is Standard American from the
eighteenth century. Excess in writing was no invention of the
Romantics, English or American, but was in fact a major legacy
from the eighteenth century.

For purposes of American literary history, the eighteenth
century is framed by sponsors of the extravagant. At the one end,
there are Edward Taylor and Cotton Mather, makers of a wilderness baroque to simulate their confidence in their election:
hyperbole is as much of the divine as the earthbound Puritan
writers dared attempt. At the other end of the period, there are
Cooper and the Gothics, especially Poe: the American frontier
is made into the Sublime, light and dark. In between, most
American writers, including those of the Revolutionary period,
participate in an aesthetic of outrageousness.

One of the legacies of the eighteenth century to American literature is the encouragement to excess. "The pure products of America," William Carlos Williams concluded, "go crazy." That axiom must be applied to the literature from the onset.

It may be important to remember that American literature, unlike most other literatures in the west, came of age in the late Romantic period. It began high. But two factors from the eighteenth century made that so, both of them connected with the emergence and the hopes following the Revolution. One was the competition with a dominating English literature, and the other was the literary energy released by the new independence. To find American writers from the beginning of the eighteenth century onward commenting on how their pure American literary products "go crazy" is a curiosity of American literary (self-) criticism which I would like to survey briefly. Extremity is the issue.

I am suggesting that early American literature should not be noticed for its plainness, piety, and patriotism, as it has often been, so much as for its excesses, its extremes, its "craziness." There is no need to talk down to early American literature, especially that of the eighteenth century, as has been done so often. In the attempt to make it respectable and therefore assimilable into classic American literature, the criticism has often focussed on that which is dullest in the tradition—the ideas, the intellectuality, the Mind of the period. One aspect of the literary theory of the period dictates otherwise.

As it is in modern American literature, aesthetic distortion in the major early writings is one of the epistemes. I would like to point to it and celebrate it, if only briefly and cursorily. In most cases it is the excesses that make it possible to refer to early American literature as literature. I realize the risk of applying belletristic standards to a place and time having few belles-lettres. But I would like to ask what one would wish to know about eighteenth-century American writers while seeking to know oneself. Do they matter at all?

"The nature of nations is the way they were born. Culture is nature," exclaimed Vico, and one of the most important features at the birth of an identifiable American literature is the need to exceed, the way in which success is linked with excess, the beginning of an aesthetic in which *most* is equated with *best*. As much as one may wish it, the eighteenth-century writers are not American in their independent-mindedness, nor in their national self-consciousness, nor in their sense of freedom to be oneself—traits of indigenousness that really came only in the middle of the nineteenth century—but in the extravagances, extravagances surprising even to a modern sensibility. The true native voice in eighteenth-century American literature, given all the imitativeness, lies in its excesses—or nowhere. Herein lies, I believe, a kind of story.

Cultural lag has been an easy (and often erroneous) way of accounting for some of the unique features of American literature of the eighteenth century. It is a staple of the best biographies of Taylor, Edwards, Dwight, Freneau, Cooper, Irving, and Bryant—selling the point that American literary uniqueness lay for two centuries in being self-consciously *behind* everybody else and therefore identifiably primitive. ("Can we ever be thought to have learning or grace," Philip Freneau complained, "Unless it be sent from that damnable place?") But lag is a factor only if one remembers the far more important issue of competition with European writers. Competition with English fathers and English betters must not be underestimated as a spur and challenge to much early American writing as well as a cause of some of the extremes to which it was driven.

Perhaps the issue of coupling native content with foreign form need not be taken very seriously anyway. As the writers sank into dependence on foreign models, a number of them still made a difference, an American difference. It is to this that I would like to point. Herein lies a new importance of the period.

Fisher Ames's worry of 1800 appears to have been a worry of the entire period. He wrote:

> Nobody will pretend, that the Americans are a stupid race; nobody will deny, that we justly boast of many able men, and exceedingly useful publications. But has our country produced one great original work of genius? If we [Americans] tread the sides of Parnassus, we do not climb its heights: we even creep in our path, by the light that European genius has thrown upon it. Is there one luminary in our firmament that shines with unborrowed rays?[1]

But if Ames had looked a little less aristocratically, he would have seen the difference the challenge made—an American difference with entertaining results. I want to cite the major writers of the century—into the period of the Revolution itself and then beyond it—to show how the early American tradition took on some of the features it did in outrageous reaction to the Europeans and in outrageous assertion of some new literary possibilities. In many ways the early writers builded better than they knew.

The first considerable American poet, Edward Taylor, for example, chose the English metaphysicals as his confrères—albeit they had been out of fashion for well over fifty years—but in the course of New Worldizing Herbert, Quarles, Wild, Wallis, and Wither, Taylor found himself trying to outdo them. His early poems parrot many of their worst features, but between 1684 and 1700 he was able to turn these features to his own advantage, using them both to grovel in his sins and to rejoice in extravagant hopes of rescue by a savior. It is significant that the first American poet of any importance should have commented on himself as self-conscious hyperbolizer: "I will . . . ." he wrote, "In Hyperboles [my] praises dress . . . with Poetick knocks . . . [and] Poetick gusts." With his verse (almost 80,000 lines of it) he said he wished to

> entertain . . . with . . . Spirituall Cheer,
> Which well Concocted will make joy up start,
> That makes thy praises leape up from my heart.[2]

Taylor had the challenge, as perhaps no other American poet has had (with the possible exception of Emily Dickinson), of agreeing to work *within* the confines of Puritan anti-aesthetics. But instead of yielding to the directive against "polishing God's altar," he concocted metaphors that both sustained his orthodoxy and pushed it to near-ludicrous extremes. One example will have to suffice. In speaking of Puritans' sins causing a destructive rainstorm, he wrote (in a poem "Upon the Sweeping Flood"):

> Were th'Heavens sick? must wee their Doctors bee
> And physick them with pills, our sin?
> To make them purge and Vomit, see,

And Excrements out fling?
We've griev'd them by such Physick that they shed
Their Excrements upon our lofty heads.

As he wrote on into the 1720s, Taylor was George Herbert as a morbid clown. His desperate spiritual needs on the American frontier made his expression extreme.

Similarly, Cotton Mather, the first American writer to concern himself seriously with style as a function of personality, took European models like DuBartas, Milton, and the then-archaic metaphysical poets and writers of prose to outdo—or, as it turned out, to *overdo*. Mather's hyperactive aspirations for himself and hopes for his writing led rather naturally to a view of language which held that all the aural, visual, structural, and metaphorical features of words had divine sanction. This inclusiveness, in his eyes, gave his American works a spiritual advantage over their English counterparts. He said he needed a style to simulate "the wonderful display of [God's] infinite power, wisdom, goodness, and faithfulness, wherewith His divine providence hath irradiated an Indian wilderness," a style written "with a variety of Projection and Contrivance to serve that Real, Vital, Solid PIETY which seems now almost wholly to have left the earth." In his General Introduction to the *Magnalia Christi Americana* (1702), he writes of the motives behind his wilderness baroque: "'Tis not possible for me to do a greater service unto the Churches on the best Island of the universe, than to give a distinct relation of those great examples which have been occurring among Churches of exiles that were driven out of that Island, into a horrible wilderness . . ." and to do this service with "a more massy way of writing, . . . provoking the whole world with virtuous objects of emulation." Mather was the first American writer to concern himself with the making of identifiably *American* works. For him to do this, he wrote, it was necessary to have "a vigor sensible in every sentence" and "composures [which] are not only a cloth of gold, but also stuck with as many jewels, as the gown of a Russian ambassador."[3] The comments confess an early American need to create by overstating, to force language forms to simulate spiritual desires, to make epical the heroic dimensions of the Puritan progress, to equate the lush with the factual.

Mather's rich baroque style, viewed semiologically, reveals such a distance between his *langage* and his *parole* (exceeded in American literature perhaps only by Emily Dickinson and Ezra Pound) that one must take the liberated space created thereby as his attempt at spiritual reach. But Mather had an additional reason for the extravagances of his prose: he had to single-handedly create an America and an American identity to match his vision of the promised millennial glory of the new land.[4] Epic scale in his style would give his America and his Americans epic proportion. Without question, Mather's is the most kinetic prose in American literature; one is involved in glory. Like Whitman, yet a hundred and fifty years off, he hoped prophetically to lead a people to a millennium, the one by idealizing an American past and the other by idealizing the American future. Mather's Puritan faith in language, faith in The Word *as words*, led, to be sure, to delusions of grandeur. The megalomania, dramatized by his "massy way of writing," was to have been contagious through being outrageous. That both Mather and Whitman failed to re-make the nation in their own image did not faze them in their prophetic roles. But the extravagant styles they worked up, while certainly giving stimulus to the progress they envisioned, have made them the two largest fools in American literature. Cotton Mather is John Milton camping it up on the right hand of God.

Jonathan Edwards's protagonists in literary history—to continue my tour of eighteenth-century American literary curiosities—are named in each of his major works; they are the many English apologists for Arminian doctrine. Edwards's writings must always be seen over against these Englishmen, now very minor figures to us, for it is from fighting them that his literary strength came. Edwards's arguments in both his theological and philosophical writings are, to be sure, in the plain style, but his anti-Arminian arguments themselves border on the baroque, for he intends to overwhelm by intricate elaboration and virtually unceasing motion: Bach was his contemporary. He is a fantasist of ideological intricacy.

In fact, Edwards's ideas are, as others have argued of him, his fictive materials. They work with each other like the materials of a fiction, an anti-fiction: movement between arguments makes a narrative, the metaphors are typologically arranged characterizations, the rhetorical rhythm is drama. Like Borges, he takes ideas to the breaking point—that is, until they are subsumed in a determinism supporting the irrevocable ultimacy of Fate, or until they are made absurd justifying the Fall. Thus Edwards the philosopher attempted to overwhelm his English Arminian contemporaries; he is a reactionary succeeding as a radical.

The same is true of Edwards the Great Awakening evangelical; his mission in that role was also to overwhelm, but now by means of a synesthetic style. In his determination to seat evidence of election in the senses, he worked on the emotions, as all other Awakeners of those two hot decades did, to gain individual submission to his arguments. Sound replaced sense in the service of Puritan fascism. An Edwards sermon, as all sinners in the hands of an angry God should know, is the perfect model of *in*decorum—the dam that is about to break upon you, the sinking wrack on which you are bound, the bow that readies an arrow at your heart, the hand that holds you over hellfire. These succeed through shock. Violence is his aesthetics. As soon as Edwards turns from Doctrine to Application in his sermons, we watch him confessing his imaginative ability to manipulate the outrageous to achieve the fantasy that salvation lies in cheap thrills. "Some talk of it as an unreasonable thing to frighten persons to heaven," he said, "but I think it is a reasonable thing to endeavor to frighten persons away from hell."[5] Edwards therefore experienced the Age of Reason mainly as an age of sensation and sensationalism.

Edwards's most remarkable contribution to an aesthetics of excess, however, goes beyond his anti-fictions and his verbal anesthetism, and is his invention of the art of equivocation; that is, getting an extra yield out of words, forcing aesthetics out of dogmatics. When, for example, in his *Personal Narrative* he speaks of the "sweet, pleasant, charming, serene, calm nature [of God's holiness], which brought [him] an inexpressible purity, brightness, peacefulness, and ravishment to the soul," Edwards cheats with the greatest kind of verbal extravagance: in his new diction, faith and taste are made to overlap, body and soul merge, objectivity and subjectivity become indistinguishable, God and man meet in a verbal equivocation—and the resulting theological-aesthetic confusion prepared for American romanticism in the nineteenth century.

In American literary history, Edwards in most remarkable, it appears to me, for his ignorance of the radical possibilities of his aesthetic positions. With Edwards, it is the excesses which are interesting; the theology he built is only a historical monument. He is John Calvin who does not know when he is an antinomian.

The New Lights that carried on Edwards's work through the period of the Revolution to the end of the eighteenth century failed almost to a man to sense Edwards's radicalism. It remained for Emerson and his Transcendentalist friends (though seriously becalmed by Wordsworth, Swedenborg, and the Bhagavad-Gita) to reveal the new aesthetics intitiated by Edwards. He was father to the American Renaissance because the gradually emerging nineteenth-century urge to make good on American Independence made taking Edwards to his extremes possible. The Revolution, as Harriet Beecher Stowe was to document in her four New England novels, liberated Edwards to this end as much as anyone.

To give further example of literary excesses in the period, the Connecticut Wits, who included two descendants of Edwards, are the only readable American poets who *enjoyed* being consciously part of the eighteenth century and the only American poets who are canonized for the power of their dullness. They are the prime eighteenth-century examples of literary overreach. The Milton-Pope-Ossian pressure to write epically hit them hard, and their attempts to match (even outdo) the English tradition—as in John Trumbull's *M'Fingal*, Timothy Dwight's *Conquest of Canaan*, and Joel Barlow's *Columbiad*—take the conventions to ludicrous extremes. Along with Brackenridge and Freneau, the Wits were, as poets, millennialists who scored by satirizing the present and idealizing a typologized future. Feeling chosen drove them to the extremities of their art. Their epics of a vernacular culture come off like wooden-dentured Washington in a toga; the result is not national pride as much as self-mocking aggrandizement. What they wrote does too much; it is by and large grandiose sentimentality and boastful prophecy, and the result is often *parody* of neoclassical literary forms. The string of tours de force make a swollen banality in the literary history of the period. These forms represented what one of them called "the rising glory of America." Because their visions for the emerging young nation were hyperbolic, their lines of verse were: their themes and metaphors are ahead of the real in order to create an America the Ideal. The rhythm of their lines is excessively orderly, even martial in their observable perfection. Their metaphors swell to symbols and their symbols to types. Their epic lengths are more nebulous than exuberant. The resulting dullness is inadvertently a form of entertaining American Primitive: thinking Greek and Roman in the muddy streets of Hartford and Philadelphia in the 1770s. American epic of the eighteenth century is static drama as political program.

Benjamin Franklin is, of course, an easy pedagogical contrast to the wild Edwards and the utopian Wits. Addison and Steele, he said, were his models, but his range was wider than the *Spectator*'s and his experimentation with cool diction made him, without question, the best American writer of a half-century. American issues took him easily beyond any one of the English contemporaries he admired and who eventually came to admire him.

The *Autobiography* is his most widely read work; it is in the tradition of literary confessions which Franklin had read in France and England. But Franklin confesses to little or nothing in it and really wrote a general manual for capitalists. The only characterization we get amid all the ideology is that of a naif constantly discovering his own greatness. Without question the flattest book canonized in the American eighteenth century, it survives into the late twentieth century as *comedy*. It is our one substantial early mock-epic; Franklin parodies Franklin on a large scale. As cineramic cliche, it and his Poor Richard go beyond contemporary autobiography and aphorism, for Franklin is largely an amateur playing with large forms and the result is highly polished primitive, even when the range of his maxims is phenomenal, from bathetically banal ("God helps them that help themselves") to the berserk ("Nine out of ten men are suicides").

The finest pieces that Franklin wrote, his satires, have English models in Swift and Churchill. In Americanizing the genre, he succeeded because of the usual exaggeration needed for a satire but more so because of a curious amount of experimentation normally excluded from polite reading abroad. His "Speech of Polly Baker" and "Old Mistress' Apologue" are pornography; his "Essay on Utility" is scatology; his "Parable on Human Rights" is a forgery of Scripture; his bagatelles are tours de force of reductio ad absurdem. In his more personal writings, as much as Franklin wishes his own rather banal ethic followed closely by an entire nation, in his satires and other pieces, he works to stretch popular morality to the point of extreme libertarianism. The deist was a closet anarchist.

And still another example of the period's curiosities. American schizophrenia showed best at that time when the Revolution had been underway and then newly accomplished and American poets turned not to progress and populism for subjects so much as to graveyards and death. Perhaps both were mainly considered democratic because great levelers. The eccentric underground English tradition of Graveyard-and-Gothic in the hands of Philip Freneau and then later William Cullen Bryant and then still later Poe, among many others, became unchurched and desanctified in the new States and made to stand as the main poetic symbol of Democracy. Perhaps only a Norman O. Brown could do justice to this schizophrenia and put that half-century on the psychoanalyst's couch to find out why the best poems of the early United States are death and escape poems—"The House of Night," "Thanatopsis," "Annabel Lee," and all the rest. We have the curiosity, for example, that Freneau wrote his escapist "The Power of Fancy" in 1770, the year of the Boston Massacre, his morbid "House of Night" in 1777-78 at the outbreak of the war, his despairing "Wild Honey Suckle" while pushing Jefferson's policies optimistically in Philadelphia newspapers.

The odd thing is that the main literary connection between the period of the Revolution and the period of the Early Republic and the American Renaissance, apart from items from the pulpit and the political press, was varieties of madness, depression, and disenchantment. These writers—all of them respected, sane journalists—escaped into the works we now read, into what Freneau called "Fancy," into the mad. American Gothic growing out of the period of the Revolution had characteristics beyond the religiosity of Young and Gray, beyond the slow sexuality of

Mrs. Radcliffe and "Monk" Lewis, beyond the cruel play-and-protest of E. T. A. Hoffmann and Mary Shelley. Freneau preceded Emerson and Thoreau in saying of his own desire to write as fully as possible as an American poet: "A real author and a man of true genius has upon all occasions a bold, disinterested and daring confidence in himself. . . . Sprightliness of fancy and elevation of soul . . . alone constitute an author."[6] Democratizing the Gothic in American led to considerable extravagance—dream visions, sophomoric ennui and suicide, necrolepsy and other porn, and experiments with insanity. Since Kafka, we can see that American Gothic was Early Absurd. The excesses endure, if not always endearingly, for us.

The Gothic thrived during the course of the Revolution and the establishment of the new nation, but so did a large body of wholly admirable political writings, of which Thomas Paine's are the best. Any mention of Paine the writer (as distinct from Paine the principled theorist and activist) must begin with his own confession about extravagant writing:

> The imagery in these books called the Prophets appertains altogether to poetry. It is fictitious and often extravagant, and not admissible in any other kind of writing than poetry . . . [but though] the natural bent of my mind was to science, I had some turn, and I believe some talent, for poetry; but this I rather repressed than encouraged, as leading too much into the field of imagination.[7]

The fascination with the extravagant, however measured, made Paine's prose a phenomenon of American literature. Like that which he wanted to achieve if he had written poems instead of polemics, his writing on behalf of reason, liberty, and the colonies has its deliberate excesses. England had to be out-rhetoricked; America had to be rhetorically created.

Paine (and the other writers of a political and utilitarian literature during the War) had to do something his English counterparts in pamphleteering and warmongering did not have to do. It is his American difference and it was very imaginative, though it took a shrill, compacted prose style to accomplish. He had to write to create a tension between libertarian hopes and his own bright fears of a nation that might fail miserably to achieve those hopes. His rhetoric is extreme because he is trying to project the extremes—high and low—that the new nation might come to. Paine's is the first American literature of conflict—or rather self-conflict, a literature of war, of a nation at war, at war with itself, the hope in an ideal warring with a fear of the real. Structurally regarded, Paine's American works are mythic: the microcosm of America at odds with itself. Pushing his hope-vs.-fear dialectic so hard made him the American Revolution's main myth-maker. It was not really (for the time) very American of Paine to work up this myth; there is no literature of ambiguity and ambivalence on American shores before him. But so successful was he that he was able to foreshadow, if not also shape, the duality into which a great deal of the literature of the early national period (the Jefferson-Adams letters, for example) and of the American Renaissance was to fit: the children of darkness (Hawthorne, Melville, Dickinson, Twain) and the children of light (Emerson, Thoreau, Whitman, James) in the same generations. In his hands the political thus became literary. Paine is Whitman's ideal American but after the Fall of Man.

Let me suggest a final set of examples of literary excess from an entirely different genre developing in America near the end of the eighteenth century and the beginning of the nineteenth. The major early American novelists are Brockden Brown and Fenimore Cooper, curious, extravagant writers to stand at the head of the illustrious history of American fiction. Brown was close to the Richardson and Gothic traditions still going (though lagging) in England in the 1790s. But whoever heard of the gothic horrors of insanity and murder growing out of such phenomena as spontaneous human combustion and ventriloquism in upstate New York—as in Brown's novel *Wieland?* Whoever heard of a seduction novel developed as a feminist tract (kill your rapist to develop backbone!)—as in his novel *Ormond?* Or whoever heard of a Gothic novel centering around a country bumpkin growing up amid a plague in Philadelphia—premature burial, city hospital as a chamber of horrors, city government as corrupt and insane, and the murder of legionnaires at local taverns—as in his novel *Arthur Mervyn?* Brown said he wanted his stories to "approach as nearly to the nature of miracles as can be done by that which is not truly miraculous" and to show "the

latent springs and occasional perversions of the human mind"—
a little kinky from a man of reasonability like Brockden Brown![8]
Using the bizarre to celebrate the Golden Mean was Brown's way
of luring readers into his moral lessons. It is literary sensationalism in the service of soft religion. Brown is our early fiction's
best example of someone driven to gothic extremes to sustain
American morality. As with Edwards and the American Gothic
poets, the awful is used in the service of awe.

Both D. H. Lawrence and Mark Twain got the other major
novelist of the period, Fenimore Cooper, wrong. Wishing him
to have written as sensibly as they did, the one called Cooper's
youth-and-wildness-myth-making dishonest (or at least acciden-
tal) and the other called Cooper's language inaccurate and high-
flown (or at least inept). But Cooper's inflations in both his frontier visions and his drawing room descriptions are really his
identifying excesses and not his awful mistakes. He is most at-
tractive in that which he overdoes: romance-writing was
American epic-writing.

The anecdote of Cooper in 1820 throwing to the floor of the
Cooperstown Hall sitting room a copy of an English novel he had
been reading, exclaiming that he could write better and there-
upon deciding on a life of writing, fixes Cooper's competitiveness
for us. Cooper was at all times extremely conscious of Americans
writing over against European accomplishments. In 1829 he
wrote:

> Man is not the same creature here [in America] as in other
> countries. He is more fettered by reason and less by laws,
> than in any other section of the globe; consequently, while
> he enjoys a greater political liberty, he is under a greater
> moral restraint than his European brother.[9]

At the same time he was extremely sensitive to his own need to
outstrip English examples. The title The American Scott both
pleased and bothered him; he wrote of Scott:

> The greatest pecularity of Scott, as a writer, is *tact* in throw-
> ing a high degree of grace around all that he did . . . [but]
> the fitness of his particular excellence for his particular style
> of writing, has induced many to give him credit for more
> general powers than he possessed. . . . I have attempted to

make my own scenes thrill and expand, while still achieving
the grace of expression Scott teaches to be of advantage to
the best epical writing.[10]

"Thrill and expand"—this is Cooper's hope for a literary
difference in which Gothic, epic, and didactic combine to make
an American style equal to American hopes. Cooper is Gothic in
his dependence on violence and large, mysterious spaces. His
expansion-compulsion with language made the Gothic epical in
scale. Cooper's religiosity expands the gestures and situations
melodramatically. The net result is an extravagant overdose of
language. His chief literary device for combining these interests
is an elaborate verbiage. A number of twentieth-century editions of Cooper bowdlerize him by cutting him down in size—to
the Natty Bumppo material, for example, or the Indian material—but Cooper had an obsession with size.

Space and scale are his real subjects—in the size of the book,
the scope of the plot, the length of the material, the reach of the
language. Knowing the frontier of the late eighteenth and early
nineteenth centuries gave his imagination size, and one must
simply have patience with all those trees, all that water, all those
Indians, all those polite manners. In all this, Cooper brought together the two features of the extravagant operating throughout
the eighteenth century: the overmatching of his Scott and the
sense of new American space to try out. When critics attacked
Cooper's work as being insufficiently realistic, he justified it by
claiming that he had "a poetical view of the subject." Cooper is
the beginning of American opera.

Now to draw some conclusions about the century of literature in America from Edward Taylor to Fenimore Cooper with
regard to this one issue—the survival of the major writers of early
America for our modern sensibilities on the single ground of
their excesses.

Straight reading of much early American literature will, I
believe, both overrate and underestimate it. Read Edward Taylor straight and you become a voyeur of poetic masochism. Read
Cotton Mather straight and you become unnerved by nervous-
ness, enervated by his annoying nerve. Read Jonathan Edwards
straight and you are awakened rudely into hypersensitive anxi-

ety, even a kind of spiritual high blood pressure. Read Benjamin
Franklin straight and you have a man sporadically bored with
being so straight, bored with being Franklin's Franklin. Read the
works of Paine straight and you have an uncontrolled/uncon-
trollable loudmouth, with what Professor Kramnick calls
"bourgeois rage." Read Fenimore Cooper straight and you are
bogged down with and bored by sheer bulk. Read Emerson
straight—to continue on in the nineteenth century—and you end
up with Zen fascism (the Esalen Institute is a cruel parody of
Transcendentalism). Read Thoreau straight and you end up with
poverty-stricken one-person communes on every lake in the
country. Read Hawthorne straight and you are ambiguized into
silence sweetly. Read Poe straight and the whole universe is on
hallucinogens. Read Melville straight and you have awkward
chunks of the universe hanging heavily over your head. Read
Emily Dickinson straight and you end up with quaint hysteria
(Julie Harris's Belle of Amherst allows women into the human
race only when cracked.) Read Whitman straight and you end
up with America the Queer, a lush queendom of heaven on earth.
And so on.

My point is that the excess must be seen as excess or we are
in trouble. The extravagance is, instead, an aesthetic factor worth
some regard, spawned to a great extent, as I have said, on paranoia of European superiority and to a great extent on the need
for and achievement of a liberated space in which to do new work
in America. The outrageous, as Kafka argued, is a territory beyond omnipotence and omnipresence.

The issue of independence is important in all of this. Surprisingly, independence was not always taken as license in the last
part of the eighteenth and early part of the nineteenth centuries, following the Revolution. But it was often enough invoked
as such by American writers to make one believe that, like quoting the Bible to justify one's private desires, it was used as an
excuse for some amazing literary experiments. The Revolution
released energy to feed the awed as well as the odd.

To reinforce my idea that "the pure products" of the American Revolution in the following several decades went just
naturally "crazy" (to misrepresent William Carlos Williams once

again), imagine Thomas Jefferson reading the extravagant comment by Emerson on the subject of revolution:

> If there is any period one would desire to be born in is it not the age of Revolution; when the old and the new stand side by side and admit of being compared; when the energies of all men are searched by fear and by hope; when the historic glories of the old can be compensated by the rich possibilities of the new era?[11]

Or imagine Freneau reading Cooper on the subject of patriotism:

> Of all the generous sentiments, that of love of country is the most universal. We uniformly admire the man who sacrifices himself for the good of the community to which he belongs; and we unsparingly condemn him who, under whatever plea of sophism or necessity, raises his arm or directs his talents against the land to which he owes a natural allegiance.[12]

Imagine Jefferson reading Thoreau's Jefferson:

> I believe,—"That government is best which governs not at all"; and when men are prepared for it that will be the kind of government which they will have.[13]

Or imagine Paine reading Whitman's version of Paine's rhetoric:

> (Not songs of loyalty alone are these
> But songs of insurrection also,
> For I am the sworn poet of every dauntless rebel the world over,
> And he going with me leaves peace and routine behind him,
> And stakes his life to be lost at any moment.)
> ....
> Then courage European revolter, revoltress!
> For till all ceases neither must you cease.
> ("To a Foil'd European Revolutionaire")[14]

In such cases, the fathers bred radicals who thought they were doing the will of the fathers but who were really making a very different kind of world. Overdoing did the deed.

I am suggesting that much that was written in the name of
the Revolution was written out of a sense that the Revolution had
been, as far as the stated ideals of liberty and unity and opportunity were concerned, a miserable failure. The writers of the
early national period and then especially of the American Renaissance had to try to do what had been promised but had not
yet, in their eyes, been brought to very full fruition. Thus, I believe, an American aesthetics of outrageousness evolved, in part,
out of the Revolution itself. The concomitant admiration for it
and revulsion against its failure moved writers to strong words.

This cursory survey of one aspect of the literary theory of
early American writers, particularly those of the eighteenth century, suggests an alternative to the existing scholarship. When
trying to look for belles lettres in the nation's middle ages, one
must go beyond the European norms for such and try to look
for that which survives and is equal to the modern—though, one
hopes, without resorting to an uncritical reliance on dredging up
a vernacular tradition. The excesses reveal a more important indigenous aesthetic.

Finally, let me admit that this tour could be much more extensive and much more particular, but I hope my selection sells
my point well enough: competing with cis-Atlantic literature and
stimulated by the new independence, eighteenth-century
America produced a body of literature of considerable interest
to the modern sensibility. It does not need apology and documentation as much as it needs precisely that which keeps us
reading American literature from 1830 to the present—the willingness to look for that which excites.

At the risk of appearing to people early Amercia with literary freaks, I see value in seizing upon certain features of the
major writers of the period for purposes of celebration, asking
reassessment on other grounds and for very modern reasons.
The Williams axiom about the pure products of America going
crazy encourages one to look for the craziness as a legacy from
the onset. When one refuses the critical requirement of disinterestedness and instead uses the advantage of one's present
critical position in time and place, then asking oneself honestly
what is endearing and enduring about the early period may yield
classics which are (to steal now a metaphor from John Gardner)

statuary not only worth dancing around but also possibly very much worth dancing *with*.

NOTES

1. Fisher Ames, "American Literature," *Works of Fisher Ames* (Boston: 1809), p. 460.
2. *The Poems of Edward Taylor*, ed. Donald E. Stanford (New Haven: Yale Univ. Press, 1960), p. 275.
3. Cotton Mather, *Magnalia Christi Americana* (Hartford: S. Andrus & Son, 1852), pp. 25-27. One listener of Cotton Mather's sermons comments on the excesses:

   Isaiah 33:17 was preached from by Mr. Cotton Mather: "Thine eyes shall see the King," whose sermon was somewhat disgust[ing] for some expressions; as "sweet scented hands of Christ," "lord high treasurer of Ethiopia," "ribbon of humility"—which [I] was sorry for because of the excellency and seasonableness of the subject and otherwise well handled (Quoted in Ralph Boas, *Cotton Mather* [Hamden, Conn.: Archon, 1928], p. 60.)
4. See Sacvan Bercovitch, *The Puritan Origins of the American Self* (New Haven: Yale Univ. Press, 1975).
5. *The Works of President Edwards* (New York: R. Carter, 1864), I, 538.
6. "Advice to Authors," *The Poems and Miscellaneous Works of Philip Freneau*, ed. Lewis Leary (Delmar, N. Y.: Scholars' Facsimiles & Reprints, 1975), pp. 42-48.
7. *The Writings of Thomas Paine*, ed. Moncure D. Conway (New York: G. P. Putnam's Sons, 1894-96; repr. New York: AMS Press, 1967), IV, 140-41.
8. C. B. Brown, *Wieland* (New York, 1962), pp. 7-8.
9. James Fenimore Cooper, *The American Democrat* (New York, 1931), pp. 54-55.
10. "Sir Walter Scott," *The Knickerbocker, or New-York Monthly Magazine* 12 (October, 1838), 363-64.
11. "The American Scholar," *Complete Works of Ralph Waldo Emerson* (Boston, 1898), I, 109.
12. Cooper, *The American Democrat*, p. 24.
13. "On the Duty of Civil Disobedience," *The Works of Henry Thoreau, ed. Henry S. Canby* (Boston, 1937), p. 789.
14. *The Collected Poems of Walt Whitman*, ed. Gay Wilson and Sculley Bradley (New York, 1965), pp. 370-71.

The Economic Debate
over the Theater
in Revolutionary America

KENNETH SILVERMAN

BETWEEN THE STAMP ACT and the inauguration of Washington, America gave birth to many features of metropolitan culture it had previously lacked. None arrived more slowly or loudly than a legally sanctioned theater. The same years that brought the first native American composer, the first American novel and epic poem, and major paintings by Copley, Stuart, West, and Trumbull, also produced the first professional staging of an American play, the first permanent American playhouses, and a new tolerance for the theater protected by the repeal or weakening of old laws against it.[1]

This tolerance ended two decades of public quarreling that raged around The American Company, the wily and determined English actors who had toured the country since the mid-eighteenth century. Managed before the war by David Douglass and after it by Lewis Hallam, Jr., the Company fended off extinction by leading a hectic double life, feigning rectitude to pacify its enemies, delivering glitter to please its friends. In the early 1760s the Company began a vigorous new effort to bring provincial American theater nearer the standard of Drury Lane and Covent Garden. It imported well-made scenery, recruited skillful actors, introduced the latest London hits, and erected a string of theaters. Its striving, especially the building of new the-

219

aters, provoked petitions, demonstrations, and legislative action throughout the colonies. Hundreds of essays and letters attacking or defending the Company appeared in American newspapers, often printed on the front page beside reports of recent taxes by Parliament or statements of Revolutionary principle. Argued frequently and passionately by many citizens before a large public, the question of whether theaters should be allowed was the chief cultural issue in eighteenth-century America.

"Theatricus," "Philander," and the other anonymous columnists who debated the issue approached it from the outside. Arguing not the excellence of the theater but its effects, they raised narrower moral and religious questions, many of them ancient: whether the theater teaches arts of seduction and encourages Sabbath-breaking or, conversely, reproves vice and supplements the pulpit. Four economic questions also arose: whether the theater undermines the business mentality; whether it drains scarce cash out of the community; whether, as a result, it increases the number of poor, widening the gap between classes; and whether it inhibits charity toward the same poor it creates.

These questions were entangled with the older moral and religious issues, but for two reasons seem unfamiliar. Their spokesmen rarely discussed them fully or distinctly, but usually in passing, as one of many arguments for or against the theater. What follows presents as virtually a point-by-point debate what in fact are brief remarks and asides by many persons across two decades, scattered among newspapers, playbills, and other documents from several colonies and states. Also, the implications and force of the questions depended on a wider, very bitter debate over problems more familiar to economic historians than to literary. Multiplying taxes, property confiscation, bankruptcies, and many sudden reversals in personal fortunes filled the debtors' prisons of Revolutionary America, left many lacking in necessaries, threatened public services, and produced unemployment.[2] Rampant gambling, drunkenness, and crime led many local legislatures to pass sumptuary laws suppressing extravagance. Like the other alleged forms of extravagance, the theater was believed to wield great economic power—so great as to suggest that provincial Americans experienced the theater as a disturbing, imposing presence in their daily lives.

The history of even the early colonial past gave reason for asking whether the theater undermined the business mentality. Since the first settlements, a shortage of labor and productive equipment relative to the country's economic potential made Industry, Frugality, and Economy an endlessly invoked slogan, and created contempt for those who lived off the hard work and thrift of others.[3] Captain John Smith, to whom the Virginia Company's supply ships brought goldsmiths and perfumers when he needed laborers, was asked by the same Company to explain why the plantation had not prospered. Smith grumbled: "There is no country to pillage . . . all you expect from thence must be by labor."[4] The lesson that America's bounty could be extracted only by hard work was intoned throughout the eighteenth century: by William Byrd of Westover, scoffing at the first adventurers for expecting to "live without work in so plentiful a country"; by Benjamin Franklin, declaring through Poor Richard that "*God gives all things to industry*";[5] by the 1769 Boston town meeting which appointed a committee to recommend methods for ending idleness, "the Parent of all Vices."[6]

Industry, according to opponents of the stage, was corrupted by playgoing. A New Yorker greeted the opening of the John Street theater in his city in 1767 by pronouncing the wisdom of a century and a half of American experience: "The most certain and permanent riches of a community, depend upon the people's industry, that being a source of wealth which cannot fail; and more especially is this the case with respect to communities in their infant state. . . ."[7] And the stage, other writers added, holds a Circean power of distraction that weakens industry, damaging the public good. It nurtures the unfocused, undisciplined "man of pleasure": "Whenever he submits to business, does he not hurry it over in a manner that betrays his aversion to it?"[8] It leads to other distractions, instilling a "turn and eagerness for *reading*" plays which causes "the loss of much time in an employment that can be of little use. . . ."[9] It contains within itself living proofs of how it muddles the head for business—an audience of gamblers and others "who despise or disregard punctuality and the faith of contracts"[10] and who sit watching actors: "How rarely do they pay their debts honorably and conduct their affairs discreetly. They are originally of the same make with others, but their seducing employment unfits them for the observance of regularity and prudence. . . ."[11] The tendency of the theater to relax the sense of responsibility was made to seem even more sinister by Republican theory, with its demand for a self-sacrificing people alert to their common interest. By "calling off the attention of our citizens from industry, frugality, and economy," a New Yorker warned in 1786, the theater would help a still-designing Britain to make America "an easy prey to herself, or some other enemy. . . ."[12]

The theater's "fatal influence"[13] on industry particularly menaced the young, whose work habits were too unformed to be slackened but could be aborted. When The American Company tried to raise a new theater in Philadelphia in 1766, citizens petitioned the governor of Pennsylvania to halt the building. It would slow trade and commerce, diverting "unwary youths from the necessary application of the several employments by which they may be qualified to become useful members of society."[14] Once diverted from the workbench to the gallery, youth would learn not "honesty, industry and oeconomy" but prodigality and a sentimental attitude toward money: "Will the merchant chuse that his apprentice should learn exactness and frugality from the stage? Do those whose generosity is strengthened by weeping over virtue in distress, make the best pay masters?"[15] And, as many writers foretold, young men softened by "virtue in distress" might end by destroying themselves. Following the hoary English argument that the theater debauches apprentices, a Philadelphian recounted how one merchant's apprentice was given money to see a few plays, and became so infatuated that he attended constantly, robbed his master, and at last married a prostitute.[16]

Defenders of the theater also extolled Industry, but denied that the stage sapped it. In their essays and petitions they often described themselves as active, responsible men "who have every endearing tie to society. . . ."[17] Members of the Philadelphia Dramatic Association, formed in 1788 to lobby for repeal of the anti-theater laws, told the legislature of their double stake in society: "As parents most of them are anxious for the happiness of posterity; and as men of property, they are generally entrusted in the order, energy and stability of government."[18] Such credentials gave respectability to the argument that instead of undermining Industry, theater going could revitalize tired businessmen and provide an alternative to far more idle amusements, such as gaming houses and taverns. A Philadelphian said: "When the tradesman could allow himself a day for pleasure, with the fruits of his labours in his pocket, he would go to see a play, it would be a novelty to him, and much more edifying than going to a public house. . . ."[19]

The edification might be particularly useful to the unformed. Countering the example of apprentices enticed by playgoing to wed prostitutes, another Philadelphian cited Lillo's *George Barnwell* as an example to apprentices of the chain of effects following sensual indulgence: debt, embezzlement, imprisonment, and early death. This "well known tragedy . . . was evidently designed," he said, "to put unwary youth on their guard, to warn and deter them, by a moving and dreadful example, from falling a prey to those very temptations. . . ."[20] A Charleston newspaper likewise commended the play to young men "trained up to the branches of mercantile business and who often have large trusts confided to their care."[21] The American Company argued its own case by keeping *George Barnwell* before the public. Shakespeare's plays aside, it became the most popular serious play in colonial America, with twenty recorded performances before 1775, against thirty performances for the most often-produced play on the colonial stage, *Richard III*.[22]

In questioning the ability of the theater to promote or discourage Industry, the debaters were not merely applying to the stage a conventional test of social utility. They were also addressing serious economic problems which beset the country throughout the Revolution, and which many blamed on a failure of industry. In the prewar period Americans went quite suddenly and deeply into debt to British suppliers. By 1760 the debt amounted to two million pounds, by 1772 to more than four million. The war itself meant a loss of markets, sources of credit, and new investments.[23] A simultaneous craving for imported goods swiftly sent available money out of the country, producing a shortage of specie to pay debts. "The scarcity of money,"

said a writer about postwar Boston, "is beyond your conception."[24] The scarcity and the chronic economic recessions raised
a second question, whether the theater did not injure the economy by taking money out of circulation. When The American
Company tried to perform in Newport in 1761, opponents
es timated their proceeds at from three to four thousand
pounds in currency weekly, with a total loss to the town of
£35,000.[25] The Company's attempt to raise by public subscription still another new theater, in Charleston in 1773, prompted
the *Gazette* to list the economic conditions that made the venture
perversely extravagant:

> It is universally acknowledged, that there is neither a Suf-
> ficiency of Currency or Specie in Circulation, to transact
> common Business . . . the Rich can scarce find Ready-Money
> to pay for what they drink and eat, and wear . . . the Public
> Treasury itself is represented as nearly in a State of Bank-
> ruptcy . . . in less than Six Months, this Province has become
> indebted to Great Britain, in a Sum little short of 300,000 l.
> Sterling, for Negroes only . . .[26]

The existence of such debts denoted a society that bought much
on credit, and whose financial health partly depended on seeming trustworthy in the eyes of its creditors. New theater buildings
and full houses made the moaning about inability to pay debts
seem fraudulent, as the *New-York Journal* observed on its front
page in 1768:

> . . . every one is complaining of the want of money—this
> scarcity of cash renders us unable to pay our debts, and yet
> one half the city are throwing away their money at the Play-
> house, as if they had no other call for it. My dear fellow-cit-
> izens, either cease going to the Play-house, or cease to
> complain of your poverty—crowded Theaters are a Bur-
> lesque upon such a complaint; the world will either not
> believe us, or if they do will laugh at us . . . if we cannot live
> without the honour and pleasure of supporting a Play-house
> . . . I had rather, to save our credit—and avoid being laughed
> at, that we should boast of our wealth and declare—our
> purses large enough to satisfy any [drafts?] that may be made
> on them—it would not be the first *untruth* that was ever told
> by people for saving their credit.[27]

The fear of seeming undependable to creditors was not unfounded. A London newspaper rebuked Americans for pleading poverty while riding in more and more carriages. "At Philadelphia a play-house is built. . . . Cock-fighting, fox-hunting, horse-racing, and every other expensive diversion, are in vogue in the colonies, yet the colonists pretend they are not able to pay towards the support of their government."[28]

One answer to the question of how people lacking cash to pay debts could build theaters was that actors picked their pockets. Alarmed at a proposed performance in their small city, petitioners to the mayor of Albany in 1785 complained that actors thrived not on Industry but on timely departures. They stay long enough in town "to support themselves on the way to another place, where they expect to meet with better friends and political connections; but in reality will drain us of our money."[20] A postwar newspaper charged members of the Company with having fled to Jamaica and elsewhere in the empire to avoid the "expence of defending their country."[30] In fact, they were driven from America by the congressional resolution of 1774 intended in part to "discountenance and discourage" the theater.[31] But critics of the theater viewed actors as itinerant economic vampires, siphoning a community's lifeblood one way or another: "The gentlemen of the stage," said an ironic Philadelphian, "have been so far from leaving us with their pockets full of money, that many of them have gone away, over head and ears in debt, so litterally [sic] have they spent and been spent for the good of the public."[32]

Whether the actors departed with cash or debts, the public paid. Either it depleted its resources for emergencies, deprived itself of civic improvements, or had to clean up what the actors left. The experience of waging a war that cost Congress some $160,000,000 made public solvency seem a matter of self-preservation.[33] Petitioners in Baltimore argued that the cost of a new theater would jeopardize their defense. Noting that they had "chearfully born their Proportion of the Taxes levied for prosecuting the war," they explained: "Should any urgent occasion oblige government to make similar applications in future [sic], it would distress us to think that, the Means of Complying with them had been destroyed or diminished by . . . an unprofitable

Extravagance."[34] Even if not subtracted from defense, money spent at the theater could always find more beneficial use. The *Pennsylvania Gazette* reprinted an item from an English newspaper pointing out that the four thousand pounds reaped in fifteen weeks by some actors in Bristol might have been "laid out in opening new Streets. . . ."[35] Petitioners in Pennsylvania described how a theater built in another English town transformed its neighborhood. Houses adacent to the theater, formerly occupied by "useful manufacturers and industrious artificers" were replaced by brothels, whose removal cost the town thirteen hundred pounds in legal fees.[36]

Defenders of the theater gave different answers to the same questions. At least one suggested that if full playhouses belied complaints of poverty, the problem might be not playgoing but poor-mouthing. The complainers exaggerated their plight, and those hostile to the theater acted "from a kind of servile fear of displeasing those gentlemen who plead poverty under a silk gown, and an enormous white wig."[37] Many others denied that actors were either tightfisted or prodigal. Far from departing America to avoid helping pay the cost of war, members of The American Company had worked in the country for twenty-six years, one writer computed, during which "they have always punctually contributed their proportion towards the expence of government. . . ."[38]

Indeed the Charleston poet Joseph Brown Ladd found actors to be "generally profuse in living; they seldom deprive a country of its cash. Hence, money in their hands is not lost: on the contrary, it is put in circulation."[39] What came in at the box office, as another writer traced its route, went out to "the numerous shopkeepers and mechanicks, which a company of actors must necessarily employ . . . . and the money left by strangers only, would be more than the actors would carry with them."[40]

The "money left by strangers" could be considerable and also significant. Many urban Americans regarded with expectant pride their swelling populations and spreading streets. They saw the theater as a necessary feature of metropolitan life, bound to increase the wealth and prominence of their cities by attracting visitors. Urging a theater in his city in 1789, a Bostonian lamented how tourists remarked "that there is no town in America so large as this, that has so few public amusements. By encouraging this establishment, we should prevent this in the future; and . . . it would be greatly ornamental to the town."[41] Philadelphians more than others saw the theater as a potential "instrument of increasing the wealth, population and literature of this metropolis. . . ."[42] The increase seemed especially desirable after the war. By then, Philadelphia's former intellectual and social brilliance had been dulled by the flight of Congress to New Jersey, and growing New York had begun to challenge that city's colonial pre-eminence. In trying to convince the Pennsylvania legislature to repeal its anti-theater law, General Anthony Wayne—like many military men, an active supporter of the stage—appealed to injured civic pride. A theater, he said, "would be no small inducement to Congress to return to this city, as there are many young fellows in that body, who do not choose to be debarred from such an innocent relaxation."[43]

A dramatic if disingenuous answer to the charge of economic vampirism came from The American Company, which offered to tax itself. Shrewdly the managers advocated a "regulated" theater, trading off a fee for theatrical licensing in exchange for the legal recognition that went with it. Douglass wrote an essay defending a licensed theater (reprinted in several American newspapers) in which he offered to pay part of his receipts into public funds.[44] The managers probably discussed their strategy with General Wayne, who assured the legislature that a theater "might be made a very lucrative and profitable source of revenue, by laying a tax on it, to supply the necessities of the State."[45]

By undermining Industry and draining cash, the theater might affect society in a third and more inhumane way. It might worsen the plight of the already poor, increase their number, and widen social inequalities. Critics of the theater observed with dismay—as visitors to London often observed with surprise—that the audience included people who could barely support their families.[46] One explanation of their presence also served to explain the contemporary rage for luxury goods and the forsaking of farms for colleges and cities: "common tradesmen, mechanics &c. . . . almost invariably have the vanity of aping their superiors in every fashionable extravagance. . . ."[47] Whether or not drawn to the playhouse by the example of the rich, the poor attended only at the cost of domestic neglect. A presentment to a Savannah, Georgia, grand jury in 1774 condemned those who spent at the theater money which "would be much better applied to the maintenance of their families . . ."[48] Theaters hurt the poor not only by taking their food money but also by paralyzing their earning power, striking at the financial resource more important to them than to any other group: "The love of pleasure naturally tends to cut the sinews of industry, and therefore if this passion [playgoing] spreads among the lower sort of people, where industry is their only means of subsistence, it must have a fatal effect upon them."[49]

By luring the marginally independent, the theater could create social chaos. According to a principle often asserted in Revolutionary America, "whatever person lives beyond his income, be it less or more, must inevitably be undone."[50] The undoing might have several effects, all unsettling to society. It might increase the alarmingly rising crime rate. A presentment to a South Carolina grand jury stated that "large Sums are Weekly laid out for Amusements, these by Persons who cannot afford it; and is a Means of promoting the frequent Robberies that are committed. . . ."[51] Also, the economic collapse of some would ripple out to many. It would shake the frail autonomy of the group from which came most of the opponents of the theater—"the mechanic, whose fortune not permitting him to be idle, is yet sufficient to preserve him from dependance, whose trade not only supports his own family, but gives bread to others. . . ."[52] Helplessly "drawn into the vortex of dissipation," some non-theatergoers would be unable to prevent "the sale of their little freeholds, the ruin of their own families, and perhaps that of their confiding friends."[53] To an age profoundly wary of ambition, such ruin meant not simple impoverishment but thralldom. Those who exhausted meager funds on playgoing purchased slavery: "Their creditors will have them in their power; a power which all mankind have been disposed to use when they had it, that is they will raise themselves to power and privileges above their debtors, and in the end reduce them to a state of vassalage." The result would be to widen the existing "great inequality, as to wealth," a condition "not a little contrary to the nature of popular government; and the native influence of it, if not carefuly counteracted, will, one day, produce a revolution."[54]

Defenders of the theater attacked such forecasts by challenging their premises, and even by granting them. Many denied or treated as theoretical the assertion that playhouses drew persons who could barely afford to feed their families. Noting that the Philadelphia theater had been open while the Pennsylvania legislature debated whether to close it, the financier Robert Morris described the house as composed largely of the hardworking. They came to the theater not to imitate their betters but seeking diversion and company:

> We have heard it asserted that the example of the wealthy will induce the lower classes to indulge themselves at the theater; and that they will thus incur a destructive expence. I admit the lower clases are too apt to ape their superiors; but instances are better than assertions. Notwithstanding the prohibitory laws heretofore passed against the theater, it has been opened with some kind of exhibitions, even during the session of Assembly. Who have been the people who attended them? . . . [they] were the industrious part of the public, who had wrought hard during the day, and who sought relaxation in the evening—[sic] people wish to assemble together, to see and be seen.[55]

Elbridge Gerry, a member of Congress, believed that the theater appealed to all classes. It worked not to estrange the classes from each other but on the contrary to "sweeten society," affording social unequals a common meeting ground: "all may partake. . . without destroying the necessary distinction of ranks. . . . all ranks are pleased at the theater, and participating alike in the pleasures appear to be of the same family and society uninterrupted by envy or malice."[56] Even granting that the lower classes attended the theater, they would stay off the street, pushing the crime rate down not up.[57] If the stage undid the marginally independent by encouraging them to live beyond their means, the same persons would probably be undone anyway: "Those imprudent people, who spend what they can't afford this way, would do it in some other way; perhaps a worse."[58] At their most combative, defenders of the theater turned their opponents' arguments around. A Bostonian proposed that instead of threatening the group which supplied the most numerous foes of the theater, the stage would give work "to many an *industrious mechanic*, that now languishes for want of employ. . . ."⁵⁹ John Henry, a leading singer in the Company and later co-manager with Hallam, answered those who argued that the opening of theaters ultimately creates unemployment. Closing the theater, he warned, meant "depriving seventy-two innocent persons, employed about the *Theater*, of their daily bread. . . ."⁶⁰

Henry's argument, however self-serving and inflated, makes evident an irony in the debate. Among the victims of the chronic recessions and cash shortages was the theater itself. Nor was it unique among cultural institutions in suffering from what its detractors said it caused. Many postwar Americans invoked Montesquieu's principle that republics survive only on virtue— that is, self-sacrifice—in order to denounce such signs of self-indulgence as the influx of foreign musicians and fashions and the launching of drawing schools and vocal academies. At the same time, these proliferating products of a rapid growth in American culture competed with each other for scarce cash, rarely continuing long and often failing quickly. The few extant letters by members of The American Company suggest that while being attacked for increasing poverty, the Company had overextended itself, building playhouses at a time when new companies had begun cutting into their prewar monopoly. In 1786 Henry found that the expense of a new playhouse in Baltimore left him unable to pay a hundred dollar debt because "the persons from whom we have had the materials workmen &c being very pressing for their money has removed it out of my power to take up the Bill. . . ."⁶¹ The Company's business in Baltimore was so bad that only one of seven performances took in a hundred pounds, and the rest, Hallam moaned, averaged "not about £10. I'll leave you to guess at our Situation with a Theater to pay for."⁶² Several times the Company lowered their prices for seats; ads for benefit nights repeatedly announced that the proceeds for some player had fallen short of expectations, requiring a second benefit.

The last large question in the controversy—whether the stage inhibited charity—arose from twin features of the American scene made scandalously visible by unemployment and by thousands of pre- and postwar insolvencies: the almshouses and debtors prisons. Those jailed were occasionally nursing mothers or indigent war veterans, and mostly poor people who owed no more than ten dollars. Often confined with criminals in tiny rooms, some hung bags or old shoes from the windows to beg food while awaiting aid from friends and relatives.[63] Hardship in the jails, and a long tradition of treating economic life as a matter of sentiment, filled American newspapers with groaning depictions of the destitute, abandoned by censorious friends and vengeful creditors:

> Oh! I have seen, and have sickened at the horrid sight, numbers of wretches, capable of being useful in the highest degree, to the public, secluded from all the privileges of men and christians, *pale famine* wasting them away by slow degrees, and grievous *oppression* grinding them to death! These are the greater number that fill our *American* prisons, and every minute with bitter anguish, curse the hour they were born, and invoke an end of their wretched beings.[64]

Such laments for the poor appeared, joltingly, near ads for The American Company ballyhooing the managers' "great expense . . . in fitting up an elegant house for the amusement of the lovers of rational entertainments,"[65] offering *Grandes Ombres Chinoises*,[66] "Spectaculum Vitae,"[67] or a version of Garrick's Shakespeare Jubilee climaxed by a Triumphal Car with banners, trophies, transparencies, and a chorus.[68]

Foes of the theater condemned the glaringly cruel contrast. The *Pennsylvania Gazette* quoted verses from a Bristol, England, newspaper, contrasting imprisoned debtors and paupers with the actors who having put them there fed on their squalor:

> . . . for more Guests our Gaol expand[s] its Gate,
> To croud its Cells, and clamour through its Grate;
> While hungry, helpless Families implore
> The falling Crumbs from Actors plenteous Store;
> Who reap, triumphant, 'midst the People's Woes,
> A golden Harvest from their Sounds and Shows.[69]

At about the same time that the Lindsay-Wall Company registered earnings of some 2,360 pounds for twenty-eight performances in Baltimore,[70] petitioners against a Baltimore theater called attention to the "abodes erected for the Reception of the unfortunate, the Poor and the Helpless. From this melancholy Situation, it would be intolerable to behold the vast Expence of a public Stage Supported."[71]

The coexistence of full playhouses and full poorhouses gave poignance and a new twist to an ancient objection against the theater. Raised continually since Calvin, it was repeated by Quakers petitioning the Pennsylvania legislature in 1788: the theater numbs "that true and unfeigned spirit of Benevolence whish [sic] is the fruit of sound christian Principle."[72] Playgoing affects charitable feelings much as it does Industry, first distracting then preoccupying. A New Yorker reminded his readers of fellow citizens "pining away under the sharpest pangs of poverty!—How many aged helpless poor!—How many as helpless innocent children, unfed and unclothed. . . ." Yet the "natural passion of benevolence," he explained, cools when opposed by "contrary" passions such as theater going:

> When the love of this pleasure, becomes a ruling passion in our minds, the principles of benevolence are not felt in all their force; for when our pleasures tax us high, there is little to be spared for charitable uses. I have heard that there has been offered in this city, fifty pounds for a box in the Playhouse during the season. The fact is hardly credible, but if it is true, it affords the strongest argument that can be urged to prove the mischievous tendency of a Theater.[73]

Conflicting American attitudes toward poverty created a variant of this argument; while making givers uncharitable, the theater also makes recipients of charity ungrateful. All the colonies extended some sort of relief to the needy, both for humanitarian reasons and to save the community the expense of caring for debtors' families. Yet according to the creed of Industry, persons incapable of sustained productive work deserved rather blame than help. In his 1768 essay "On the Laboring Poor," for instance, Benjamin Franklin questioned poor relief, however compassionate, because it "tends to flatter our natural indolence, to encourage idleness and prodigality, and thereby to promote and increase poverty, the very evil it was intended to cure. . . ."[74] Like recent welfare measures, the soaring cost of public taxes for poor relief incensed many who found the poor living above a subsistence level, much less sitting in the gallery. A front page article in the *New-York Journal* reported that many of the "necessitous poor" who had been aided by benevolent citizens and tradesmen had turned up at the playhouse, including

> some who with all their care and industry can scarce hope to escape the terrors of a gaol. For such persons to throw away their money on play-tickets! What compassion! What mercy can they expect? Some of those debtors we are assured have already been sued. How many more have deserved it? Is this properly requiting the generosity of their benefactors? Will this be a future recommendation for the like beneficence?[75]

Revealingly, the same newspapers which published the texts of new laws to assist debtors also published attacks on the theater addressed, with begrudging righteousness, to "fellow-citizens who must work hard to support your families."[76]

To the charge that theaters dissolve or discourage the instinct for charity, The American Company and its supporters gave a single reply. They turned the theater itself into a charitable agency. Appeals for relief went out from the stage. The prologue to a Philadelphia performance explained that although actors are too poor to give money, their empathy and mimetic talent might move the affluent to give:

> . . . I can feel, ye rich, but not redress;
> Oh could each generous heart whose tears will flow
> For others' griefs, but mitigate the woe![77]

Rather than ignoring the difference between actors and prisoners, a Pennsylvanian emphasized the "odd contrast" in the columns of a recent newspaper: "On the one side, we were pathetically recommended to a view of misery in the inhabitants of the Jail, and on the other, had a tempting invitation to the Play-House."[78] The contrast could be made less oppressive, he suggested, by playing benefit performances for the prisoners. The managers of the Company promoted this idea. The licensing bill drawn up by Hallam himself obliged him to give two performances each year for poor relief, and one for prisoners confined for debts under forty shillings.[79] His proposed legislation of course did little more than formalize his existing practice. To display a sense of social concern and obligation, the Company had always given benefits for the needy, followed by such announcements in the newspaper as "The Donation received from Messieurs *Hallam* and *Henry* . . . will be delivered out in BREAD to the Poor of the city . . . by the overseers of the poor . . . at the Court-House."[80]

The announcements fail to tell how much economic relief the benefits afforded. In the Company's absence during the full-scale combat, charity productions were mounted by amateur groups and by British and American military actors, who advertised their performances, typically, as "for the Benefit of Families who have suffered in the War for American Liberty."[81] General Clinton's actors during their first season in occupied New York provided £291 for army widows and orphans; but they disbursed over £1,000 for wardrobe alone.[82] Perhaps such stingy ratios were well enough known to create suspicion. In any case, foes of the theater often eyed charity benefits as maneuvers to gain the public's indulgence by manipulating its conscience. In giving the first play by professional actors in New England—in Providence in 1761—Douglass and Hallam raised over a thousand pounds old tenor to buy corn for the poor. The distrust aroused by their generosity appears in the remark of an apologist in a local newspaper, who insisted that the deed "can not without an uncommon degree of malevolence be ascribed to an interested or selfish view."[83] During one of its postwar tours, the Company offered the commissioner of an almshouse forty pounds; the city council directed him to return it.[84]

Argued in newspapers, to grand juries, and before legislatures for two decades, The American Company's long campaign to make the theater permanent and comfortable in America ended with the repeal of the Philadelphia anti-theater laws in 1789 and the opening of the Boston Federal Street Theater five years later. Which side more often spoke economic realities remains unclear, mostly because of the scarcity of surviving box office receipts, letters, and other documents of theatrical life in Revolutionary America. Perhaps theaters operating three or four times a week to audiences of eight hundred or so, in towns of fifteen or twenty thousand, did strain available cash, tempt the poor to spend necessary money, and lure people often enough to disturb vital patterns of work. Perhaps, on the other hand, the theater did spur the growth of cities and benefit many citizens by exciting business, creating employment, and affording relaxation.

Whether playhouses nurtured softhearted paymasters or clearheaded apprentices is something else. The remoteness or fancifulness of some arguments suggests that the economic issues in the debate often served as a vehicle for moral or religious prejudice, class envy, and other more general antagonisms to the theater. The theater itself to some extent served as an instance of larger grievances—resentment against poor relief, for instance, or fear of social change. Like the friends of the theater, those who wished to encourage native manufactures urged that factories would attract the lower classes, preventing crime by keeping the poor and unemployed off the streets.[85] The arguments on both sides often seem contending visions of America couched in terms of specie or charity—one side preferring an accustomed provincial life and disdaining European luxuries, the other desiring the country to rise in glory and rival by imitating the great transatlantic capitals.

Whether the theater seriously threatened American economic life or merely brought into focus other problems which did, or both, those who questioned "the vast Expence of a public Stage" attributed to the theater what our own time attributes to TV, advertising, movies, and other mass media—an enormous power to influence society. Perhaps the sophisticated entertainments of the metropolis, transported to the provinces, invariably become mass media. Everyone goes. For whatever reason, the theater was the most visible and controversial form of cultural life in Revolutionary America, an inescapably felt presence, an unsettling force.

NOTES

1. These assertions are documented in my *A Cultural History of the American Revolution* (New York: Thomas Y. Crowell, 1976). The essay before the reader grew out of the *Cultural History*, where I have described the debate over an American theater, but without detailed treatment of the economic issues.

2. See Robert A. East, *Business Enterprise in the American Revolutionary Era* (1938; Gloucester, Mass.: Peter Smith, 1964), *passim*.

3. See Virgle Glenn Wilhite, *Founders of American Economic Thought and Policy* (New York: Bookman Associates, 1958), pp. 171-208.

4. John Lankford, ed., *Captain John Smith's America* (New York: Harper & Row, 1967), p. 162.

5. William Byrd, *The History of the Dividing Line* and Benjamin Franklin, *The Way to Wealth*, in Kenneth Silverman, ed., *Literature in America: The Founding of a Nation* (New York: The Free Press, 1971), pp. 244, 305.

6. Quoted in Carl Bridenbaugh, *Cities in Revolt: Urban Life in America, 1743-1776* (New York: Alfred A. Knopf, 1955), p. 319.

7. *New-York Journal; or, the General Advertiser*, 11 February 1768.

8. Ibid., 21 January 1768.

9. Ibid., 11 February 1768.

10. Quoted in Norman Arthur Benson, "The Itinerant Dancing and Music Masters of Eighteenth Century America," unpub. doct. diss., Univ. of Minnesota, 1963, p. 210.

11. *New-York Packet*, 20 October 1785.

12. Ibid., 16 February 1786.

13. *New-York Journal; or, the General Advertiser*, 21 January 1768.

14. Quoted in George O. Seilhamer, *History of the American Theater: Before the Revolution* (Philadelphia: Globe Printing House, 1888), p. 152. The quotations in this book are sometimes inaccurate, but I have been unable to locate the original.

15. *New-York Packet*, 20 October 1785.

16. *Freeman's Journal: or, the North-American Intelligencer*, 25 February 1784.

17. *Pennsylvania Packet*, 10 February 1789.

18. *Federal Gazette, And Philadelphia Evening Post*, 17 February 1789.

19. *Freeman's Journal: or, the North-American Intelligencer*, 18 February 1784.

20. *Pennsylvania Gazette*, 5 March 1767.

21. Quoted in Eola Willis, *The Charleston Stage in the XVIII Century* (Columbia, S. C.: The State Company, 1924), p. 125.

22. As tabulated in Susan Armstrong, "A Repertoire of the American Colonial Theater," typescript notebook, Colonial Williamsburg Research Institute, 1955. At the English patent theaters too, *Barnwell* appeared more frequently than any other serious play except *Jane Shore* and *The Orphan*. See George Lillo, *The London Merchant*, ed. William H. McBurney (Lincoln, Neb.: Univ. of Nebraska Press, 1965), p. xii.

23. James A. Henretta, *The Evolution of American Society, 1700-1815: An Interdisciplinary Analysis* (Lexington, Mass.: D.C. Heath and Company, 1973), pp. 138ff.

24. Quoted in Curtis P. Nettels, *The Emergence of a National Economy 1775-1815* (New York: Holt, Rinehart and Winston, 1962), p. 61.

25. Bridenbaugh, p. 370.

26. *South-Carolina Gazette*, 25 August 1773.

27. *New-York Journal; or, the General Advertiser*, 11 February 1768.

28. Quoted in Bridenbaugh, pp. 371-72.

29. Quoted in H. P. Phelps, *Players of a Century: A Record of the Albany Stage* (1880; New York, Benjamin Blom, Inc., 1972), p. 24.

30. *New-York Packet*, 16 February 1786.

31. Jack P. Greene, ed., *Colonies to Nation: 1763-1789* (New York: W. W. Norton & Co., 1967), p. 248.

32. *Freeman's Journal: or, North-American Intelligencer*, 18 February 1784.

33. E. James Ferguson, *The Power of the Purse* (Chapel Hill, N.C.: Univ. of North Carolina Press, 1961), p. 333.

34. Undated petition "To the Honorable the Governor and Council of Maryland," Massachusetts Historical Society, ca. 1783.

35. *Pennsylvania Gazette*, 13 August 1767.

36. George O. Seilhamer, *History of the American Theater: During the Revolution and After* (Philadelphia: Globe Printing House, 1889), p. 253.

37. *Daily Advertiser: Political, Historical, and Commercial*, 12 January 1786.

38. *Pennsylvania Packet*, 16 February 1789.

39. Joseph Brown Ladd, *The Literary Remains of Joseph Brown Ladd, M.D.* (New York: H. C. Sleight, 1832), p. 227.

40. *Massachusetts Centinel and the Republican Journal*, 15 August 1789.

41. Quoted in Van Carl Kussrow, Jr., "On with the Show: A Study of Public Arguments in Favor of Theater in America during the Eighteenth Century" (unpub. doct. diss., Indiana Univ., 1959), p. 239.

42. *Federal Gazette, And Philadelphia Evening Post*, 28 February 1789.

43. *New-York Packet*, 6 February 1786.

44. See *Pennsylvania Journal*, 19 February 1767; *Pennsylvania Chronicle*, 2 March 1767; *Pennsylvania Gazette*, 5 March 1767.

45. *New-York Packet*, 6 February 1786. Provision for an annual payment into the public treasury was made in an amendment to the bill of repeal, but the amendment was defeated. See *Federal Gazette, And Philadelphia Evening Post*, 3 March 1789.

46. Harry William Pedicord, *The Theatrical Public in the Time of Garrick* (New York: King's Crown Press, 1954), pp. 23-24.

47. *Connecticut Journal,* 4 February 1778.

48. Quoted in Jack W. Broucek, "Eighteenth Century Music in Savannah, Georgia," unpub. doct. diss., Florida State Univ., 1962, p. 121.

49. *New-York Journal; or, the General Advertiser,* 28 January 1768.

50. *Pennsylvania Journal; and Weekly Advertiser,* 22 October 1767.

51. Quoted in Willis, p. 66. For a time in 1765 the *South-Carolina Gazette* reported a robbery "almost every night." See Bridenbaugh, p. 303.

52. *Federal Gazette, And Philadelphia Evening Post,* 20 February 1789.

53. Ibid.

54. *New-York Packet,* 2 March 1786.

55. Ibid., 6 February 1786.

56. S. E. Morison, "Two 'Signers' on Salaries and the Stage, 1789," *Proceedings of the Massachusetts Historical Society,* 62 (1928-29), 60.

57. *Daily Advertiser: Political, Historical, and Commercial,* 14 January 1786.

58. *Pennsylvania Gazette,* 5 March 1767.

59. *Federal Gazette, And Philadelphia Evening Post,* 18 February 1789.

60. *New-York Journal; or, the General Advertiser,* 26 January 1786.

61. John Henry to Gilmore, ALS, Baltimore, 19 September 1786, Historical Society of Pennsylvania.

62. Lewis Hallam, Jr., to Thomas Bradford, ALS, no place, undated, Historical Society of Pennsylvania.

63. Peter J. Coleman, *Debtors and Creditors in America: Insolvency, Imprisonment for Debt, and Bankruptcy, 1607-1900* (Madison, Wis.: The State Historical Society of Wisconsin, 1974), p. 113.

64. *Pennsylvania Chronicle, and Universal Advertiser,* 6-13 April 1767.

65. *The Independent Gazetteer; or, the Chronicle of Freedom,* 15 November 1783.

66. Seilhamer, *History of the American Theater: During The Revolution,* p. 168.

67. Thomas Clark Pollock, *The Philadelphia Theater in the Eighteenth Century* (Philadelphia: Univ. of Pennsylvania Press, 1933), p. 44.

68. *New-York Journal; or, the General Advertiser,* 17 May 1788.

69. *Pennsylvania Gazette,* 30 April 1767.

70. "A List of the Plays with their Gross Proceeds," MS, 1782, Maryland Historical Society.

71. "To the Honorable the Governor" (see note 34).

72. *Pennsylvania Archives,* lst Ser., XI (Philadelphia: J. Severns & Co., 1855), p. 343.

73. *New-York Journal; or, the General Advertiser,* 7 January 1768.

74. Silverman, *Literature in America,* p. 313.

75. *New-York Journal; or, the General Advertiser,* 21 January 1768.

76. Ibid., 28 January 1768.

77. Quoted in Seilhamer, *History of the American Theater: Before the Revolution,* p. 328.

78. Postscript to *Pennsylvania Chronicle and Universal Advertiser,* 30 March 1767.

79. *New-York Packet*, 9 February 1786.
80. *Freeman's Journal: or, North-American Intelligencer*, 14 February 1787.
81. Quoted in Pollock, p. 38.
82. "New-York, Theater, 1782" (broadside).
83. Quoted in George O. Willard, *History of the Providence Stage 1762-1891* (Providence: The Rhode Island News Company, 1891), p. 6.
84. William Dunlap, *History of the American Theater and Anecdotes of the Principal Actors*, 2d ed. (n.d.; rpt. New York: Burt Franklin, 1963), p. 111.
85. Joseph Dorfman, *The Economic Mind in American Civilization*, (New York: Viking Press, 1953), I, p. 254.

The French Image of
American Society to 1815:
Some Tentative Revisions

DURAND ECHEVERRIA

MONTAIGNE'S COMMENTS in his *Essais* on the ethnocentric bias of contemporary accounts of the American Indians indicate that as early as the sixteenth century some thinkers were aware that the European image of the New World not only was flawed by factual errors but also was being shaped by the preconceptions of European observers and that it was revealing perhaps as much about these observers as about the Americas.[1] Similarly two hundred years later, though Franklin and Jefferson assiduously disseminated documents and data in an effort to clean up what John Adams called the "Augean stables" of French misconceptions of the United States, these first American ministers to Versailles were nonetheless sensible of the extent to which the French image of their country was being colored by cultural, political, economic, and philosophical influences that factual information could little affect. Yet it was not until Gilbert Chinard published in 1911 his *L'Exotisme américain dans la littérature française au XVIe siècle* that a concerted scholarly effort was begun to discover and analyze the processes by which one culture or society conceives an image of another. Many have followed in Chinard's revered footsteps, yet it may be fair to say that the results have been less satisfying than we might have expected, and this despite the great concern of all governments with their national images abroad. One reason for this putative failure to make better progress in understanding the formation of intersocial and intercultural images may be that the problem is an interdisciplinary one requiring the collaboration of scholars in literature and the other arts, historians, psychologists, sociologists, anthropologists, economists, and political scientists, yet it has attracted the attention mainly of students of literature and of ideological and cultural history. It is also possible that, because of our predominately literary, and sometimes anecdotal and impressionistic, approaches to the problem, and our concern with formulas of literary criiticism, we may have unwittingly created distortions not dissimilar in nature from the distortions we were explicating—that we may sometimes have dreamed *rêves* of *rêves exotiques*, mythologized myths, and conjured mirages of mirages. Be that as it may, the following pages offer a *mea culpa* for some of the misinterpretation I believe I myself have made or endorsed, and a few tentative suggestions for what may be production lines of investigation.

First of all, I should venture to suggest that in the interests of greater rigor and objectivity in our analyses of intercultural and intersocial images we might do well to renounce some of the eye-catching terms we have been using, such as *rêve, dream, mirage, impact,* and perhaps even *myth*. On the covers of our books and the programs of scholarly conferences they are indeed more striking than more precise and prosaic terms, but it is possible that they too often imply or denote falsifications and confuse our thinking.

The latest in vogue, *impact*, which appeared in the titles of a conference and a series of essays in which I myself participated, is perhaps the most misleading. It suggests that something concrete and objective struck the eyes and ears of Europeans, like a projectile, or the sound waves generated by Ralph Waldo Emerson's "shot heard round the world"; it obscures the fact that the European idea of America was subjective, that the image was essentially created by the viewing mind, not by an external reality.

Rêve and *dream* sin on the other side, for they mean a *chimère*, an imaginary vision totally disjoined from reality. This is equally inaccurate. Pennsylvania was certainly not the scene of a renewal of Hesiod's golden age nor was it situated south of

Maryland, as Voltaire said and presumably believed, but it nevertheless existed. *Mirage*, the emendation that Gilbert Chinard was the first to offer, is better, for it suggests delusion and distortion rather than pure fantasy, but again there is the connotation of a vision of something that did not in fact exist. Washington's army existed in objective reality and was no mirage, though it was not as large or as effective as Vergennes believed.

Of course these words *impact, rêve, dream,* and *mirage* have all been intended as metaphors, not scientific terms, and indeed they do suggest valid comparisons: *impact,* that the discovery and development in the New World had an explosive effect on the thought and culture of the Old; *rêve* and *dream,* that America came to symbolize a complex of European aspirations, that Americans represented, for Turgot and many other Europeans, "the hope of the human race"; and *mirage* connotes belief in the truth of the illusory. But metaphor is a treacherous device for the historian; it often suggests not only the intended truth but also unintended untruths.

The word *myth* presents difficulties of a different sort. Since myth as a phenomenon of language and literature has been so thoroughly and carefully analyzed for so many years, we must assume that any use of the term in the study of the European image of the Americas must be with one or another of the precise meanings it has been given, and that it is not to be taken, like the other words I have mentioned, as metaphoric.

It would be idle, of course, to deny the existence of a mythology of America, that is, of a complex of narratives prevalent at various times among various peoples which have dramatized the psychological and cultural meanings of the American experience. Myth is one of the linguistic and literary forms in which the image of America has been conveyed.

Yet it is only one of a number of such forms, and it seems to me that there has sometimes been a certain laxness in qualifying as myth any part of the image of America that was fictitious or inaccurate, and in even referring to the entire image as *le mythe américain*. Where and if myth occurs, let us so note, but with a precise definition of the term (which is still under debate), and a precise application to particular cases.

Whatever else a myth is, it is a story, a narrative involving characters, a universe in which they exist, and a series of related events in which the characters and their universe interact. The distinction has been made between the myth itself, the vision conceived by what Philip Wheelwright has called the "mytho-poeic mode of consciousness," and the "myth-artifact," the specific tale in which the myth is given form.[2] This is a valid point, for the same myth may be voiced in a number of more or less different stories. Yet the myth itself cannot exist except in and through the story, and it is in the story that its meaning is found. As Claude Lévi-Strauss has said, the "substance" of a myth "does not lie in its style, its original music, or its syntax, but in the *story* it tells."[3]

For this reason, which may seem too obvious to insist upon, we cannot, for instance, properly speak of the "myth" of the good savage. The good savage is a literary type which played various roles in many plays, novels, *contes*, and accounts of travel and exploration in many different parts of the world and often with quite different significations—the Brazilian *cannibale* of Montaigne, the Canadian Indian of Lescarbot, the Chactas of Chateaubriand, the Tahitian of Diderot, and the black *bon sauvage* of Bernardin de Saint Pierre.

The same may be said of the figure of the Good Quaker— in Voltaire's *Lettres anglaises*, in Chamfort's play *La Jeune Indienne*, or in Brissot's *Nouveau voyage*—and likewise of the American military hero, the enlightened American, the American yeoman, the American frontiersman, and later, the American businessman. These are archetypal literary figures deliberately created to symbolize and at the same time to validate a particular idea—primitivism, deism, toleration, libertarianism, ruralism, or the inferiority of American culture. They are not properly speaking mythic, for these figures never become the protagonists of stories that achieve the mythic function and they are not produced by the mythopoeic mode of consciousness.

Of course a myth is more than a story, and not all stories are myths. Here I venture into an area in which I can claim no special competence, but I think it would be generally accepted that a myth is a paradigm or a recapitulation of the experience of a people within a certain universe, a poetic or figurative expression through a narrative of a believed truth about this experience in this universe. The requirement of the particular *universe* is most important for our purposes here. When the universe is common to all mankind and when the myth is an attempt to explain fundamental conditions of life and psychological situations which are shared by all men, then we have what has been called a universal archetypal myth. No doubt the universal archetype is essential to myth, for all myths must link and relate the experiences and problems of the culture in which they are generated to the fundamentals of human psychology and to the universal conditions of human existence. Yet we must also acknowledge the existence of *cultural* myths, that is, of variants of the universal archetypes which attempt to explain a special experience of a particular people of a particular culture in a particular universe at some moment in their history, and which are intelligible only within this special context.

Thus the phrase "mythology of America" can refer—I am assuming we are not concerned here with Amerindian myths—only to such cultural myths generated by the experiences of Europeans in the American universe. Examples are the New England Puritan captivity myth, epitomized by Mary Rowlandson's *Narrative*, and the Daniel Boone myth of the eighteenth century, which Richard Slotkin has so well anaylzed,[4] or the Spanish chivalric myth of quest and conquest, as in Bernal Díaz del Castillo's *Historia Verdadera de la Conquista de la Nueva España*. These were the direct products of the experiences of European explorers and colonists in America and were American in that their universes were specifically American and in that the myth was created and maintained by participants in the American experience. It is true that these myths entered the literatures of the mother countries, for instance in the English publications of the Puritan captivity narratives, but they were European versions of the myth only to the extent that there was a continuing cultural identity between Puritan England and Puritan New England.

The French experience in Canada may have generated similar myths, but it is obvious, I think, that the French experience in the British colonies or in the United States could not possibly have produced a mythology, limited as it was to the brief sojourns of a few soldiers, travelers, and diplomats. Those French who remained permanently and their descendants, notably the Huguenots, for instance the Bartrams, became Americanized and could participate only in generating native myths.

The only possible French myths about non-French America were those which arose out of the experiences of Europeans in Europe confronted with the new moral, economic, and political situations created by the sudden appearance of a New World beyond the Atlantic. An example might be the Inkle and Yarico story, which first appeared in Jean Mocquet's *Voyages* of 1611 and was frequently retold in various versions and genres during the next two centuries.[5] It is the tale of a shipwrecked English sailor whose life is saved by an Indian maid with whom he falls in love but whom he abandons—in some versions sells into slavery— when he is finally rescued. In heartbroken fury she seizes their child and tears it to pieces before his eyes. Perhaps this can be called a genuine myth, for it seems to give an archetypal expression to the collective sense of vicarious guilt that Europeans since Las Casas felt for the exploitations of the Indians and the Blacks. But is belongs to what Philip Wheelwright has called the stage of the "romantic" myth, the "deliberately contrived story."[6] It is a literary, self-conscious myth, which expressed a vision meaningful and true in a French salon, but which would have been absurd and false in seventeenth-century New England. It is a European myth, for it is an expression of the reactions of Europeans to European colonialism.

We may speculate that similar European myths might have arisen out of French participation in the American War, perhaps a French counterpart to the American myth of Lafayette. As it happened, however, the rapid course of events, the deluge of the French Revolution, and the anti-Americanism of the 1790s all frustrated this possibility. In short then, while I stand open to correction, I find it difficult to identify in any part of the abundant French literature on this country before 1815 any narratives that seem qualifiable as mythic in the scholarly sense of the word.

What we do find, as I have said, is something quite different, the archetypal *figure*—the figure of the city of brotherly love, of secularism, toleration and enlightenment, Philadelphia; the figure of the enlightened American, Franklin; of the Roman patriot, Washington; of the military hero, John Paul Jones; of the virtuous yeoman; and later of the degenerate frontiersman and of the materialistic American businessman. Behind each figure stands an easily identified idea or ideology or political cause of some sort—secularism, or Physiocracy, or the theory of American degeneration. The reasons for the existence of these ideas in France are not our present concern. What is of immediate interest is the explication of the reasons why the French used first the British colonies and later the United States as figures for these ideas. What motives caused the image? It seems to me that we shall make more progress in explicating the image by paying less attention to literary modes like dream or mirage and more to the cultural and psychological causes. There is no reason to assume that the motivations for the figuring of America were any different from those which created all the other images of alien societies generated by Western peoples since the Renaissance. It is even possible that these motivations may be universal in human nature and may operate whenever any society or culture comes in contact with another.

The deepest origins of this phenomenon of image-making are, I think, in two essential but contradictory drives in man: one is the centripetal instinct for socialization, the desire to promote and preserve the welfare of the group; the other is the centrifugal force of individualism, the urge to promote and preserve the interests of the self, regardless or in spite of the interests of society.

The first, the socializing drive, is obviously manifested in the creation of pejorative or honorific images of those alien societies which seem to present dangers or benefits to the viewing society. They serve as it were as banners under which the people muster to repel enemies or welcome allies. Less obviously, the same socializing drive operates in the construction of comparisons by the viewers between their own societies and cultures and those of others. When such comparisons are made to bolster the viewers' collective self-esteem, the images are invariably pejorative, but when they are rationally and deliberately constructed, as was frequently the case in eighteenth-century France, as propaganda in support of internal political or social reforms, then the images may be of all sorts and become very complex. Of this phenomenon more will be said later.

The second motive, the individualistic one, as it affected the French image of this country, seemed to grow stronger as the eighteenth century drew to its tumultuous close and as what is called romanticism became more prevalent. It manifested itself principally in exoticism and primitivism, by which terms I mean attitudes deeply rooted in human nature, more fundamental than merely Chateaubriand's description of the Mississippi or his *bon sauvage*. Both exoticism and primitivism are individualistic and potentially antisocial because both express rejection of existing cultural patterns and social institutions.

The least important, in relation to our present problem, seems to be exoticism. Lovejoy and Boas have defined exoticism as the "love of strangeness, and the revolt against the familiar."[7] There seem to be two contradictory urges in humans: one, to repeat and habitualize cultural inventions, to create and perpetuate traditions, to cling to familiar scenes, institutions, and patterns of behavior; and the other, to invent new artifacts, new institutions, new patterns of living and to seek new environments—in short, the desire for variety, boredom with the familiar. Indeed, one is tempted to wonder whether this "divine discontent" may not be what makes man the preeminently inventive animal, what gives him what Rousseau called his fatal "faculté de se perfectionner." It may be that inventions are initiated more frequently by the desire to do a familiar task differently than by the deliberate intent to discover a better technique. In any case, this need for variety, for change, for *divertissement*, is, as I think Voltaire rightly maintained against Pascal, essential in man's humanity and it may be satisfied in many ways. Certainly it must be the basis of the appeal of the literature of fantasy, of accounts of unfamiliar worlds, either imaginary or exotic. This general cultural, psychological, and literary phenomenon may properly be designated basic exoticism. It seems to occur in all peoples and in all periods, in new fashions of dress and in the invention of new slang, and in all literatures—in the Chinese, for instance, in the tales of the Tang Dynasty and the cycle of stories originating in the seventh century around the legendary journey of the Buddhist priest, Tripitaka, to India.[8] In the West this literature of fantasy and exotic adventure extends from the *Odyssey* to the medieval epic.

With the Renaissance, however, this basic exoticism found a new and different focus in alien and unfamiliar cultures and societies, and in their environments, in their geography and flora and fauna. Thus the appeal of the strange was heightened by a documented authenticity. As Erich Auerbach points out in *Mimesis*, this kind of exoticism was new to Western literature. "The exotic appeal," he says, "which Venice, Verona, and the like had for an English audience in the year 1600 is an element that was virtually—not to say completely—unknown to the theater of the ancients. . . . During the Middle Ages all practical acquaintance with alien forms of life and culture was lost. . . . There was . . . such a lack of historical consciousness and perspective that the events and characters [of past cultures] were simply transferred to the present forms and conditions of life: Caesar, Aeneas, Pilate became knights, Joseph of Arimathaea a burgher, and Adam a farmer, of twelfth- or thirteenth-century France, England, or Germany."[9] This cultural revolution Auerbach attributes to what he calls the new "historical perspective in depth" produced by humanism, to the great discoveries, to the new sense of national identity, and to the schisms in the Church. To these causes one might add the scientific curiosity engendered by the Renaissance and also the invention of printing, which made possible the diffusion of hundreds of voyage narratives after the end of the fifteenth century.

French interest in the British colonies in North America, as in all regions of the globe, was of course augmented by this new sort of cultural and social exoticism and the great vogue of literature of travel and exploration. Yet such exoticism, in so far as it was a factor, directed French attention not so much toward the cultural and social institutions of the colonies themselves as toward the adventures of discovery and toward the land, its animals and plants, and its aboriginal inhabitants, the Indians. This was particularly true during the earliest period from Bigge's *Voyage de Messire Drake* of 1588, the first French publication related to British North America, until about the 1670s, but the same bias continued to be apparent throughout the rest of the seventeenth and the eighteenth centuries and was evidenced in works on the natural history of the region, such as Catesby's *Histoire naturelle de la Caroline, la Floride et les Isles Bahama* of 1731, in the translations of accounts of explorations and adventures in the wilderness by Long, Timberlake, Bouquet, William Bartram, and others, and in *contes* and plays about the Indians by Saint Lambert, Chateaubriand, and many more.

Exoticism as a psychological motive does not seem to have directed French attention to life in the settled colonies or to the United States until the heightened social and political tensions in France began to produce a desire to escape and serious plans of emigration. When this did occur in the last third of the eighteenth century, exoticism, hitherto no more than sporadic boredom or uneasiness with the familiar, was sharpened to a very real anguish and fear, and even a desperate desire to escape. Perhaps one of the first expressions of this modern need for *évasion* was, significantly, that voiced by Rousseau himself, who in 1768 said he was thinking of finding sanctuary in America.[10]

He was soon echoed by others, and not only by his own disciples. In 1776 the hardheaded and cynical Abbé Galiani wrote Mme d'Epinay, "The total collapse of Europe is upon us, and the time has come for emigration to America. Everything here is falling into decay and corruption: religion, the law, the arts, the sciences. And everything will be built anew in America. . . . So don't buy your new house on the Chaussée d'Antin. Buy it in Philadelphia."[11] As the French Revolution became imminent such plans for escape became more numerous. In 1787 Dr. Guillotin, soon to be immortalized by his efficient contrivance, wrote Benjamin Franklin, "We are all of us enemies of the tumult, disorder, intrigue, and extravagance now consuming our cities. We are revolted by the unreasonableness of our laws and their contradictions of our customs and traditions, which often put a man in the cruel dilemma of either appearing ridiculous or committing a crime. . . . Hence we have resolved to flee this poisoned land where one can find only trouble, disgust, worry, disappointment, and danger. We have formed the plan of establishing a settlement in the United States, and specifically in the region of the Ohio."[12]

After the Bastille, escapism became epidemic, even before the so-called "forced emigration," to the profit of less than scrupulous American land speculators, and thousands of French fled to hastily organized asylums in the United States, of which the Scioto colony was the most famous, or infamous. It is very significant, however, that these projected refuges were on the Ohio or the banks of the Susquehanna or in Kentucky or upper New York State, beyond the frontiers of American society. Like Chateaubriand, the best known of these seekers of asylum, French escapists found Philadelphia too European. It is true that many emigrés did settle in American cities, mostly in Philadelphia, but these men had usually not left France for psychological reasons or out of true exoticism, but simply to save their skins, and most shared the feelings of Talleyrand, who later wrote, "I arrived [in the United States] full of repugnance for the new sights which usually interest travelers. I found it very difficult to awaken in myself any curiosity."[13] Asylum was in the wilderness, not in American society.

In summation, the conclusion must be that important as exoticism was in forming the French image of other areas of the Americas, it contributed to the concept of the colonies and the United States little if anything except the negative idea of asylum from the 1770s to the early 1790s, disjoined from or loosely linked to other features of the image, which had different origins.

Similarly primitivism had a late and relatively minor part in shaping French opinion of the society and culture established here by persons of European origin. I am referring of course not to what Lovejoy calls "chronological primitivism," the idea epitomized by Hesiod's legend of a golden age in the remote past, which of course was inapplicable and in any case had few if any true proponents in the seventeenth and eighteenth centuries,[14] but rather to that which Lovejoy has distinguished as "cultural primitivism," an eighteenth-century commonplace. This may be defined as the belief that men are happier and more virtuous, not in the pure state of nature, which Rousseau and Monboddo equated with the condition of the orangutan, but in a merely less complex society and culture.

The motivation of primitivism seems to be another inconsistent and apparently perverse tendency which, if it is not natural to man, has at least been apparent throughout Western history. Man is, as I have said, the preeminently inventive animal, and, as Robert A. Nisbet has insisted, there has undoubtedly existed in the western consciousness since the Greeks a "sense of the progressive development of culture," Lucretius' *pedetemptim progredientis*, the belief in "an advancement caused by man's own faculties, leading to a present that, in cultural and technological terms, was clearly and incontestably superior to anything that had been known in remote antiquity."[15] Yet we must also acknowledge the existence since the earliest times, as Lovejoy and Boas amply documented in their great work on *Primitivism and Related Ideas in Antiquity*, the persistent though not universal idea that the undeniable progressive accumulation of technological and social inventions has not been on the whole a good thing for mankind. The process of civilization is, after all, nothing more than the accumulation of inventions, technological, artistic, and social, which have formed cultures and societies of greater and greater complexity, hence exerting greater and greater pressures on the individual. The sense of the threat to humanity in man's fatal aptitude for civilization, today manifested in the efforts to protect ourselves from offshore oil and the other attacks on our environment, was expressed in antiquity by the chronological primitivism figured by the myth of the golden age and in the eighteenth century by the wave of cultural primitivism.

In fact perhaps the greatest debate of the Enlightenment was on whether the Enlightenment itself was a good thing. On the one side there were Voltaire and the other apologists of *luxe*, Condorcet and the other dogmatists of the theory of progress, and De Pauw and the other proponents of the theory of American degeneration, which was an attempt to turn primitivism upside down. On the other side there was the Rousseau of the First Discourse, who attacked the evils of intellectual and artistic invention, the Rousseau of the Second Discourse, attacking the evils of technological and social invention, and the Rousseau of the *Nouvelle Héloïse* and the *Lettre sur les spectacles*, offering the solution of ruralism and de-civilization, and around him all his disciples and ideological allies, who ranged from Marie Antoinette in her Hameau to the Physiocrats. This cultural primitivism was powerfully reinforced by association, partly by semantic confusion, with two other concepts. One was the complex of ideas denoted by the word *nature*, for the idea of nature as the innate, the instinctive, the not-learned, and hence the non-cultural and pre-social and therefore primitive, became unconsciously blended with the idea of nature as the ethical norm, as in natural law and natural rights, with nature as the healthy and vigorous condition of human life, and with nature as the divinely planned cosmic order.[16] Second, primitivism as a negative reaction to the existing conditions in French culture and society was inevitably associated with historical pessimism, which was probably an even stronger and more pervasive current in French eighteenth-century thought than Vyverberg indicated in his stimulating study.[17]

As is well known, the primitivists found ready-made images and demonstrations of their thesis in the Americas. The *bon sauvage* became the archetypal figure of the virtues of un-civilization. Yet he had no real or apparent relation to the British colonies, or to the United States. The *bon sauvage* was a Huron in Canada, or he was an Iroquois or a Natchez beyond the Anglo-American frontier, depicted virtually always without significant reference to the British settlements, as in Saint Lambert's *Deux Amis* or Chateaubriand's *Atala* and *René*. Though the American myth of the frontiersman's initiation into the nature of the wilderness and his partial Indianization was offered to French readers through translations, notably that of Filson's *Kentucke*, the sense of the myth does not seem to have been understood by the French, even by Filson's translator Parraud, and it was not voiced by French writers.

Instead French primitivism used the British colonies and the United States as the source of the figure of the bucolic American yeoman of the Atlantic seaboard. For instance, in 1771 the ultra-Rousseauist Gaspard de Beaurieu dedicated the latest edition of his popular *L'Élève de la nature* to the inhabitants of Virginia, writing, "In the land which you inhabit and cultivate there are no cities, no crimes, no sickness. . . . You are as Nature would have us all to be." In the same edition he reprinted a letter originally published in 1769 by the Physiocrat Pierre Samuel Du Pont de Nemours, also written in praise of a Virginia unspoiled by cities: "In no country in the world are women more beautiful, even at an advanced age, or men handsomer or more robust, or minds

more lofty, or characters more gentle, or hearts more in-
trepid."[18] Similarly in 1781 Hilliard d'Auberteuil wrote, "In
general the inhabitants of these colonies live in happiness and
innocence, occupied with farming, hunting and fishing, and the
tranquil pleasures of rustic life";[19] and two years later the Abbé
Brizard, evoking Hesiod, said, "The golden age sung by the poets
seems to be realized in that happy land."[20] Of course the best-
read exponent of this figure of the rural, arcadian American was
Saint John de Crèvecoeur, whose *Lettres d'un cultivateur américain*
gave a touching picture of the simplicity and innocence of the
life he had led on his farm in Orange County, New York.

Yet this primitivistic figure, which flourished from the late
1760s to the mid-1780s, never became dominant over its pro-
gressionistic counterpart. Indeed, the figure of the enlightened
and civilized American functioned as a most effective counter to
primitivism, for he was used to show that the Rousseauistic di-
chotomy was an error, that the American example demonstrated
that progress in the arts and sciences was not incompatible with
simplicity and virtue and that enlightenment and philosophy
could flourish in a rural environment. The learned American
had appeared in Paris long before the American farmer, in the
persons of Dr. Benjamin Rush and Dr. William Shippen and in
the works of Cadwallader Colden, John Dickinson, John Bartram, Benjamin West, and the American Philosophical Society.
Of course the prime figure was Benjamin Franklin, scientist, in-
ventor of lightning rods and stoves and constitutions, *Economiste*,
salon wit, academician, and man of letters, the very epitome of
the civilized man. It is true that in the 1770s he was given in addition—and consciously assumed—the functions of a
primitivistic figure. He arrived in Paris in his tall fur hat and
spectacles, the very picture of the rural philosopher, he took no
pains to correct the French notion that he was a Quaker, and he
was well aware of the effect his plain brown coat made in the
midst of the brilliantly costumed courtiers at Versailles. Mme Du
Deffand wondered whether his white hat was a symbol of liberty; she should have realized it was a symbol of moral purity.
Yet Franklin always remained, in the French vision, primarily a
scientist, a diplomat and a Philosophe, not a pseudo-Quaker.
Crèvecoeur himself compliantly fell in with this curious synthe-

sis of the contradictory theses of progress and primitivism, and
when he translated his letters into French he presented the simplicity and moral purity of the young rural society of the United
States as a providentially created ground on which mankind was
to find "a new birth," "a second creation," which was to become
"the theater on which the liberated forces of the human mind
will acquire all the energy of which they are susceptible—the
theater on which human nature, so long confined, so long reduced to the measure of pigmies, will achieve it final and greatest
honors in all the arts and in all the sciences."[21]

Thus the figure of America as a new Arcadia was, as it were,
swallowed up by the figure of America as a new Athens, a Greek
colony, a new Salente, where the best of European civilization was
being transplanted to a fresh, pure, and fertile soil. And of course
once the figure of the mercenary and materialistic American
businessman entered the image in the 1790s, the bucolic American vanished virtually completely.

For these reasons it does not appear that it was the individualistic anti-social urge, manifested either through exoticism
or through primitivism, that determined the French vision, but
rather the socializing motive. This drive was closely associated
with the new nationalism.

There is little doubt that French attitudes towards the colonies and towards the United States until 1783 were to a large
extent the by-products of French attitudes to England. It is true
that the *anglomanie* of the eighteenth century certainly predis-
posed the French to receive Anglo-Saxon ideas and values.
Franklin, member of the Royal Society and Oxonian doctor, appeared a companion figure to Locke and Newton.

But at the same time there existed in France the contradictory prejudice, an inveterate Anglophobia, still not extinct.
England's long-standing role as France's traditional enemy on the
Continent, on the seas, and in the colonies had, in this case, two
effects. We find, particularly in the officially sponsored anti-
British propaganda during the Seven Years War, the identification of Americans with the English as enemies of French
national interests. British soldiers from both sides of the Atlantic
figured in atrocity stories, such as the one of the treacherous
murder of M. de Jumonville, a French officer carrying a flag of

truce, by soldiers under the command of an American major by the name of George Washington, an incident made well known to the French reading public by Thomas's poem "Jumonville."

On the other hand, however, the revolt of the colonies against England became early in the eighteenth century a dream cherished by the French ministry of foreign affairs, the hope for a providential compensation for the long series of defeats by English arms. As I have noted elsewhere, this prophecy that the colonies would resist the restrictions of the Navigation Acts and eventually revolt and achieve independence was voiced as early as 1703 in Du Bos' propaganda piece, *Les Intérêts de l'Angleterre malentendus* and was repeated in following years by men like Montesquieu, the Marquis d'Argenson, Turgot and Maurepas, and it spread to Italy and probably to other Continental countries.[22] After the Seven Years War Choiseul sent spies to the British colonies in search of signs of the expected revolt and he invited Franklin to Paris with the hope (as Franklin astutely saw and said) "to blow up the coals between Britain and her colonies."[23] Thus Lexington and Concord merely confirmed a long-standing French expectation, and this fact, together with the new theory of the battle superiority of a citizen militia, explains Vergennes' overestimate of the military effectiveness of Washington's small and badly equipped army, his assumption of an eventual American victory, and his decision first to supply arms and then to sign the treaty of alliance, in the confident hope of sharing in a cheap victory with lucrative military, colonial, and commercial rewards. It likewise explains the disposition of both the government and the public to cheer every American victory. Much of the pro-Americanism after 1775, particularly in Lafayette and the other volunteers and among Rochambeau's officers, was, initially at least, merely the obverse of their chauvinistic and nationalistic hostility to England.

Once the United States became an independent nation in 1783 the situation charged, but the same motives continued to operate, though in different ways. The *arrêt* of August 1784, reluctantly issued by the Conseil d'Etat du Roi at the insistence of French-West-Indian planters, opening the ports of Santo Domingo to certain urgently needed imports from the United States, provoked a flood of protests from the merchants in French ports who had hitherto enjoyed a privileged monopoly in this trade. They were shocked to realize that this new nation that France had helped to bring to independence with the expectation of opening a profitable market for French exports was going to be a redoubtable competitor in world trade. During the first years of the French Revolution, when France was surrounded by a hostile royalist coalition, the National Assemblies and the Convention issued repeated statements of solidarity with the only independent ally they seemed to have in the world. Yet as soon as Washington's rebuff of Genet, the American policy of neutrality, and the signature of Jay's treaty with Great Britain made apparent to the French that the United States were going to pursue their national interests at the expense, if necessary, of France, anti-Americanism became predominate and the Undeclared War ensued.

Thus it is obvious—though the point has perhaps been obscured by the concepts of dream, mirage, and myth—that the French image of the United States and the colonies was always and inevitably modified by the apparent benefits or dangers this country presented to the French government and the French people.

Lastly we come to a much more complex set of effects of the socializing drive on the image, those which resulted from efforts by Frenchmen to modify and reform their own society and culture by employing the device of socio-cultural comparison. The new sense of historical perspective appearing in the Renaissance generated, as we have seen, not merely an exotic interest in alien societies and cultures but also a new awareness of the manifold differences between the diverse institutions and patterns of behavior discovered in various parts of the globe. At the same time, the revolutionary forces created by the Renaissance and the Reformation were producing profound social changes and spawning new ideas and movements, such as the theories of divine right and the contract, secularism, religious separatism, corporatism, and the like, and consequently stimulating new proposed solutions to the new problems. It was the coincidence of these two phenomena, the new historical perspective and the movement for cultural and social reform, that initiated socio-cultural comparisons.

There was nothing new in the construction of such comparisons between the present, immediately experienced
structures and patterns of existence and some ideal or superior
model, for there were the precedents of Plato's Republic and
Saint Augustine's Heavenly City. Indeed, the utopian genre took
new life with the Renaissance, from Thomas More onwards, and
European readers were presented with a congeries of imaginary
societies which became more and more thinly disguised satires
of contemporary real society and parabolic proposals for specific reforms. For polemic purposes, however, utopias never
could be fully effective, because as obvious fictions and ideali-
zations they were not persuasive demonstrations of the
immediate practicality of the reforms they suggested. Real, documented examples from other contemporary societies would be
far more convincing arguments of the feasibility of new proposals.

In France the literary genre of the comparison, explicit or
implied, between France and other contemporary societies and
cultures seems to have first appeared during the last third of the
seventeenth century. Such works found their documentation
initially in the Jesuit *relations* of China, in accounts of travels to
the Near East, particularly those by Tavernier and Chardin, and
in Huguenot and English reports on the colonies in British North
America. Among the first works were Marana's *L'Espion turc dans
les cours* of 1684, the *Lettre sur la morale de Confucius* of 1688, and
Charles de Rochefort's *Récit de l'estat présent des clébres colonies de
la Virginie, de Marie-Land, de la Caroline, du nouveau Duché de York,
de Penn-sylvania, et de la Nouvelle Angleterre* of 1681. Then in the
eighteenth century comparisons began to be made with European societies as well as those on other continents; Voltaire's
Lettres anglaises is the best-known example. From these beginnings the genre has continued and flourished to the present day
and has produced such masterpieces as Tocqueville's *De la dé-
mocratie en Amérique.*

Usually the image created by these comparisons has been of
models to be admired and imitated, but just as Orwellian anti-
utopias are possible so are either mixed images such as Voltaire's, which urged imitation of English inoculation but not of

Shakespeare, or wholly negative images like Georges Duhamel's.

I should perhaps emphasize that the motives and nature of
what I have been calling a socio-cultural comparison are quite
different from those of exoticism and primitivism. For an alien
society to provide useful lessons it must have enough in common
with that of the viewer to make its institutions and practices susceptible of imitation or at least of adaptation. Therefore the less
exotic the object the more useful it may be to the subject. England, distinct yet scarcely exotic to a Frenchman and faced with
problems analogous to those in France, was perfect material for
Voltaire, and he succeeded in drawing a long list of useful lessons for his compatriots in psychology, physics, medicine,
political organization, toleration, secularism, and literature.

By the same token the more primitive the object the less its
usefulness. The *bon sauvage* was a suitable figure for a theory of
human nature and as an effective expression of a generalized
uneasiness with the tensions and pressures of a complex society,
but he never could be a model to copy. Rousseau had no intention, Voltaire to the contrary, of crawling about on all fours and
eating grass, or of persuading his readers to do so, and Diderot
had to conclude, albeit a bit wistfully, that though it would be
agreeable to live like a Tahitian in Tahiti, in Paris one had to live
like a Parisian.

For a socio-cultural comparison to be useful it has to be made
with a civilized nation which has apparently found practical solutions to familiar problems, such as inoculation in England or
unicameralism in Pennsylvania. The three best candidates for
French writers were England, China, and the United States, and
all three were used, but the latter was obviously the most suitable. It was neither a hostile power like England nor exotic like
China, yet it was distant and new and thus a plastic object that
could be shaped to whatever comparison was ideologically or
politically suitable.

While one society may be more easily and effectively used
than another, for socio-cultural comparison to occur at all there
has to be the uniformitarian assumption that humanity is essentially one, that the same psychological principles, the same values,
the same artistic forms, the same ethic, the same political prin-

ciples are equally valid for all peoples. This uniformitarianism
underlies the aesthetics of Boileau, the deism of Voltaire, and the
political philosophies of Condorcet and Brissot. Without this assumption the supposed success of Physiocratic principles in
China or of freedom of expression in England or of religious
toleration in Pennsylvania would have been to the French mean-
ingless curiosities.

The contrary assumption, which Lovejoy has called diversitarianism, conceives the world as a series of closed systems, of
unique societies, each possessing its own cultural values and governed by special laws. In this view, the formulas applicable to a
given society would elsewhere be impractical absurdities. This
was the relativism of Montesquieu, of Mme de Staël, and of some
other romantics.

The French alternately looked at America through the
prisms of these two contrary philosophies, and inevitably they
saw different images. The uniformitarians dominated until about
1795, which explains why the Physiocrats, the Philosophes, and
the révolutionnaires believed that America could be "the hope
of the human race," that it was serving as a sort of laboratory in
which were being conducted social experiments whose results
would be equally applicable in Europe. For such men the American Revolution was in truth, as Brissot, Chateaubriand and
others said, the mother of the French Revolution, in the sense
that it provided the theoretical justification.

For the American image to serve as a figure for propaganda
in support of social and political reforms, that is, for a socio-cultural comparison to work, faith in uniformitarianism was a
prerequisite. For America to be an example of a good to imitate
or of an evil to avoid it was necessary to believe that what was
happening across the Atlantic could be repeated in Europe. This
was the thesis of Tocqueville, who saw in the United States the
first appearance of the wave of providential democracy that was
to sweep across the Western world, and of Duhamel, who likewise had witnessed in America, he believed, "*scènes de la vie
future.*"

The contrary assumption of relativism and diversitarianism
began to become more common in French thought after 1789.
From this date reactionaries began to say that the success of the

American Revolution proved nothing since conditions in the United States were so different from those in France. Necker wrote in 1792 that "it would be a great error to imagine that liberty, equality, and all our other new institutions will make us similar to the Americans."[24] Joseph de Maistre maintained that traditions and circumstances in France and America were so disparate that it was impossible to draw any useful analogies.[25] Malouet stated flatly that "it was insane to think the example of the American Revolution and its fortunate outcome . . . could be applied to us."[26]

Such relativism may produce two results. In a period of social maladjustment, of *mal du siècle*, of escapism, as in the early nineteenth century, the very otherness of the image enhances the exotic appeal, and thus the America of Franklin and Washington was replaced in the popular eye by the American of *Atala*, of the Leatherstocking Tales, and *"le Far-West."* Alternatively, for those who felt no need for escape, or who sought escape in other ways, the United States became simply an object of indifference. Bibliographical analysis reveals dramatically the abrupt decline in interest in the 1790s and early 1800s.

The most striking feature of the history of the French image of the colonies and the United States is the rhythmic alternation of americomania and americophobia, if I may use these terms, of grossly overstated favorable and unfavorable images, of inordinate sympathy and admiration that was indeed a mirage and a dream, and of outraged antipathy that delighted in every perceptible or imaginable American defect. The history of this pendulum-like process has been thoroughly studied up to the latter part of the nineteenth century: first, a slowly developing positive image that became clear by 1768, suddenly increasing in intensity in 1776 and continuing to about 1795; next, an extremely negative image until Brumaire; then a moderately favorable image during the Consulate and the First Empire, followed under the Restoration by strong pro-Americanism in all groups except the Ultras and the royal government; next, after the July Revolution, a brief prolongation of this sympathy until 1832, succeeded by a generally negative image until the fall of the Bourgeois Monarchy; then in 1848 a vigorous but brief burst of Americanism quickly replaced by an anti-American reaction; lastly, during the Second Empire a broadly based positive image, especially in the liberal opposition, though the supporters of the regime were decidedly anti-American.[27]

Clearly these fluctuations were unrelated to corresponding transformations in American culture. The United States were changing rapidly, it is true, but the nation so admired by Condorcet in 1786 was not radically different from the nation ten years later on which De Maistre heaped his scornful contempt. The significant variations were in the distortion of the object, not in the object itself, and were typically manifested, on one hand, in the unwarranted praise of a mediocre poet like Joel Barlow or, on the other, in condemnations of America as a nation of vulgarians incapable of producing any literature at all.

The explanation, which of course can be valid only for those I have called uniformitarians, seems to lie in the purposes for which the comparisons were drawn, in the political and social philosophies of the comparers, and in the political position of the regime of the moment. The periods of pro-Americanism were those when the government in power was to the right of the real or apparent position of the American state and of American society. At these times the opposition to the left, which (because of the progressive leftward movement in France) generally included the most articulate and intelligent writers, found in the colonies and later in the United States ready-made figures which served to exemplify the reforms they were proposing and which could provide extremely effective contrasts with existing French institutions. Thus Voltaire could compare the religious toleration practiced in Pennsylvania with French theocracy; the Physiocrats, American championship of economic liberty with French *dirigisme*; Condorcet, Brissot, and Mme Roland, American political liberty with the tottering absolutism of the Bourbons; the Ideologues, American liberalism with Bonapartism; and the opposition during the Restoration and the Second Empire, American republicanism with the anachronistic royalism of Charles X or the inept imperialism of *Napoléon le petit*.

Once these liberals came to power, however, as happened in 1789, 1830, and 1848, the previous pro-Americanism continued for a while, either by inertia or because it served to justify the new regime. But as soon as the French came to see no material difference between the American government and their own, whether it was the Directory or the July Monarchy of the Second Republic, the comparison became for the rulers more embarrassing than useful, and the opposition, on both the right and the left, saw in the United States a hostile figure. Thus the Directory denied the American example, the opposition to the left, men like Babeuf, despised it, and the royalist émigrés to the right denounced it. The same postures were taken during the July Monarchy by the Orleanists, the legitimists, and the socialists, and under the Second Republic Americanists such as Tocqueville were soon reduced to an ineffective handful of moderates in the center.

Of course once these political and social factors fixed the essential axis, the image was free to spin out in all directions and extend to non-political aspects of the culture such as the American character, the American mind, and American art and literature, which were rendered supportive of the essential political thesis. Thus De Maistre sourly predicted that the projected capital at Washington would never be built, and Brissot dogmatically asserted that not a single case of adultery had ever been known in the fair city of Philadelphia.

These explanations of the French image of American society to 1815 which I have offered are admittedly generalizations, and I acknowledge in advance many exceptions which might be cited. Nevertheless, my tentative opinion is that they may be useful and point toward the historic truth. In any case, I hope the points I have been attempting to make are clear: that in our study of the French image of America, or indeed of any intercultural or intersocial image, it may be misleading to give too much attention to the literary form and expression of the image; that we may achieve a better understanding of the problem by examining the psychological, social, and cultural motives that generated the image; and that in all cases, at least in modern Western history, these motives seem to have been either individualistic, namely, the primitivistic reaction against the tensions of civilization or the desire for exotic variety or escape, or else the socializing drives to promote the self-esteem and welfare of the viewing society by denigrating others or by constructing comparisons with others which would support needed internal reforms. In any particular historic case, any one of these motives may dominate. In the case we are discussing, the French image of America up to the fall of Napoleon, the evidence seems to indicate that it was the socializing drives which happened to prevail, especially the desire to draw useful comparisons for purposes of propaganda.

NOTES

1. The present text, which has also been published in the *French-American Review*, 6 (1982), 196-216, contains some revisions of the paper read at the Bicentennial Conference in Philadelphia in November 1976.
2. Philip Wheelwright, "The Semantic Approach to Myth," and Claude Lévi-Strauss, "The Structural Study of Myth," *Myth: A Symposium*, ed. T. A. Sebeok (Bloomington: Indiana Univ. Press, 1958), pp. 95-96, 50-66; Richard Slotkin, *Regeneration through Violence: The Mythology of the American Frontier, 1600-1860* (Middletown: Wesleyan Univ. Press, 1974), p. 8.
3. Lévi-Strauss, p. 52.
4. Slotkin, pp. 94-145, 268-312.
5. See Lawrence M. Price, *Inke and Yarico Album* (Berkeley: Univ. of California Press, 1937).
6. Wheelwright, P. 96.
7. Arthur O. Lovejoy, George Boas, et al., *Primitivism and Related Ideas in Antiquity* (Baltimore: The Johns Hopkins Univ. Press, 1935), p. 8.
8. Li Kung-tso, "Governor of the Southern Tributary State," *The Dragon King's Daughter: Ten Tang Dynasty Stories*, tr. Yang Hsien-Yi and Gladys Yang (Pekin: Foreign Language Press, 1962), pp. 44-56; Glen Dudbridge, *The Hsi-yu chi: A Study of Antecedents to the Sixteenth-Century Novel* (Cambridge: Cambridge Univ. Press, 1970). Wu Ch'êng-ên, *Monkey*, tr. Arthur Waley (New York: John Day, 1943).
9. Erich Auerbach, *Mimesis: The Representation of Reality in Western Literature*, tr. Willard Trask (New York: Doubleday, 1957), pp. 281-82.
10. *Correspondence générale*, ed. Dufour (Paris, 1932), XVIII, 338.
11. *Correspondence*, ed. Perey and Maugras (Paris, 1881), II, 442-43.
12. J. F. McDermott, "Guillotin Thinks of America," *Ohio State Archeological and Historical Quarterly*, 47 (1938), 133.
13. *Mémoires* (Paris, 1891-92), I, 232.
14. See Arthur O. Lovejoy, "The Supposed Primitivism of Rousseau's *Discourse on Inequality*" and "Monboddo and Rousseau," *Essays in the History of Ideas* (New York: Putnam's Sons, 1960), pp. 14-61. Cf. Lovejoy and Boas, *Primitivism and Related Ideas in Antiquity*, pp. 1-11.
15. Robert A. Nisbet, *Social Change and History: Aspects of the Western Theory of Development* (London: Oxford Univ. Press, 1972), pp. 46-47.

16. See Lovejoy and Boas, pp. 11-16, 447-56.

17. Henry Vyverberg, *Historical Pessimism in the French Enlightenment* (Cambridge: Harvard Univ. Press, 1958).

18. *L'Elève de la nature, nouvelle édition* (Amsterdam, 1771), III, i-iii; II, 241-59.

19. M. R. Hilliard d'Auberteuil, *Essais historiques et politiques sur les Anglo-Américains* (Bruxelles, 1781-82), I, 53.

20. Gabriel Brizard, *Fragment de Xénophon* (Paris, 1783), p. 16.

21. Hector Saint John de Crèvecoeur, *Letters d'un cultivateur américain* (Paris, 1784), I, 31-32.

22. Jean Baptiste Du Bos, *Les Intérfets de l'Angleterre malentendus* (Amsterdam, 1703); Montesquieu, "Notes sur l'Angleterre," *Oeuvres complètes*, ed. Laboulaye (Paris, 1875), VII, 194; *Journal et mémoires du marquis d'Argenson*, ed. Rathery (Paris, 1859), I, lv-lvi; Turgot, "Recherches sur les causes des progrès et de la décadence des sciences et des arts" and "Tableau philosophique des progrès successifs de l'esprit humain," *Oeuvres*, ed. Schelle (Paris, 1913-1923), I, 141, 222; Condorcet, "Eloge de Maurepas," *Oeuvres*, ed. O'Connor and Arago (Paris, 1847-1849), II, 493. For the appearance of the idea in Italy, see Antonio Genovesi, *Lezioni di Commercio* (Bassano, 1769), pp. 290-291. This work was first published in Naples in 1766.

23. Durand Echeverria, *Mirage in the West: A History of the French Image of American Society to 1815* (Princeton: Princeton Univ. Press, 1957), pp. 21, 23.

24. Jacques Necker, *Du Pouvoir exécutif dans les grands étate* (Paris, 1792), II, 7.

25. Joseph de Maistre, *Considérations sur la France* (Londres, 1797), p. 118.

26. P. V. Malouet, unsigned essay in J. B. A. Suard, *Mélanges de littérature* (Paris, 1803), III, 170.

27. See René Rémond, *L'Amérique devant l'opinion française, 1815-1852* (Paris: Armand Colin, 1962).

INDEX